T0355046

2 Peter
Growing in Christ
amid False Teaching

HARRY UPRICHARD

WESTBOW
PRESS®
A DIVISION OF THOMAS NELSON
& ZONDERVAN

WestBow Press books may be ordered through booksellers or by contacting:

WestBow Press
A Division of Thomas Nelson & Zondervan
1663 Liberty Drive
Bloomington, IN 47403
www.westbowpress.com
844-714-3454

Unless otherwise indicated, Scripture quotations are from the English Standard Version Anglicised
(ESVUK) ® Bible (The Holy Bible, English Standard Version®), copyright © 2001 by Crossway,
a publishing ministry of Good News Publishers. Used by permission. All rights reserved.

Excerpts from: *Exposition of James, Epistles of John, Peter, and Jude* by Simon J. Kistemaker,
copyright © 1996. Used by permission of Baker Academic, a division of Baker Publishing Group.

Excerpts from: *The NIV Application Commentary: 2 Peter, and Jude*, by D.J. Moo. (U.S.A.,
Zondervan, Grand Rapids, Michigan, 1996). Used by permission of Harper Collins Publishers Ltd.

Anglicised edition

Scripture quotations are from the ESV® Bible (The Holy Bible, English
Standard Version®), copyright © 2001 by Crossway, a publishing ministry
of Good News Publishers. Used by permission. All rights reserved.

Scripture quotations taken from The Holy Bible, New International Version® NIV® Copyright ©
1973 1978 1984 2011 by Biblica, Inc. TM. Used by permission. All rights reserved worldwide.

Scripture taken from the NEW AMERICAN STANDARD BIBLE®,
Copyright © 1960,1962,1963,1968,1971,1972,1973,1975,1977,1995 by The
Lockman Foundation. Used by permission. www.Lockman.org

Scripture taken from the New King James Version® Copyright © 1982
by Thomas Nelson. Used by permission. All rights reserved.

Scripture taken from the King James Version of the Bible.

ISBN: 978-1-6642-3966-1 (sc)
ISBN: 978-1-6642-3968-5 (hc)
ISBN: 978-1-6642-3967-8 (e)

Library of Congress Control Number: 2021913694

Print information available on the last page.

WestBow Press rev. date: 07/27/2022

Contents

Preface

Peter's second letter is about growing in Christ amid false teaching so that Christ's character will be reflected in Christians' lives. Peter begins by explaining true knowledge of God, for he wants his readers to enjoy the same salvation that he himself enjoys. It is a saving, growing, fruitful, assured and remembered knowledge. Above all, the source of this true knowledge of God is in Scripture. Scripture comes from God. Men spoke from God carried along by the Holy Spirit. That is why true knowledge of God is so completely dependable.

Peter next contrasts false knowledge of God with true knowledge of God. There are false teachers among the churches Peter addresses, whose precursors are the false prophets of the Old Testament. Arrogance, sensuality, and emptiness characterize these false teachers. They not only deny the truth but also live immoral lives. False knowledge of God leads nowhere but to God's condemnation and to eternal death.

Peter finally writes of practical knowledge of God. He reminds them, as earlier, of the predictions of the prophets and the commandment of their Lord and Saviour through the apostles. The point at issue is Christ's Second Coming, which the false teachers deny. But Peter assures the truth of his promise and calls Paul's Scripture to corroborate this. Practical knowledge of God produces godly living and assures that God fulfils all his promises in Scripture. True knowledge of God leads to salvation. False knowledge of God brings destruction. Practical knowledge of God confirms growth in grace and knowledge of our Lord Jesus Christ. All of this is possible through Scripture. Let's together see how Peter explains in detail how to grow in Christ amid false teaching.

Harry Uprichard

Harry Uprichard is a retired minister of the Presbyterian Church in Ireland. He has authored: A Son is Given – Christ in Isaiah, A Son is Promised – Christ in the Psalms, A Son is Revealed – Christ in Mark and a Study Commentary on Ephesians, all published by Evangelical Press; What Presbyterians Believe published by: The Oaks; Characters in Acts, A Matter of the Heart, published by Day One and 1 Peter Living for Christ in a Suffering World published by WestBow Press. He spends his time preaching and writing. His interests include music, sport, walking and detective thrillers.

KEYNOTE:
Peter's first letter encourages Christians to live for Christ in a suffering world, His second letter instructs them how to grow in Christ amid false teaching.

Acknowledgements

Sincere thanks are expressed to my dear friends Daniel and Mary McKee for extensive work in typing, correcting and preparing the manuscript for publication, to Joy Conkey of Union Theological College Library Belfast, to Westbow Press for undertaking editing and publishing the project and to many friends, who have encouraged me in writing, among whom I mention my good friend and colleague, the Rev Professor Edward Donnelly formerly Minister of Trinity Reformed Presbyterian Church, Newtownabbey and Emeritus Professor of New Testament at Reformed Theological College, Belfast. I dedicate this work to the memory of my beloved wife Maisie.

Every attempt has been made to acknowledge dependence on source and authority. If, in any way, this had been overlooked or omitted, I apologize unreservedly. I trust that what is written will be of blessing to many and, above all, to God's great glory.

Harry Uprichard.

Chapter 1

TRUE KNOWLEDGE

AUTHOR

2 PETER 1:1[A]

INTRODUCTION

The main theme of First Peter is that of suffering and how the Christian is to cope with it. In Second Peter, it is knowledge of God and how the Christian is to continue in this and, at the same time, combat false teaching. In Second Peter, true knowledge of God is portrayed in Chapter 1, false knowledge in Chapter 2 and practical knowledge in Chapter 3. This progression itself is instructive.

Second Peter opens in the normal fashion of letters of the day. First, the author is stated, then the readers are designated and, finally, greetings are brought. The letter itself claims to have been written by Simon Peter, Christ's disciple. There is the striking self-address, Simeon (or Simon) Peter, a servant and an apostle of Jesus Christ (1:1). The author, further, claims how the Lord had revealed to him the approach of his own death (1:14), and represents himself as an eyewitness of the Transfiguration, recalling the voice that addressed

1

him on "the holy mountain" (1:18). He also mentions a previous letter, which he had written to the same people (3:1) and refers with intimacy to "our beloved brother Paul" and to his letters (3:15, 16). Obviously, Peter claims to be the author, an author whose great personal authority and position within the disciples substantiates a true knowledge of God.

However, of all the New Testament books, Second Peter is the one whose authorship has, perhaps, been most disputed. Indeed, it has been suggested that, it is 'pseudepigraphous' in form, that is, written by one other than the claimed author in the name of Peter, but not a 'forgery', as the pseudepigraphous form was said to be an accepted mode of writing of the day and occurs also in early Christian literature. Pseudepigrapha is a Greek word that literally means "false writings". Thus, it describes a document written by someone in the name of another person, in this case, Peter, not so much with malicious intent as to express the views of the other person, who may, indeed, have died. At that time, it was, in some cases, an acceptable form of literature.

Grounds on which Petrine authorship has been challenged include:

1.	External Evidence	The external evidence of the early Church Fathers indicates a late acceptance of Second Peter into the canon of the New Testament. Nonetheless, while the acceptance was late, there is nothing suggesting that the letter is spurious, even though there was a marked hesitancy regarding its acceptance.
2.	Personal Allusions	Personal allusions within Second Peter, such as those noted

above, are taken by some not to authenticate Petrine authorship but rather the contrary. They are said to substantiate the pseudepigraphous nature of the writing, a form claimed, as already noted, and quite acceptable in the literary practice of the day. However, some of these personal details would be unusual, if not intentionally misleading, if the letter is regarded as pseudepigraphous. Furthermore, pseudepigrapha, as a viable and acceptable form of Christian literature, is not at all proven. In particular, with regard to Second Peter, it is difficult to substantiate the 'testamentary' nature, as a last letter of Peter just prior to his death, claimed by some on the basis of 1:14-16 as supportive of a pseudepigraphous form.

3. Historical Problems

Certain features in Second Peter are said to presuppose a date later than Peter's lifetime. These include references to Paul and "all his letters" (3:16); the allusion to the "second letter" (3:1); a claimed Gnosticism behind the false teaching more germane to the second century; the reference "ever since the fathers fell asleep" (3:4) as an allusion to the death of the apostles and "your apostles" (3:2) as being much too cold or general a term to have come from Peter himself. On the other hand, the "all" in connection with Paul's letters (3:16) may simply refer to those extant at the time of writing; the "second letter" may well imply that First Peter was, in fact, the first and that Second Peter is, in fact, the second; evidence of a developed Gnosticism in Second Peter is by no means proven; "ever since the fathers fell asleep" (3:4) could refer and, more probably does in view of the context, to the patriarchs rather than to the apostles; while the expression "your apostles" (3:2) might simply be Peter stressing his authority among his friends as the founder of the church.

4. Literary Problems

These include a claimed dependence on Jude, which would require a time later than Peter's lifetime. But there may not be this dependence of Second Peter on Jude. Indeed, the dependence may be the other way around, that of Jude on Second Peter, or, as some claim, that Second Peter and Jude both depend on another written document. Furthermore, Jude need not necessarily be dated as later than Peter's death. Linguistic differences are also said to be notable between Second and First Peter and also with the Pauline corpus. These, however, could be largely peripheral and not fundamental. Similarly, stylistic differences, on this same score, may simply reflect a different mood in the temperament of the author in his writing or a variation of his attitude in the light of a different situation addressed.

5. Doctrinal Problems

Differences in doctrine are said to exist between Second and First Peter, as well as with the rest of New Testament teaching. For example, major themes in First Peter are said not to occur in Second Peter at all – the cross, the resurrection, ascension, baptism and prayer while the primary emphasis in Second Peter is on the Parousia or return of Christ. It is even suggested that Second Peter portrays an inferior view of Christ, who is no longer regarded as redeemer. Apart from the fact that there are biblical features, which both First and Second Peter hold in common, these criticisms are somewhat overdrawn. As is the case generally in the New Testament and in the letters in particular, the subject matters addressed will largely determine the biblical and doctrinal material alluded to. In Second Peter, since false teaching is being combated, it is natural to expect allusions to Peter's authority. Subject matter also, in large degree, accounts for any variation in doctrinal emphases that may occur in the letter. Although Second Peter may have what might be described as "omissions" doctrinally, there are no contradictions and certainly no features are present in Second Peter, which are foreign to the biblical and apostolic gospel.

In conclusion, there is as good, if not a better, case to be made out for Petrine authorship of Second Peter than for the contrary and we trust that this will be substantiated as we look in detail at this letter.[1] This true knowledge of God, then, is there from the very beginning of Second Peter. It is evident in the author, Peter, and in his credentials for writing the letter.

EXPOSITION

AUTHOR

"Simeon Peter, a servant and apostle of Jesus Christ" (1:1ª).

---

[1]   See D. Guthrie, *New Testament Introduction,* pp814-863, for authorship and other introductory matters.

"Simeon Peter" The letter begins with the normal address of the day opening with the author's name and credentials. **"Simeon"** is perhaps better than "Simon", the name referring to the same person with the manuscripts being fairly equally divided on the issue with the former being the more difficult reading and preferable. **"Simeon"** is a transliteration of the Hebrew and strongly Palestinian in nuance. It is used only elsewhere of Peter in the account of the Jerusalem Council (Ac. 15:14), though "Simeon" also in the New Testament designates one of those in Jesus' ancestry (Lu.3:30), also the person who pronounced a blessing and prophesied about the infant Jesus (Lu.2:25, 34) and the name is also used of one of the New Testament prophets (Ac. 13:1). The significance of this Semitic form **"Simeon"** has been used as evidence both supporting Petrine authorship on the one hand, and of pseudonymity on the other. The former seems more probable, as it would be exceedingly crude and clumsy for the pseudonymist to choose a self-designation so different from that of First Peter, while, in addition, the form **"Simeon"** never occurs in pseudo-Petrine literature of the second century.[2] The name **"Simeon"** tends to support rather than deny Petrine authorship.

"Peter" was that name given by Christ to Peter after his confession at Caesarea Philippi of Jesus as "the Christ, the Son of the living God" (Mt. 16:16), just as Simeon represents the name given of his entry to the Old Covenant at birth. **"Peter"**, the Greek form, recalls the Aramaic Cephas, meaning a 'rock': "Blessed are you, Simon Bar-Jonah! For flesh and blood has not revealed this to you, but my Father who is in heaven. And I tell you, you are Peter, and on this rock I will build my church, and the gates of hell shall not prevail against it. I will give you the keys of the kingdom of heaven, and whatever you bind on earth shall be bound in heaven, and whatever you loose on earth shall be loosed in heaven" (Mt. 16:17-19). "Peter" emphasizes markedly Peter's New Covenant name.

---

[2]   M. Green, *2 Peter and Jude*, p.68.

Despite Peter's shaky start at the outset leading eventually to his denial of Jesus, his subsequent restoration heralded great developments in his life. Luke's account shows how the first half of Acts is dominated by Peter's prominence: the evangelization of Jerusalem, the inclusion of the Samaritans within Christ's Kingdom, the admission of Gentiles to the faith and that settlement ushering Gentile believers into the Church debated and decided at the Jerusalem Council (Acts Chapters 1-15). Recognized as "an apostle to the Jews" (Ga. 2:7, 8^{NIV}) just as Paul to the Gentiles, Peter is also involved in the evangelization of Corinth, Pontus-Bithynia, and Antioch and, by the time of writing First Peter, he is resident at "Babylon", which is probably a reference to Rome (cf. Ga. 2:7, 8; 1 Co. 1:12; 1 Pe. 1:1; Ga. 2:11-14; 1 Pe.5:13). The later story of Peter's life is certainly impressive.

The combination **"Simeon Peter"** or "Simon Peter" could well be significant. **"Simon Peter"** is a repeated form in the Gospels and Acts occurring as such or with variations such as "Simon who is called Peter" (Mt. 16:16; Lu.5:8; Jn. 6:68 cf. Mk. 3:16; Ac. 10:5). This combination seems to be the form, with its Greek nuance Peter, commonly used among Gentile Christians in the early Church. Of the twenty-two occurrences in John's gospel, seventeen are in this combined format, the other five introducing Simon (1:41, 42) or categorizing his reinstatement when the name "Peter" would have been inappropriate (21:15, 16, 17). Significantly, too, it is the form of address used of Peter's visit to the Gentile home of Cornelius! "Simon who is called Peter" (Ac. 10:5, 18, 32; 11:13). There was certainly no doubt as to the person designated by **"Simeon Peter"**. The dual name recalls both an Old and a New Testament context.

Some have suggested the combination pointed to those addressed in Second Peter as being much more of a Gentile Christian audience than those Jewish Christians addressed in First Peter. These distinctions are, however, not particularly as defined as is

8

often suggested. Much more probable is the simple fact that, in a letter dealing with authentic knowledge of the faith in the light of false teachers and false teaching, this combination vividly and appropriately recalls the dynamic change which Peter's authentic encounter with the living Christ involved – the transformation from the Galilean fisherman fishing for fish to the Christian apostle fishing for men. M. Green puts it well:

> Others think, with more probability, that the double name, if significant at all, is meant to draw the reader's attention from the Jewish fisherman to the Christian apostle, from the old life to the new, from Simon, the name given him at his entry into the Old Covenant, to Peter, his distinctively Christian name.[3]

"A servant" Humility was a mark of the servant and this is here stressed by the fact that the word is not the Greek *diakonos,* the "household servant", but *doulos,* the "bond-slave". In Hebrew and particularly in Roman society the *doulos* had little or no rights at law and was, literally, in the hands of his master completely. He had no significance as to his own person but existed purely for the well-being of his overlord. However, honour and dignity were also a feature of servanthood particularly in Hebrew society. It was an honour and privilege to serve one's master. In the Old Testament, prominent men who served God were called his "servants"; Abraham, Isaac and Jacob (Ex. 32:13, De. 9:27); Moses (De.34:5; Jos. 1:1-2; 1 K. 8:53, 56); Samuel (1 S. 3:9, 10) and David (1 S. 17:32; 2 S. 3:18; 7:5, 8, 19-21, 25-29). Judges, kings, and prophets were similarly described as God's "servants", especially in view of their obedience to the divine will (Jud. 2:8; Ps. 89:3; Je.26:5; Amos 3:7). In the New Testament, Paul (Ro. 1:1; Ga. 1:10; Ph. 1:1; Tit. 1:1), James (Ja.1:1) and Jude

---

[3]   M. Green, *2 Peter and Jude,* p.67.

(Jude 1) introduce themselves in their letters as *doulos* or servant of God. One aspect of the honour of servanthood, which climaxes all, is depicting the Messiah as God's perfect Servant (Is. 49:1-7). Peter was not only expressing his abject humility in service to God in addressing his readers, as a **"servant of Jesus Christ"** he was also stressing his authority and calling for their attention, since he wrote to them as a servant of the Lord, as **servant** had also this context of honour. That same attention continues to be the implication of Peter's words to believers today.

"Apostle" Apostle, *apostolos,* derives from the Greek *apostellein* "to send". It connoted an official commissioning and was used in secular Greek for the sending of a naval fleet or the directing of an army on a particular expedition. In the Old Testament, some of the great leaders were personally commissioned or sent by God to accomplish their tasks: Moses (Ex. 3:10), Gideon (Jud. 6:14), Isaiah (Is. 6:8), Jeremiah (Je.1:7) and Ezekiel (Ez. 2:3). In each of these cases, significantly, the verb "send" is employed. They are commissioned for the task in hand by God himself.

In the New Testament, **"apostle"** can have a more general term of reference describing messengers, delegates, and missionaries, leading Christian workers. In this broad sense, for example, Barnabas, Silas, Titus, Timothy, Epaphroditus, are described as apostles (Ac. 14:14; 1Th. 1:1; 2:6, Ph. 2:25). Such workers are messengers or apostles (Greek) to the churches (2 Co. 8:23).

"Apostle" is, however, used in a much more restricted and technical sense in the New Testament of those specifically appointed by Christ to bear witness to his life and resurrection and to lead the church authoritatively. Jesus appoints the Twelve, who are designated apostles, among whom prominently is Peter (Mt. 10:1-4; cf. Mk. 3:13-19; Lu. 6:12-16). The replacement for Judas was significantly described as "one of the men who have accompanied us during all

10

the time that the Lord Jesus went in and out among us, beginning from the baptism of John until the day when he was taken up from us – one of these men must become with us a witness to his resurrection" (Ac. 1:21-22). Matthias was chosen by lot, so that, by implication, he was divinely appointed: "to take the place in this ministry and apostleship from which Judas turned aside to go to his own place" (Ac. 1:25). Merely to have seen the risen Jesus was not sufficient but specific appointment by Jesus to the office was necessary. More than five hundred brothers who saw the risen Christ are not called "apostles" (1 Co. 15:6). Paul claims to be an apostle on account of his extraordinary commission by the risen Christ on the Damascus Road, an appearance described as to "one untimely born" (1 Co. 15:8). Paul substantiates his claim to apostleship over against false apostles who also claimed to be numbered among this selected band (2 Co. 11:1-15). As with "servant", the apex of apostolate is epitomized by Christ himself: "Jesus, the apostle and high priest of our confession" (He.3:1).

The New Testament leaves us in little doubt as to this special and restricted category of the office of **"apostle"** in the church. It also becomes clear, on this Old Testament background, why Paul describes the church as "built on the foundation of the apostles and prophets, Christ Jesus himself being the cornerstone" (Ep. 2:20). **"Apostle,"** is, then, in this restricted sense an extraordinary office, appointed by Christ to bear confirmatory testimony to his life, death and resurrection and to direct the church by his commissioned authority. As such, we might rightly speak of today's church as apostolic but, at the same time, deny the existence of present-day apostles within the church in this restricted sense.

The combination of **"servant and apostle of Jesus Christ"** is not without significance too. When Christ washed his disciples' feet he significantly said: "Truly, truly, I say to you, a servant *(doulos)* is not greater than his master, nor is a messenger *(apostolos)* greater than the one who sent him" (Jn. 13:16). Calvin admirably sums up the dual yet diverse authority of this combination and prepares us to listen to Peter's words as the living and abiding word of God, when he comments:

> Why he called himself the *servant and an apostle* of Jesus Christ, we have elsewhere stated, even because no one is to be heard in the Church, except he speaks as from the mouth of Christ. But the word *servant* has a more general meaning, because it includes all the ministers of Christ, who sustain any public office in the Church. There was in the apostleship a higher rank of honour. He then intimates, that he was not one from the rank of ministers, but was made by the Lord an apostle, and therefore superior to them.[4]

APPLICATION

In today's postmodernism, when everything is relative and nothing absolute, there is the tendency for the church to think in the same way. Doctrine is deprecated in principle and anything that smacks of definitive truth is frowned upon. It is significant, then, in a letter that deals primarily with true and false knowledge of God, as Second Peter does, that we find such an authoritative introduction from Peter at the very outset. It is noteworthy also that, in what was probably Paul's final letter, Second Timothy, the same authoritative greeting opens the letter and continues throughout in emphasizing the knowledge of God evident in Scripture as fundamental, defined, and absolute. Authority stands clearly in this introduction.

The doctrine of regeneration is one authoritative note struck at

---

4   J. Calvin, *Commentaries on II Peter*, p.366.

the very outset by Peter in this second letter. The name which alerts our attention at the very start is two-fold – Simeon Peter. "Simeon" recalls his place from birth largely formal, as it would seem, within the Old Covenant. It is the name of a Jew fishing for fish and plying his trade in his own strength. "Peter" marks that dramatic change as the New Covenant in Christ bursts into his life and portrays a new man fishing for men and that, in the event, with notable success. This combined name suggests the progression of Jewish fisherman to Christian apostle. And it does so truly and definitely. It recalls not only the divine call, sovereign conversion but also the indifferent beginning and yet glorious finale of the man, now near the end of his life. The name beckons us to listen to what he says, because not only has he met Christ but has lived with Christ from start to finish. The name Simeon Peter, which speaks of regeneration, makes absolute demands on our attention in this postmodern world, for it is down to earth, defined, and real.

The doctrine of revelation, too, comes at the very outset of Second Peter. Peter is a servant and apostle of Jesus Christ. Not only his name but also the nature of his person is involved. Personal humility has now replaced early arrogance, for Jesus' words about his being "old" (Jn. 21:18) have now become a reality. There is, however, more to his being a servant than that. There is the honour of Jesus Christ, whom he served. Peter takes his place unashamedly amid all the great servants: Abraham, Moses, David, Isaiah, Paul, Barnabas, Silas – an innumerable host – who all obeyed and that gladly. But more, Peter is an apostle, "an apostle to the Jews" (Ga. 2:8 NIV). He is sent specifically to his fellow-countrymen at the commission of Jesus himself. Peter is to be heard not simply because of his name but because of his nature, neither of which he derived from himself but from Jesus Christ. Peter is to be heard, too, by a postmodern world and a questioning church because he is "Simeon Peter, a servant and apostle of Jesus Christ". Christopher Green puts it exceedingly well:

The reason for Peter's importance and authority today lies not in his intellect or personality, but in the one who sent Peter to us as an apostle, the one of whom he is now a servant, Jesus Christ.[5]

We need to listen to Simon Peter and learn from him as well, today, as a church. The authority of Peter the apostle immediately confronts us with genuine regeneration and authentic revelation. It is a fitting introduction to the true knowledge of God portrayed in Chapter 1 of Second Peter.

---

[5]   D. Lucas & C. Green, *The Message Of 2 Peter & Jude*, p.33.

Chapter 2

READERS

2 PETER 1:1^B

INTRODUCTION

As in letters of the day, after the author is named, the readers are designated. Originally, the 'Catholic Epistles' was a term used to describe the Epistles of James, First and Second Peter, the Epistles of John and Jude, because, apart from Second and Third John, they were not specifically addressed to a local congregation or to an individual but "generally" to a wider group of Christians. Later, the term 'Catholic Epistles' was used of all letters accepted within the New Testament canon.

This original definition seems a fair one. Paul's letters were largely directed quite specifically to local churches or stated individuals, with the exception, perhaps of Ephesians which has been taken by some as a 'circular letter' for distribution among a number of congregations as well as that at Ephesus. The designation of readers in Second Peter is noticeably vague so far as geographical area or definition of addressees is concerned: "To those who have obtained a faith of equal standing with ours by the righteousness of our God and Saviour Jesus Christ" (2 Pe.1:1ᵇ). This stands in stark contrast with the geographical definition of those believers addressed in First Peter. Are there any other hints in Second Peter as to the definition of the readers? It would seem so. The author claims to have personal knowledge of his readers. He writes as a witness of the Transfiguration who had instructed his readers in "the power and coming of our Lord Jesus Christ" (1:16). He declaims false teachers apparently active in the present among his readership and also warns his readers against them in the future (2:1f). He has already written to them previously and describes this present as his "second letter", accepting the traditional understanding of this description (3:1). So apparently, he has a definite readership in view. At the same time, as with many New Testament letters, many of his remarks are general and could apply to others than to his immediate addressees, and of course, as to subsequent generations of believers including ourselves. If as some, including the present writer, accept that Peter is the author and that Second Peter is his "second letter" of which First Peter is the first, then the problem largely resolves itself and the addressees are probably the same as in First Peter. The fact that the author quotes from the Old Testament in First Peter and, merely alludes to it in Second Peter is no real problem, for it seems reasonable to assume that the readership in both letters was a mixture of Jewish and Gentile Christians rather than exclusively Jewish or Gentile believers.

However, even if the question of readership of Second Peter remains "open", it makes little practical difference to the burden of Christian teaching here. Just as in First Peter, readers are 'spiritually' defined: "elect exiles of the dispersion in Pontus, Galatia, Cappadocia, Asia, and Bithynia, according to the foreknowledge of God the Father, in the sanctification of the Spirit, for obedience to

Jesus Christ and for sprinkling with his blood" (1 Pe.1:1, 2), this also is the case in Second Peter.

When Peter writes: "To those who have obtained a faith of equal standing with ours by the righteousness of our God and Saviour Jesus Christ" (2 Pe.1:1^b), he is flagging up the most important feature about his readers. Peter is setting out his stall as he writes to them of the true knowledge of God and introducing key themes in the letter which he will develop: "faith", "righteousness", "our God and Saviour Jesus Christ". For it is in the standing of that faith, the nature of that righteousness and the definition of that God and Saviour that his readers will discover or, indeed, rediscover the foundation of true knowledge of God. That is infinitely more important than where they are or to whom or to what area he writes. A grasp of readership at this level confirms the apostolic authorship and enhances the authority of the letter as the living and abiding word of God.

EXPOSITION

READERS

"To those who have obtained a faith of equal standing with ours by the righteousness of our God and Saviour Jesus Christ" (1:1^b).

FAITH

"Faith", *pistis*, is the first of those themes that Peter will develop in his letter relating to true knowledge of God. **"To those who have obtained a faith"**. Faith is clearly portrayed as a gift of God to the believer. Peter introduces his first letter majoring on God's part in salvation – divine choice and election. In his second letter, he begins by stressing man's response in faith. Yet here also faith is set in a divine context. God's sovereignty and man's responsibility are essential elements in salvation. **"Obtained"** is *lachousin*. The verb is rare in the New Testament, a further usage being at John 19:24. It means, "to obtain by lot". Roman soldiers cast lots for Jesus' clothing (Jn. 19:24). Similar in thought but not in language, Zechariah, the father of John the Baptist, obtained by lot the task of offering incense in the temple (Lu. 1:9) and Judas had been allotted to share the apostolic ministry, just as Matthias was chosen by lot to replace him as exemplifying divine direction (Ac. 1:17, 21-26): "To obtain by lot" implies ultimately that God did the choosing. In the secular world, the verb also had a political context. Government officials were "of persons who have a post assigned to them by lot"[6]. It was an appointment "from above". H. Hanse comments: "In this sentence the point of *lagchanein* is that faith has come to them from God with no co-operation on their part".[7] The implication is clear. Faith is received from God as a divine gift. The responsibility is ours to receive, the initiative God's to give. Faith is sovereignly given.

"Of equal standing with ours" Faith is a gift common to all believers. *isotimon* is perhaps better translated as "equal standing" rather than "as precious as". "Compounds of *timē* 'invariably borrow their meaning from *timē*, *honour*, and not from *timē* in the sense of price'".[8] The former translation stresses rightly the standing of the faith rather than the latter, which majors on its value. The term is found only here in the New Testament, though well-known from other Greek literature. It is used as a political word implying equal

---

6   H.G. Liddell and R. Scott, *Greek-English Lexicon,* ninth edition, revised by H.S.Jones and R. McKenzie (Oxford: Oxford University Press, 1940) p1022 cf. Acts 1:17 cited by D. Lucas and C. Green, *The Message Of 2 Peter & Jude,* p34.

7   H. Hanse, *lagchanō, Theological Dictionary Of The New Testament,* 4.2. cited by T.R. Schreiner, *1, 2 Peter, Jude* p 285 footnote 7.

8   J.B. Mayor, *The Epistles of Jude and II Peter,* Grand Rapids: Baker [1901], 1979), p80 quoting Field cited in Peter H. Davids, *The Letters Of 2 Peter And Jude,* p161 footnote 8.

status or rank in civil life. Josephus specifically uses the term to refer to civic equality.[9]

It is important to assess to whom does this equal standing refer. It could, simply, be a general statement implying the equality of all believers having a common faith, similar to Paul's claim that in Christ is neither Jew nor Greek, slave nor free, male nor female (cf. Ga. 3:28). But something more specific seems to be implied here. It could refer to Gentile believers being on exactly the same standing, in terms of faith as Jewish believers. J.N.D. Kelly notes as a similar expression 'the same gift' *(isēn dōrean)* upon the Gentiles 'as upon us' at Acts 11:17, where Peter is amazed at events taking place in Cornelius' home.[10] Certainly, the acceptance of Gentiles as of equal standing with Jews as Christians was a mighty leap for the early church (cf. Ac. 10:1-48; Ep. 2:11-13). However, there is little mention of Jewish/Gentile conflict in Second Peter and the main controversy of that issue might well have been in the past. More probably, the contrast implicit in **"ours"** is between Peter the apostle and the believers to whom he is writing. He has just stressed his apostleship, refers clearly to this contrast when he mentions the Transfiguration (1:16-21) and reflects strongly on this in a context where contemplating his own death, he wants to assure his readers of these abiding truths after he has died (1:12-15). Nor is this contrast limited to this immediate context but has implications for us today in our present experience as believers. We look back to the apostles in their unique situation and function, but are assured that in terms of our faith there is absolute equality with them. Peter was here probably preparing his readers not to feel in the least inadequate, inferior or under-confident as they faced the threat of false apostles

9   Josephus, *(Antiquities* 12. 119) referred to by T.R. Schreiner, *1, 2 Peter, Jude,* p285.

10   J.N.D. Kelly, *A Commentary On The Epistles Of Peter and Of Jude,* pp296-297.

both in the present or in the future. They had a faith "of equal standing" with the very apostles.

"A faith" Faith is a subjective action based on objective facts. Commentators are divided as to whether "faith" here means an objective body of doctrine or that trust in the gospel exercised personally and subjectively. Those who support an objective faith here quote Jude 3: "Beloved, although I was very eager to write to you about our common salvation, I found it necessary to write appealing to you to contend for the faith that was once for all delivered to the saints" together with Paul's usage frequently in his Pastoral Letters of "the faith" as a deposit or body of teaching (cf. 2 Ti.1:13, 14). However, in contrast to both Jude 3 and many of Paul's references particularly in the Pastorals, Peter here does not use the definite article, so personal trust in the sense of subjective faith seems the more appropriate understanding. Furthermore, this subjective aspect of faith fits more easily with the concept of a faith **"of equal standing"** and Paul frequently uses this subjective sense when speaking about "faith". That is not to say that there is no objective side to faith. Indeed, there is, and the idea of faith as personal trust being mutually exclusive of faith in terms of a body of doctrine is something alien to the New Testament, at least as far as genuine faith is concerned. The subjective personal action involved in saving faith is based on the objective facts of faith as represented in the biblical doctrines of the gospel. M. Green puts it well when he writes:

> The *faith* in question appears to be, *pace* Boobyer, not the faith as a body of doctrine, which would scarely make sense in the context, but the faith or trust which brings a man salvation as he grasps the proffered hand of God.[11]

---

[11]   M. Green, *2 Peter and Jude*, p68.

There is nothing inconsistent here with "the faith" conceived as a body of doctrine, as long as it is not perceived as requiring merely barren intellectual assent devoid of personal will and individual commitment. Faith like grace is God's sovereign gift to be received and appropriated.

RIGHTEOUSNESS

"By the righteousness" **"Righteousness"**, *dikaiosunē*, is a second major theme, which Peter develops in his letter relating to true knowledge of God. Many take **"by the righteousness"** as qualifying the preceding **"of equal standing"** and attribute to God's righteousness the equality of privilege among believers of which Peter writes. This means taking this **"righteousness"** as God's justice and fairness not in the more accepted sense of God's making right that which is wrong. M. Green writes:

> Peter's use of *righteousness (dikaiosunē)* has none of the forensic overtones which we find in Paul. As in 1 Peter (2:24, 3:12, 14, 18; 4:18), so in this Epistle (2:5, 7-8, 21, 3:13) the word has the ethical associations which we find given to it in the Old Testament; here it means the fairness, the justice of God.[12]

However, **"by the righteousness"** can alternatively be linked with **"obtained"** and so attribute to God's righteousness the righting of the wrong of sin through our God and Saviour Jesus Christ. This maintains a forensic sense of legal imputation similar to Paul and is the view we hold for the following reasons:

1. The concept of **"righteousness"** demands it. Consistently, in both Old and New Testament God's righteousness carries with it the implication of making right what is wrong and is not simply an attribute of God's character in terms of

---

12   M. Green, *2 Peter and Jude*, p68.

justice. Many of the references to "righteousness" quoted in both letters have forensic and legal implications even within context.

2. The syntax suggests it. The phrase **"by the righteousness"** is obviously instrumental and it seems much more probable to be instrumental to the creation of faith itself rather than simply the equality of faith among believers.

3. The context requires it. The entire context is one of grace rather than justice or fairness. Faith is *obtained* by lot (v1[b]). *Grace* along with peace is to be multiplied to Peter's readers (v2). Both all things that pertain to life and godliness together with those precious and very great promises mentioned are *granted* to believers (vv3, 4). Thomas R. Schreiner significantly comments: "The emphasis on God's grace and gift in the context (cf1:3-4) suggests that fairness is not the most natural meaning in context. The gift of faith given by God is not understood in the New Testament to be "fair" but entirely of grace. Hence, God's righteousness here does not denote his fairness but his saving righteousness".[13]

4. The Old Testament predicates it. In the Old Testament, God's righteousness is synonymous with his "salvation" and, hence, a communicable attribute of God to the believer, (Pss. 22:31; 31:1; 35:24, 28; 40:10; Is. 42:6; 45:8, 13; 51:5-8; Mi. 6:5; 7:9).

5. The uniqueness of the expression implies it. This is the only place in the New Testament where we read of the **"righteousness of . . . Jesus Christ"**. Everywhere else it is attributed to God[14] It is unlikely that such an affirmation

---

13   T.R. Schreiner *1, 2 Peter, Jude*, p286.

14   D. J. Moo *2 Peter, Jude*, p35.

of Jesus' divinity and saviourhood would simply relate to righteousness as justice or fairness alone.

6. The later reference to Paul's letters (3:15, 16) may well imply that Peter not only knows but also thoroughly accepts as his own what has been described as Paul's forensic view of righteousness.

Calvin sums it up succinctly:

> For the efficient cause of faith is called God's righteousness for this reason, because no one is capable of conferring it on himself. So the righteousness that is to be understood, is not that which remains in God, but that which he imparts to men, as in Rom. iii. 22. Besides, he ascribes this righteousness in common to God and to Christ, because it flows from God, and through Christ it flows down to us.[15]

JESUS, GOD AND SAVIOUR

"Of our God and Saviour Jesus Christ" The third theme Peter will share with his readers in this letter is that of the person and work of Christ. This is introduced here by this fulsome ascription of divinity and saviourhood to Christ. There are a number of places where these ascriptive titles build up through his letter painting a rich picture of Jesus' person and work (1:1, 2, 8, 11, 14, 16; 2:1, 20; 3:2, 18). This is the first and it designates Jesus as both God and Saviour.

Jesus is God. The form of this statement is intriguingly significant. It literally reads: "of the God our and saviour Jesus Christ", *tou theou hēmōn kai sōtēros Iēsou Christou.* There is difference

---

[15]   J. Calvin *Commentaries on II Peter*, pp366 – 367.

of opinion as to whether Peter is here distinguishing God from Jesus or saying that Jesus is God. Hence, an alternative translation to that above is: "of God and our Saviour Jesus Christ". The reading **"of our God and Saviour Jesus Christ"**, implying that Peter is saying, in effect, that Jesus is God, is preferable on the following grounds: Grammatically in Greek when one definite article connects two nouns of the same case, it relates to the same person. Had Peter wanted to distinguish Christ from the Father he would have inserted an article before the noun **"Saviour"**. In the other four instances where "Lord and Saviour" occur in the letter, it refers in every case to the same person, Jesus (1:11; 2:20; 3:2, 18). One of the main reasons for rejecting this reading has been the claim that the New Testament rarely explicitly calls Jesus God. To a degree this may be so, perhaps to guard against ditheism. Yet quite clearly there are a number of instances where Jesus is called God explicitly or the implications of statements are such that it is beyond reasonable doubt but that this is the case. (Jn. 1:1, 18; 20:28; Ro. 9:5; Tit. 2:13; He. 1:8 cf. Col. 2:9). 2 Peter 1:1, on this interpretation, could join these august ranks. By way of confirmation, the doxology of 2 Peter 3:18 is in the same form with the difference that there, "Lord" takes the place of **"God"**, so that the format may be seen as *inclusio,* that is, Peter starts and finishes his letter with the affirmation of Jesus' deity. It would also be most unlikely that Peter is using **"God"** merely in the general and weak sense as of pagan deities, since that would be contrary to the whole spirit of his claims in the letter. For Peter, as for us, our great affirmation is the deity of Christ.

Jesus is Saviour. **"Saviour"** *sōtēr* was used of pagan gods and of the emperor within the Caesar cult. However, there is little evidence in the letter that Peter is combating either cultic deities, even allowing for incipient Gnosticism, or Caesar worship. It is rather the false teachers who are the focus of his attention. On the other hand, saviour and salvation are integrated biblical themes in both testaments. Saviour is one of the great names for God in the

Old Testament. While salvation in both testaments is seen both individually and corporately as deliverance or rescue from great human disasters such as illness, calamities in nature or defeat in battle, it also connotes rescue from sin and deliverance from God's judgement. God in the Old Testament is known by his character as Saviour, indeed exclusive Saviour and Saviour is used as a divine title (Ps 106:21; Is. 43:3, 11; 60:16) reaching its climax in the Suffering Servant of Isaiah (45:15, 21; 49:26). **"Saviour"** occurs twenty-four times in the New Testament, apart from other references to salvation. Its usage is significant. It continues the Old Testament title of God. The preponderance of references to Jesus as Saviour, though also referred to in the Gospels, Acts and letters, come in the later books like the Pastorals and Second Peter. It is, in fact, in Second Peter where Saviour occurs plentifully. It is significant here, as in the Pastorals also that Jesus is described as both God and Saviour.

Peter mentions Jesus as Saviour five times in his second letter (1:1, 11; 2:20; 3:2, 18) but not at all in his first letter. Apart from 1:1, in each of the other four, there is the combined title "Lord and Saviour". It is highly probable that the title "Lord" is used of Christ's divinity in these instances, even though it can simply mean ruler or master. Consequently, in this dual title "Saviour and Lord", we have again a stress on Christ's deity.

Peter relates the saviourhood of Christ in his letter to his readers in a number of important ways. The righteousness of their Saviour affords them saving faith on a standing equal to the apostles (1:1). The kingdom of their Saviour awaits their glorious entry at the end of the day as mature believers (1:11). The knowledge of their Saviour provides escape from the defilement of the world and participation in divine promises and in a divine nature (2:20 cf. 1:4). The commandment of their Saviour stimulates them to wholesome thinking as they recall it on the journey of faith and growth in grace, and knowledge of their Saviour gives them personal stability as believers and glorifies their Lord and Saviour as well (3:2,18). There could be little else they would either want or need from Jesus their God and Saviour, nor ourselves either.

Peter, then, sets out his stall in anticipation of his readers enjoying true knowledge of God – the standing of faith, the nature of righteousness and the definition of Jesus as God and Saviour. What a rich preview of things to come.

APPLICATION

Righteousness stands out clearly in this resumé of themes toward the true knowledge of God, with which Peter introduces his second letter. This is the usual slot, at the beginning of letters of the day, for address to readers and Peter goes directly to the spiritual substance of his readers' needs, just as in First Peter, Peter is describing his readers' spiritual condition (cf. 1Pe.1:1, 2). Amid a confusing world of false teaching, which they encountered, they needed a firm foundation to guide them in the direction of true teaching, to keep them there and to stimulate their growth positively as over against the negative misrepresentations, which would undermine their faith. Our situation in postmodern church-life of the twenty-first century is little different. Peter, then, in both letters goes directly to his readers' spiritual standing and in due course accommodates this to their needs under circumstances of trials and of false teaching.

We must be careful on two scores, in particular, in considering Peter's teaching on righteousness. We must not import into Peter's words about righteousness ideas which would remove his distinctive emphasis, as some fear might be done with forensic views from Paul's presentation. On the other hand, we must preserve in expounding Peter's words on righteousness the biblical emphases germane to righteousness as depicted throughout Scripture.

From October 6, 1946, to March 30, 1947 Dr D.M. Lloyd-Jones preached twenty-five sermons on Second Peter at Westminster Chapel, London. Though preached in post-war Britain amid difficult years, they were the first extensive series of sermons in any one book of Scripture undertaken by him. His preaching, arising from the magisterial importance of the doctrine of justification at the Reformation and subsequently, comes to us from then till now with equal significance. The recent exploration into this great doctrine of justification, if biblically orientated, can do nothing but good to the church:

> Not only that, Peter becomes still more specific – 'You have obtained like precious faith with us through the righteousness of God and our Saviour Jesus Christ'. Now that is Peter's way of putting in a phrase the great doctrine of justification by faith which is expounded so wondrously by the apostle Paul in the Epistle to the Romans. That is the essence of the Gospel. The message is, that there is only one way whereby man can be right, or righteous, in the sight of God; and that is by the righteousness that is given to us in Christ.[16]

The importance of that righteousness is that it provides for us a faith, which we obtain from God as a gift, a faith of equal standing with the apostles, that this righteousness is not only an attribute of Almighty God but a communicable attribute that is offered to us in the gospel and that this righteousness comes to us from Jesus Christ who is God and Saviour. What a blessing to any reader of Second Peter, whether of Peter's day or ours. What a foundation for a true knowledge of God.

---

[16]   D.M. Lloyd-Jones, *Expository Sermons on 2Peter*, p.8.

Chapter 3

TRUE KNOWLEDGE

GREETINGS

2 PETER 1:2

INTRODUCTION

The general salutation of Second Peter, as in other New Testament letters follows the pattern of letters of the day: Writer to the readers, greetings. The greetings, in particular, follows a similar format. For Greek letters of the day, the typical opening address was "Greetings" *chairein*, as in James 1:1. It expresses good wishes and happiness to the reader, somewhat like our modern "cheers". In Hebrew letters, the usual salutation was "peace" *shalom*, a request that the reader might know well-being, health, happiness and prosperity in daily life.

This greeting is "Christianized" in Second Peter in two ways, the first of which is common to many New Testament letters. First, the secular tone is transformed by the two biblical terms "grace" *charis* and "peace" *eirēnē* with Greek and Hebrew cultures respectively in view. Secondly, the verb "multiplied" *plēthuntheiē* is added to intensify and enlarge the Christian sentiments of writer to

29

readers. Peter is urgent to express wishes for spiritual well-being in abundance. Hence, the form, initially, is the same in both First and Second Peter: "May grace and peace be multiplied to you."

In Second Peter, however, the greeting is further extended by the words: "in the knowledge of God and of Jesus our Lord". This seems to have reference particularly to the subject matter of this second letter of Peter, namely, the knowledge of God. Peter, again, is setting out his stall. He has already mentioned "faith", "righteousness" and "our God and Saviour Jesus Christ" (1:1ᵇ). Now, he adds "the knowledge of God and of Jesus our Lord" to the list. Indeed, he will major on this "knowledge" in his letter. This knowledge is not just academic and factual, though it includes those aspects, but personal and relational as well, the knowledge that leads to a relationship with a person, that is, God. It is knowledge both of head and heart, as it were. This is the keynote of Second Peter.

Peter develops this theme throughout the letter. He writes of the means of obtaining this relationship through knowledge (1:3), the nature of its growth (1:8), the possibility of rejecting it (2:20, 21) and the overriding demands of its priority (3:18). Peter starts and finishes his letter on this note (1:2 cf. 3:18). It is his storyline and main message. Here, at 1:2 in his greeting to his readers, he lays the foundation. Knowledge of God in terms of a personal relationship with God is the essence of Peter's second letter.

EXPOSITION

> **"May grace and peace be multiplied to you in the knowledge of God and of Jesus our Lord" (1:2).**

"Grace and peace" "Grace" *charis*, which replaces the usual greeting of best wishes introducing Greek letters, connotes the condescending favour of a superior toward an inferior and, in Scripture, is used of God's approach to man. Grace is God's undeserved favour reaching down as a gift to man. In the Old Testament, it was fundamental to survival as far as Noah and Moses were concerned (Ge. 6:8; Ex. 33:13). In the New Testament, God's grace rests upon Jesus as a growing boy and upon the infant church, as it developed in faith and fellowship (Lu. 2:40; Ac. 4:33). **"Grace"** becomes virtually a synonym for salvation as the means whereby God blesses mankind – a means not of works but of grace (Ep. 2:8-10). Peter longs that his readers may enjoy this saving grace.

"Peace" *eirēnē* replaces the typical *shalom* of Jewish address, a longing for well-being in terms of health and prosperity. Even in the Old Testament, **"peace"** exceeds this human aspiration: "Great peace have those who love your law; nothing can make them stumble. I hope for your salvation, O Lord, and I do your commandments" (Ps 119:165, 166). In the New Testament, **"peace"** like grace, is axiomatic of salvation. God's **"peace"** follows justification, surpasses all understanding and characterizes the salvation that Christ is, brings and proclaims (Ro. 5:1; Ph. 4:7; Ep. 2:14-18). Peter prays this peace upon his readers. **"Peace"** in the New Testament often characterizes the cessation of war-like activities and in the Old Testament emphasizes a continuing state of well-being.

"Be multiplied to you" Greetings which in Greek and Hebrew letters would be separately expressed are combined here by Peter. The significance of this is not only that the terms are **"grace"** and **"peace"**, full of biblical import, but, now that Gentiles are admitted to the body of Christ on an equal standing with Jews, the combined linguistic and cultural formula reflects their oneness in Christ. They are all one in Christ and so Peter wishes for them, whether Greek or Jew, these fulsome blessings of God in Christ.

This fulsome nature continues in the expression **"multiplied"**, *plēthuntheiē*. The passive voice of this verb, appearing in the form of a wish, emphasizes both the depth and extent of Peter's wishes for his readers. Precisely the same expression "multiplied" is listed in First Peter. Thus, continuing longings motivate Peter as he writes. John McArthur puts it well:

> **Grace** *(charis)* is God's free, unmerited favor toward sinners, which grants those who believe the gospel complete forgiveness forever through the Lord Jesus Christ (Rom. 3:24; Eph. 1:7; Titus 3:7). **Peace** *(eirēnē)* with God and from Him in all life's circumstances is the effect of grace (Eph. 2:14-15; Col. 1:20), flowing out of the forgiveness God has given to all the elect (cf. Ps. 85:8; Isa. 26:12; 2 Thess. 3:16). 'Grace upon grace' (John 1:16) is an expression that defines the boundless flow of divine favor, while peace comes with such fullness that it is divine and beyond human understanding (John 14:27; Phil. 4:7). Believers receive surpassing **grace** for every sin (Ps. 84:11; Acts 4:33; 2 Cor. 9:8; 12:9; Heb. 4:16) and abundant **peace** for every trial (John 14:27; 16:33)".[17]

KNOWLEDGE

"In the knowledge" The additional words referring to knowledge occur only in Second Peter as compared with First Peter, and are probably added, as we have already noted, because knowledge forms the main subject of Peter's second letter. **"Knowledge"** here at 1:2 is the compound form *epignōsis*. Peter uses both the simple and compound forms in both verb and noun in developing the theme of knowledge in his letter. The simple verb as a participle appears at 1:20 and 3:3, the compound verb at 2:21 (twice); the simple noun at

---

[17]   John MacArthur, *2 Peter & Jude*, p24.

1:5, 6, and the compound noun at 1:2, 3, 8; 2:20. The simple verb is *ginōskō,* the compound verb is *epiginōskō.* The simple noun is *gnōsis,* the compound noun *epignōsis.* The simple form is converted to the compound by the addition of the prepositional prefix *epi,* (meaning in English, 'upon'), which some maintain intensifies the meaning, that is, to 'know fully', a 'full knowledge'.

As far as the meaning of "knowledge" in the Bible is concerned, there are two main aspects: knowledge of facts, that is, cognitive knowledge and knowledge of persons, that is, relational knowledge. The two are not mutually exclusive, though are used in contexts where one sense or other is clearly predominant. Throughout the Bible however, there is a tendency to prioritize the latter, without necessarily excluding the former.

In the Old Testament, we find the idea of knowledge (Hebrew *yadah)* used in a personal and relational way of man and God. Knowing was used of the intimate sexual relationship between Adam and Eve (Ge. 4:1). Eli's sons were wicked men; they did not know the Lord (1 S. 2:12). Samuel, by way of contrast, did not yet know the Lord. The word of the Lord had not yet been revealed to him (1 S. 3:7). Jeremiah foretold a time when a man would no longer teach his neighbour saying 'Know the Lord', for they would all know God from the least of them to the greatest, for God would forgive their wickedness and remember their sins no more (Je. 31:34). This knowledge was personal, relational and, certainly in the case of the last three references, also was synonymous with revelation from God leading to a relationship with God.

The on-going story of "knowledge" in the New Testament is similar. In his teaching, Jesus makes it clear that no one knows the Son but the Father, no one knows the Father but the Son and those to whom the Son chooses to reveal him (Mt. 11:27). In prayer, Jesus defines eternal life as knowing God as the only true God and

Jesus Christ whom God has sent and recalls the way in which he communicates this knowledge to his disciples – he gave them words God had given him; they accepted these words, knew for a certainty that Jesus had come from God and believed that God had sent him (Jn. 17:3, 8). Not only the relational nature of the knowledge is clear, but also the revelatory means by which the knowledge was communicated, namely, Scripture, words from God, is evident.

Peter, even in the early insecure days of his faith, was learning this: To whom else could he and his friends go but to Jesus, for Jesus had the words of eternal life – they believed and knew, and obviously because of these words, that Jesus was the Holy One of God (Jn. 6:68, 69). John reflects the same perspective: that Christians know that they have come to know Jesus Christ, if they obey his commands. To say that they know him and not to do what he commands is to be a liar, indeed, devoid of the truth. Christians also have an anointing from the Holy One and all know the truth (1 Jn. 2:3, 4, 20). Paul is equally and passionately adamant about the nature of this knowledge: he assures Philippian believers that he considers everything a loss compared to the surpassing greatness of knowing Christ Jesus his Lord. Indeed, he wants to know Christ at every level of experienced relationship possible (Ph. 3:8, 10). He also longs that those to whom he writes at Ephesus, or wherever, might know Christ better (Ep. 1:17). In his second letter to Timothy, the same passion, assurance and wisdom, and for the same reasons, pervade: "That is why I am suffering as I am. Yet I am not ashamed, because I know whom I have believed, and am convinced that he is able to guard what I have entrusted to him for that day" (2 Ti.1:12^{NIV}).

It was not that Peter, John and Paul were on some esoteric trip of mystically communicated "knowledge" coming to them as initiates into a cultic sect. They all affirm, within context and elsewhere, that this knowledge is related to "the truth", based on the objective facts that Jesus has taught them. **"Knowledge"**, in this sense, both from

Old and New Testament perspectives, is predominantly personal. Based on knowing facts, it leads to a knowledge of relationship. It is relational knowledge based on word revelation.

As far as the distinction between simple and compound forms of this "knowledge" is concerned both in noun and verb (*gnōsis / epignōsis; ginōskō / epiginōskō*), as well as within Second Peter in particular and the New Testament in general, there has been much discussion. Some assessment of this debate is both necessary and relevant to our understanding here.

Some have suggested a Gnostic background with a degree of polemic implicit. Gnosticism was an early Christian heresy, which made a severe and unbiblical distinction between physical and spiritual entities and ultimately advocated belief in a dual godhead of good and evil, an extreme asceticism and a truncated version of the Scriptures interpreted to suit such views. The very language of *gnōsis* and its occurrence in later New Testament writings such as Second Peter, the Pastorals and, perhaps, exceptionally at Hebrews 10:26, led to the view that the *epi* formula in the compound form stressed true as opposed to false knowledge. However, while it is true that incipient Gnosticism may have been present before the second century, it was only in the second century that Gnosticism as a heresy really came to the fore and it is doubtful whether evidence exists that Gnosticism was an issue in any of the New Testament writings, including Second Peter.

A much more persuasive theory was that the compound formula *epi* reflected inceptive force, giving the sense of "to come to know" or "coming to knowledge of" as in conversion to Christianity, while the simple form indicated an on-going developing and maturing faith, subsequent to initial conversion. This view has certainly much to commend it. It fits in with the compound usage in 2 Peter at 1:2, 3, 8; 2:20 and at 2:21 (twice as a verb), where Peter may well be using the term in the sense of being converted or coming to faith and where the compound is regularly linked with the fulsome title of Jesus as Lord, Christ and Saviour or combinations of the same. The simple form, moreover, is used in contexts where growth in faith is implied or where instruction in faith is involved as at 1:5, 6, 16, 20; 3:3, 17-18.

However, there is also a danger in limiting simple and compound forms too severely or exclusively to these two categories. The major force of the compound prefix *epi* is to intensify the concept of the knowledge, and while the simple form is used for the development or communication of that knowledge, the compound form also explains the means of that knowledge (1:3), embraces its development (1:8) and defines its rejection (2:20). The use of the simple form in closing the letter (3:18) may not so much refer to confirmational as to relational knowledge, for the full title Lord Jesus Christ is used there. The theme of knowledge, thus, opens and concludes the letter (1:2 cf. 3:18). The closing exhortation forms a fitting climax to Peter's theme, where by now at the close of the letter, he uses *gnōsis* as a virtual synonym for *epignōsis*. "But grow in the grace and knowledge of our Lord and Saviour Jesus Christ" (2 Pe.3:18). Whatever our understanding of the term, the glorious truth of knowing him, whom to know means eternal life, pervades the letter from start to finish.

"Of God and of Jesus our Lord" These words further define **"knowledge"**. It is a knowledge both of God and of Jesus our Lord. As Jesus taught, that knowledge of the living and true God and of Jesus Christ whom God has sent, which is eternal life, only comes by means of Jesus and only to those to whom Jesus chooses to reveal God (Mt. 11:27). It is, in this sense, exclusive knowledge, knowledge of God exclusively revealed through Jesus. Both persons within the godhead are thus stressed in respect of this "knowledge".

This comports with the previous verse (1^b), where the "righteousness" of which Peter writes is specifically attributed to Jesus, thus stressing Christ's deity: "by the righteousness of our God and Saviour Jesus Christ". The distinctive emphases on both "righteousness" and "knowledge" respectively enhances the import of their combined meaning. Peter, thus, implies by this double usage that Jesus is God.

"Grace and peace", which Peter longs to be multiplied in the experience of his readers comes through or **"in the knowledge of God and of Jesus our Lord"**. That knowledge is true knowledge, it is personal and relational, but it comes by means of a knowledge that is factual and informational. The knowledge of God that leads to a relationship with God is founded on and continues by means of word-revelation.

Douglas J. Moo sums it up well with an informative caveat:

> But we must be careful not to evacuate the biblical concept of 'knowing' of all cognitive value. 'Knowing God' does mean having a warm, intimate relationship with our Creator; but it also means understanding who he is, with all its implications. Peter, we remember, is warning his readers about some heretical teachers. To avoid their errors, these Christians must not only have a 'warm and fuzzy' feeling toward God; they also need to know some specific things about him, what he has done, and what he demands of us. One of the things they need to know, Peter hints, is that Jesus is God. (v.l; see explanation above).

In our day we are rightly warned about the danger of a sterile faith, of a 'head' knowledge that never touches the heart. But we need equally to be careful of a 'heart' knowledge that never touches the head! Too many Christians *know* too little about their faith; we are therefore often unprepared to explain how our 'God' differs from the 'God' of Mormonism or of the Jehovah's Witnesses. Again and again the New Testament makes plain that our very salvation can depend on confessing truth about God and his revelation in his Son. The biblical writers demand a 'knowledge of God' that unites head and heart. We must be careful not to sacrifice the head in favor of the heart.[18]

APPLICATION

Peter writes to refute false teachers who are spreading a false knowledge of God. He combats this by defining true knowledge of God. The false teachers arise within church circles. Their teaching is alien to God's law and is driven by the philosophy of the world around them. A similar situation exists with us today. Postmodernism, with its rejection of authoritative moral structures – everyone doing what is right in his own eyes – has invaded even the church. Human opinion is valued more highly than God's word and is taken as the norm. What the Bible says is of relative importance and is to be reinterpreted in the light of twenty-first century human wisdom. Knowledge of God has not escaped this infection. We need to affirm true knowledge of God on two complementary biblical levels at the very least, if we are to make any headway against this modern insidious heresy.

True biblical knowledge of God is 'heart' knowledge. It is personal and relational. Biblical theology both Old and New

---

[18]   D.J. Moo, *2 Peter, Jude,* pp38-39.

Testament affirms that we must know God, not just know about him. Our knowledge of God must involve a relationship with God, where we hear what he says, respond to that in a meaningful way, get or come to know him on this level and continue to grow and mature in that relationship. It must be warm and personal, living and active, relational and growing.

True biblical knowledge of God is also 'head' knowledge. It must be informed, structured and educative. This is often disparaged today. Doctrine divides, it is claimed. Theology should be left to the theologians, it is said. 'Head' knowledge is academic, theoretical, and impractical and produces a barren, sterile, cold type of faith devoid of reality. This, of course, often happens. But the separating of 'heart' knowledge from 'head' knowledge misses the biblical point, which is that both aspects are involved, interrelated but also interdependent.

Our brief overview of 'knowledge' in Old and New Testaments makes this clear. The 'knowledge' that is warm, personal and relational — 'heart' knowledge arises from a 'knowledge' that is factual, informed and cognitive — 'head' knowledge. Scripture never divorces the two, because they belong together. The Westminster divines, were correct when they spoke of effectual calling or regeneration in terms of "enlightening our minds" and "renewing our wills" so as "to embrace Jesus Christ, freely offered to us in the gospel"[19]. They got their biblical theology of the knowledge of God right. So should we in today's church. Peter very early in Second Peter gets to grips with the nature of the true knowledge of God like this.

---

[19]   Westminster Shorter Catechism 31, *Westminster Confession of Faith* (Free Presbyterian Publications), pp295-296. [a]. Acts 26:18; 1 Cor. 2:10, 12; 2 Cor. 4:6; Eph. 1:17-18. [b]. Deut. 30:6; Ezk. 36:26-27; John 3:5; Titus 3:5. [c]. John 6:44-45; Acts 16:14. [d]. Isa. 45:22; Matt. 11:28-30; Rev. 22:17.

Chapter 4

SAVING

2 PETER 1:3, 4

INTRODUCTION

Peter has introduced his second letter in a way typical of letters of the day: writer, to the readers, greetings. He has also, however, set out his stall in doing this. As a writer, his name brings to the fore the doctrine of regeneration. His office as servant and apostle recalls the doctrine of revelation (v1[a]). His address to his readers emphasizes the doctrine of righteousness as an agent of salvation (v1[b]). His actual words of greeting stress the doctrine of knowledge, which leads to a personal relationship with God (v2). Peter mentions all this before starting his letter proper.

Usually, after normal greetings, letters of the day would have an exordium or word of thanks to introduce sentiments. Peter, however, goes straight to his subject: true knowledge of God. The particular aspect of that subject he first deals with is its saving nature. Peter outlines saving knowledge in three ways: its power (v3[a]), its means (vv3^b, 4^a) and its results (v4^b). He uses the same emphatic Greek term for knowledge *epignōsis* in verse 3 as he does in verse 2. It is knowledge of God at its deepest level, not just knowing about God but also knowing God personally and relationally. This lies at the very heart of the Christian doctrine of knowledge. Peter starts his letter by emphasizing these three important aspects of the saving knowledge of God:

POWER OF SAVING KNOWLEDGE	(v3^a)
MEANS OF SAVING KNOWLEDGE	(vv3^b, 4^a)
RESULTS OF SAVING KNOWLEDGE	(v4^b)

EXPOSITION

> **"His divine power has granted to us all things that pertain to life and godliness, through the knowledge of him who called us to his own glory and excellence, by which he has granted to us his precious and very great promises, so that through them you may become partakers of the divine nature, having escaped from the corruption that is in the world because of sinful desire" (1:3, 4).**

POWER

"His divine power has granted to us" The punctuation presents a problem in verse 3, since the original begins with the Greek particle *hōs,* "according as". This may mean that the connection is primarily with verse 2 and that grace and peace are multiplied according as the divine power has granted all things or that, alternatively, a new section begins at verse 3 and the "according as" picks up the *kai auto touto de,* "for this very reason" at verse 5, so that according as this divine power has granted all things, so Peter's readers are to make every effort to add to their faith. The resolution is somewhat academic, for whatever way the punctuation is taken, and my own preference is for the latter: a new section beginning at verse 3, the overall sense emphasizes the divine power as fundamental to the saving knowledge. Some translations as, for example NIV, ESV. simply omit translating *hōs*, while others retain it: AV, NKJV. It makes little difference to the sense either way.

But to whom does **"his"** refer – to Jesus or to God? While undoubtedly God's "power" is constantly and rightly emphasized in many New Testament contexts and, sometimes, as a circumlocution for God (Mt. 10:28; 22:29 = Mk. 12:24; Lu. 1:35; Ro. 1:16, 20 cf. Mt. 26:64 = Mk. 14:62), the fact that Jesus is the immediate antecedent grammatically, his divinity stressed already and constantly throughout the letter and that "power" is later at verse 16 attributed to Jesus' Transfiguration, it seems reasonable to take "power" here as belonging specifically to Jesus. Again, to some extent, the matter is somewhat academic, since it is the same divine power. That Jesus manifested divine power is indisputably clear throughout the New Testament (Mt. 14:2 = Mk. 6:14; Mt. 24:30 = Mk. 13:26; Mk. 5:30; 6:2; Lu.4:14, 36; 5:17; 6:19; Ac. 2:22; 10:38; Ro. 1:4 cf. Ac. 3:12; 1 Cor. 5:4; 2 Cor. 12:9; He.1:3 cf. 1 Cor. 1:24). Jesus himself emphatically claims exclusive authority by virtue of this, power given to him by God his Father: "All authority *(exousia)* in heaven and on earth has been given to me" (Mt. 28:18). Jesus' divine power as Son of God seems to be highlighted here also in Second Peter, where the equally frequent New Testament Greek word for power, *dunamis,* is used.

"Divine" is *theias.* As an adjective, it occurs only three times in the New Testament (Ac. 17:29; 2 Pe. 1:3, 4), nine times in the LXX (Greek Old Testament) but is much more frequent in Hellenized Jewish writers as in 4 Maccabees and Philo. It was very much used in pagan Greek sources, which gave it a polytheistic or pantheistic flavour. It is, perhaps, for that reason mentioned very little in the New Testament or Christian literature generally up to the time of Justin. It is a notably "Greek" word, but Peter in this letter on occasion used these kinds of terms. Some see this as an argument for pseudonymity against Petrine authorship. But Peter may well use these terms to communicate with the society of the day or to combat effectively the wrongful use of these words and ideas by the false teachers. The idea, of course, of divine power was thoroughly biblical, normally expressed in the term "power of God", even if this particular expression is unusual.

"Granted to us" "Granted", *dedōrēmenēs,* is a very strong verb, which could be translated "bestowed". It connotes royal, official, or divine bounty, lavishly and solemnly granted. It is a perfect, passive participle in form meaning a gift granted specifically in the past with continuing results in the present and future. This enhances the "divine power" as a gracious and permanent gift from God. In sum, Jesus' divine power is sovereign and unilateral in its nature, gracious and lavish in its bestowal. C. Bigg puts it well when he writes: "The *dunamis,* power and authority of Christ, is the sword which St. Peter holds over the head of the false teachers".[20]

"To us" It seems unnecessary to restrict this to Peter and the apostles. Peter is probably referring to all Christians here, since they have all equal standing in their faith.

"All things that pertain to" The saving power is not only unilateral but also universal. **"All things"** is emphatic in its position in the sentence. All things necessary for justification and sanctification are to be found in Christ's power. Sinners need neither special preparation nor good works for salvation. Nor should Christians

---

[20] C. Bigg, *The Epistles of St. Peter and St. Jude* (International Critical Commentaries, Edinburgh, T. and T. Clark, 1901) p253 cited by D. Lucas & C. Green, *The Message Of 2 Peter & Jude,* p46 n10).

seek post-conversion experiences, instant means, private revelations, tongues, healings, health and wealth gospel or deliverance teaching to confirm their faith. They do not need to pursue special themes such as "second blessing", "spirit baptisms". "self-crucifixion" or "deeper life" schemes to aid their growth in grace. All they have and need is in Christ's power and gift. Just as through Scripture, they are "thoroughly equipped for every good work" (2 Ti. 3:17 ᴺᴵⱽ), so in the Christ of Scripture they have **"all things that pertain to life and godliness"**. A proper use of the right means is the Christian's complete answer for sanctification.

"Life and godliness" "Life" is *zōē* not *bios*. *Zōē* is better taken as referring to the life of special rather than common grace, that is, to eternal life, with which it is usually associated in the New Testament. **"Godliness"** is *eusebeian*. *Eusebeia* is another of these special Greek terms found in Second Peter. It occurs only nine times in the LXX (Greek Old Testament) but is frequent in 4 Maccabees (47 times), Philo and Josephus. In Second Peter, it is also found at 1:6, 7; 3:11 (cf. *eusebeis*, 2:9) interestingly in Peter's speech at Acts 3:12 (cf. *eusebēs*, Ac. 10:2,7) and some eight times in the Pastorals. It means piety toward the gods in pagan thought and in Jewish and Christian circles respect for God's will in moral living, including such attributes as decency, honesty, trust and integrity, namely the results of religious belief in observable holiness (cf. 2 Pe. 3:11). It is remarkable that Peter, addressing the crowd after healing the lame man at the Temple should use both terms "power" *dunamis* and "godliness" *eusebeia* to reject any idea of his own contribution to this healing: "Men of Israel, why does this surprise you? Why do you stare at us as if by our own power *(dunamei)* or godliness *(eusebeia)* we had made this man walk? The God of Abraham, Isaac and Jacob, the God of our fathers, has glorified his servant Jesus . . . It is Jesus' name and the faith that comes through him that has given this complete healing to him, as you can all see" (Ac. 3:12-16 ᴺᴵⱽ). Calvin comments: "For Peter here, by attributing the whole of godliness, and all helps to salvation, to the divine power of Christ, takes them away from the common nature of men, so that he leaves to us not even the least particle of any virtue or merit".[21]

MEANS

"Through the knowledge of him who called us" "Knowledge" is the fuller *epignōsis*, not only knowledge of facts but knowledge of a person in a deep and relational way. This saving knowledge comes about through the means or agency of the one who calls. But to whom does **"him who called"** refer – to Christ or God? Normally in the New Testament, God the Father is the one who calls people into a relationship with himself (Ro. 8:28, 29; Ep. 1:18). Yet here, the emphasis does seem to be on Christ who calls. Peter has already in his letter stressed the role of Christ in salvation. Christ's deity also has been underlined (v1[b]). Jesus Christ is the object of this "knowledge" (1:8; 2:20, 3:18 – it is both "God" and "Jesus our Lord" at 1:2) and, as we hope to show, "his own glory and excellence" refers specifically to Christ. This in no way detracts from God the Father's role in salvation, but simply underscores God the Son's deity and saviourhood, who, in his own teaching laid claim to "call" to salvation: "I came not to call the righteous, but sinners" (Mk. 2:17).

The calling itself does not seem to be limited to Christ's call to Peter and the apostles (Mk. 1:14-20), which would involve taking "us" here as referring to the apostles. Earlier, however, in verse 3 "us" seems more properly to have a wider range of meaning including Peter's readers and, indeed, ourselves today. So it is here also. Nor would the calling seem simply to refer to the merely 'external' call of the gospel, but rather to the 'effectual' calling to salvation as verse 10 would indicate: "Therefore, brothers, be all the more diligent to make your calling and election sure". It is Christ in his person, then, as Son

---

[21]   J. Calvin *Commentaries on II Peter*, p369.

of God who calls to saving knowledge. Within a triune salvation, knowledge of him as Saviour comes through the agency of his calling.

"To his own glory and excellence" Jesus calls to or by "his own" glory and excellence. "His own" – "own" *idia* is a characteristic word in Second Peter occurring seven times – refers not to a change of subject from Jesus to God, but is emphatic of the God-Man's own intrinsic nature. **"Glory"**, *doxē,* a favourite word of Peter's coming ten times in First Peter and five in Second Peter, recalls the Hebrew *kabod,* literally, the "heaviness" of the divine splendour. It speaks of the majesty of God's presence, such as Isaiah saw in the temple (Is. 6:1-5). Christ, as God, partakes of that same glory (2 Co. 4:4; Ep. 1:12; Ph. 3:21; He.1:3; 2:7; 1 Pe.1:21). John in his gospel attributes this glory to Jesus as of the only begotten of the Father (1:14). Peter in his first letter claims that God gave Christ glory in his resurrection (1:21) and in his second letter witnesses to that glory in the Transfiguration (1:17). Jesus "glory" magnificently displays his divine nature.

"Excellence" translates *aretē.* It is another of these specialized Hellenistic words and, indeed, combined with "glory" appears frequently in Greek literature. It connotes achievement, wealth, celebrity, fame, virtue and excellence. In the Old Testament the combination of glory and excellence belong to God (Is. 42:8, 12 LXX). Peter has already used the term in his first letter to describe the virtues or praises of God evident in his calling his people out of darkness into light, where obviously the active aspect of God's saving work is emphasized (1 Pe.2:9). Here, it specifies Christ's excellence of character, his purity of life, his active obedience, his sinlessness – in whom was no sin, who knew no sin, who was without sin. All these are included here. Jesus' "excellence" evinces the perfection of his human nature. Jesus as God-Man calls by the glory and excellence of his deity and humanity. The person of Jesus Christ becomes the means of saving knowledge, which persuasively attracts sinners to himself (cf. Jn.12:32).

"By which he has granted to us his precious and very great promises". The royal bounty which bestows all things pertaining to life and godliness now confers precious and very great promises "**Precious**", *timia,* is a favourite word of Peter's in both letters. Peter describes faith as more precious than gold (1 Pe. 1:7), Christ's blood as precious (1 Pe. 1:19), Christ as cornerstone, elect and precious (1 Pe. 2:4, 6), Christ as the object of believers' faith as precious (1 Pe. 2:7), a faith in Christ which is similarly precious or of equal standing (2 Pe. 1:1) and, here, promises which have great value and worth, "**Very great**" *megista,* the normal Greek superlative, is found only here in the New Testament and endorses the value of the promises. "**Promises**" are *epaggelmata,* the less common word, occurring only here and at 3:13 in the New Testament, the more usual word being *epaggelia* found fifty-two times in the New Testament including 2 Peter 3:4, 9. The occurrence of this less common word for "promise" at 1:4 and 3:13 acts as a sort of *inclusio* for Second Peter; presenting the substance of the whole letter, start to finish within these perimeters as one great and glorious promise. If there is any difference in meaning in these two words, it may be that the former stresses more the content of the promise. Hence, J.B. Philipps translates, "God's greatest and most precious promises have become available to us men."[22] As to the content of these promises, various suggestions have been made; promises particularly pointing to conversion – partakers in the divine nature – or, more generally, promises already fulfilled in Christ or anticipating the false teaching of Chapter 3, that is, promises relating to the "end times". Of all these, the first seems the most probable, though all the Old Testament promises relating to Christ may be in view, as Paul put it: "For no matter how many promises God has made, they are 'Yes' in Christ. And so through him the 'Amen' is spoken by us to the glory of God" (2 Cor. 1:20 ᴺᴵⱽ). At any rate, it is indisputably clear that not only is the person of Christ the source of saving knowledge but

---

[22]   J.B. Phillips, *The New Testament In Modern English,* p468.

also the promises of Christ as well. Intriguingly, Peter mentions both aspects, person and promises, man and message, as he introduces the gospel in the Gentile home of Cornelius. The correspondence is striking:

> "You know the message God sent to the people of Israel, telling the good news of peace through Jesus Christ, who is Lord of all. You know what has happened throughout Judea, beginning in Galilee after the baptism that John preached — how God anointed Jesus of Nazareth with the Holy Spirit and power, and how he went around doing good and healing all who were under the power of the devil, because God was with him" (Ac. 10:36-38^{NIV}).

RESULTS

"so that through them you may become partakers of the divine nature, having escaped from the corruption that is in the world because of sinful desire"

The results of saving knowledge through these "precious and very great promises" is put first positively: **"that through them you may become partakers of the divine nature"** and, secondly, negatively: **"having escaped from the corruption that is in the world because of sinful desire"**.

Peter uses language here, as we have noted earlier, which was current in the Greek philosophy of his day. The idea of participating or sharing in the divine nature was well established in Greek language and literature. The Stoics and Plato thought this participating was achievable through *phusis* (nature) or *nomos* (law) respectively. Hellenistic Jews such as Philo, Josephus and the author of 4 Maccabees also expressed similar ideas. In all, these views bordered on the concept of divinization or deification. Because of this language and its implications, Second Peter has been regarded as pseudonymous. E. Käsemann went as far as to claim of this verse:

> It would be hard to find in the whole New Testament a sentence which, in its expression, its individual motifs and its whole trend, more clearly marks the relapse of Christianity into Hellenistic dualism.[23]

However, this claim is somewhat sweeping. Peter, as we have noted before, is here using Greek language and concepts, which were the common coinage of the day, to communicate his message to the society of his day and to combat false teaching harmful to the church. A number of considerations will help demonstrate how Peter, far from aiding the relapse of Christianity into Hellenistic dualism was, in fact, defending the apostolic gospel and presenting it in a form, vital and fresh, and well accommodated to defuse any counterfeit misrepresentations:

1. Peter uses the biblically oriented noun *koinōnoi*, "**partakers**", rather than the Greek philosophical verb *metechein* "to participate", "to share" used in secular literature.

2. Peter attributes the means of participating in the divine nature neither to the igniting of the divine spark in human nature nor to the rewarding of keeping the law on the part of man but to God's grace. It is "**through them**", *dia toutōn*, that his readers are made partakers of the divine nature, where "**them**" refers more probably to the immediate direct antecedent "precious and very great promises" and, perhaps

---

[23] E. Käsemann, *Essays on New Testament Themes* (London: SCM; Naperville: A.R. Allenson, 1964) pp179-180 cited in D. Lucas & C. Green, *The Message Of Second Peter and Jude*, p51 n29.

as well, additionally to the whole context of divine power as the means of granting this saving knowledge. It is all of God, nothing of man.

3. Peter's aorist participle "**having escaped**", *apophugontes*, makes it clear that the escape from corruption precedes the participation in the divine nature. The removal of sin is necessary to the importing of salvation. This negative/ positive thrust in respect of sin and grace is fundamental to the biblical portrayal of salvation and quite alien to Greek philosophical thought.

4. Peter also shows quite pointedly that "**the corruption**", *phthoras*, is not the Greek concept of the baseness of the material over against the purity of the spiritual but the biblical doctrine of fallen human nature, flawed by sin. It is a corruption "**in**" *en* not "of" the "**world**" a *kosmos* of sinful mankind, "in" *en* or through "**desire**", *epithumia*, which in the biblical context can be either good or evil, but is obviously evil in this case.

5. Peter, later in this letter, expresses the idea of escaping defilements by knowing Jesus Christ (2:20), but has already in his first letter mentioned his readers participating in the sufferings of Christ (4:13) and himself and his readers anticipating being sharers in the glory to be revealed (5:1). It is entirely natural, then, that Peter should conceive of salvation as an escape from the corruption of sin and a participating in the divine nature. Further, again in his first letter, Peter has described his readers as having purified themselves by obeying the truth, having been born again through the imperishable seed of God's word, that is, needing to rid themselves of all kinds of sin so that like new-born babies they might crave the milk of God's word and grow up in

their salvation (1:22-2:2). There is the same negative and positive thrust regarding salvation here in Peter's first letter and just as much dynamic or radical in this imagery as in that of escaping the corruption of sin and partaking in the divine nature in his second letter. Both kinds of expression in his first and second letters are similarly vivid.

Peter is not claiming for the believer divinization or deification but simply expressing what the Bible as a whole teaches, that in salvation, man as a creature can share the blessings of God his Creator, who is willing to communicate some of his attributes to him in grace. As Calvin puts it: "But the word *nature* is not here essence but quality . . . they (i.e. the apostles) only intended to say that when divested of all the vices of the flesh, we shall be partakers of divine and blessed immortality and glory, so as to be as it were one with God as far as our capacities will allow"[24]. In all of this, Peter is saying in language which suits his day and combats the attacks on the church of his day nothing more radical than what Paul wrote to the Galatians: "I have been crucified with Christ. It is no longer I who live, but Christ who lives in me. And the life I now live in the flesh I live by faith in the Son of God, who loved me and gave himself for me" (Ga. 2:20) or how John summarized the gospel he was about to write: "But to all who did receive him, who believed in his name, he gave the right to become children of God, who were born, not of blood nor of the will of the flesh nor of the will of man, but of God" (Jn. 1:12, 13).

M. Green sums up the matter masterfully:

> But is the idea, of being partaker of the divine nature, too advanced for Peter? It is intrinsically no different from being born from above (Jn. 3:3; Jas 1:18; 1 Pet. 1:23), being the temple of the Holy Spirit

---

[24]   J. Calvin *Commentaries on II Peter*, (Addition mine), p371.

(1 Cor. 6:19), being in Christ (Rom. 8:1) or being the dwelling-place of the Trinity (Jn. 14:17-23). In this whole introductory paragraph of his Epistle, the writer is putting his Christian doctrine into Greek dress for the purposes of communication, without in the least committing himself to the pagan associations of the terms. Indeed, in 1:3-4 he makes a frontal assault on Stoic and Platonic presuppositions, who taught, respectively, that by *phusis* (nature) or *nomos* (law) a man became partaker of the divine. No, says our author; it is by grace, by the gospel promises, that this comes about (1:3-4).[25]

APPLICATION

When around the year 1646 the Westminster Fathers wrote, "The Sum of Saving Knowledge", they tabled the contents under four headings:

1. Our woeful condition by nature
2. The remedy provided in Jesus Christ
3. The means provided in the covenant of grace
4. The blessings conveyed by these means.[26]

There follows a biblical exposition of those four headings incorporating the relevant theology of their Westminster Confession and Catechisms. Peter in Second Peter 1:3, 4 is doing substantially the same – "The Sum of Saving Knowledge." Peter's letter, which follows, expounds this saving knowledge.

25   M. Green, *2 Peter and Jude*, p26.
26   *Westminster Confession of Faith*, (Free Presbyterian Publications) pp322-343.

John Wesley, looking back on his spiritual crisis early in the morning of 24 May 1730 wrote in his diary for 4 June:

> All these days I scarce remember to have opened the New Testament, but upon some great and precious promise. And I saw, more than ever, that the gospel is in truth but one great promise, from the beginning of it to the end.[27]

From two somewhat different theological perspectives, from great men of faith in the past, the sum of saving knowledge as epitomized in 2 Peter 1:3-4 emerges. Peter's grand description here, in language and thought equal to the philosophical views of his day, communicates with society, addresses a pagan world, and protects the church. The doctrine of this biblical summary complements the many glorious descriptions of the doctrines of grace throughout Scripture. It is as dynamic in proclaiming the gospel to New Agers, humanists, and atheists of our day, as it was to the Stoics and Platonists of Peter's day. We must continue to meditate on its glories, use it as an apologetic for today's culture, employ it to preach the gospel and feed on it to enable us to grow in grace and in the knowledge of our Lord and Saviour, Jesus Christ. For it is the sum of saving knowledge of God's glory in Christ. It comprises the power, means and results of salvation in a superlative way. It emphasizes the person and promises of our Lord and Saviour to a dynamic degree and in a vitally relevant manner for the world of the day, Peter's world, and ours.

---

[27]   Cited in D. Lucas & C. Green, *The Message Of 2 Peter & Jude*, p54, from J. Moffatt, *The General Epistles: Peter, James and Judas, The Moffatt New Testament Commentary* (London: Hodder and Stoughton; New York: Doubleday, 1928) p179 *(Peter)*.

Chapter 5

TRUE KNOWLEDGE

GROWING

2 PETER 1:5-7

INTRODUCTION

After laying the foundation of true knowledge in underlining its saving nature (vv3, 4), Peter goes on to describe its growth (vv5-7). The form in which he describes this growth is technically known by the Greek terms *prokopē*, "progress", "advancement", "furtherance", and *sōreitēs*, literally, "a heap". One description of sorites as a figure of speech explains its meaning:

> A set of statements which proceed, step by step, through the force of logic or reliance upon a succession of indisputable facts, to a climactic, conclusion, each statement picking up the last key word (or key phrase) of the preceding one.[28]

---

[28]   H.A. Fischel, "The Uses Of Sorites *(Climax, Gradatio)* in the Tannaitic Period". *Hebrew Union College Annual* 44 (1973) 119, cited in R.J. Bauckham, *Jude, 2 Peter*, p175.

Other New Testament examples of sorites as a list of ethical qualities required of Christians occur at Romans 5:3-5, where the subject is the development of Christian character under suffering, at James 1:3-4, where testing of faith results in growth in grace and at Galatians 5:22-23, where Paul describes the fruit of the Spirit. In these, common ethical terms such as faith or faithfulness, self-control, and endurance along with others recur. There are other New Testament lists which do not quite follow a sorites formula. Similar lists in the form of sorites are found in Stoic and other Hellenistic ethical writers, in Jewish literature such as in Philo, the Wisdom of Solomon, and Rabbinic writings as well as in some later Christian apocryphal books such as 1 and 2 Clement and Hermas.

Peter's list here at verses 5-7 is similar in sorites form to those of the New Testament, Jewish and later Christian writings mentioned above. These verses are a chain-like list of specifically Christian marks of character beginning with faith and ending with love, where steps in the chain in between are logically linked. This provides a "growth pattern" in Christian character for Peter's readers. Another interesting feature is Peter's language here. As we have already noted, Peter uses some words that have a strongly Greek, indeed, philosophical nuance, such as "godliness" and "excellence" (v3). Peter uses similar language at verses 5-7 and even perhaps "knowledge" (v2). He may well use these terms apologetically in defence of the true gospel, as it were, since some of them were part of the common coinage of secular, philosophical language of the day. Peter then introduces them with a transformed Christian meaning. He may well do this particularly in the light of the false teachers and their teaching, which he combats in his letter. For, frequently, as we shall note, some of the positive qualities Peter asserts in this chain of Christian growth are lamentably missing in the lives and behaviour of the false teachers he later berates.

But how far are we to take the figure of sorites? A number

of suggestions have been made as to the logical links within the chain-like steps of a ladder, but intriguing as these are, they seem sometimes a little too contrived or artificial. It would, for example, be going too far to claim that each step as instructional growth had to be completed before going on to the next, for it might be seriously questioned as to why "virtue", "excellence"[29] should precede "knowledge", or "godliness" precede "brotherly affection" and "love". Each value is, to a degree, an entity on its own. But there is merit in the layout. "Faith" necessarily is the foundation and "love" consistently the climax in New Testament protocol. Some pattern may rightly be seen within the chain, whether "pairing" of words or concepts, as often happens with Peter in this second letter, or logical gradation is the keynote. J. A. Bengel makes an insightful comment at this point, which is not too extreme but catches the atmosphere of sorites sufficiently to drive us with interest and excitement to the text and appreciate the living and growing nature of true Christian faith: "Each step gives birth to and facilitates the next. Each subsequent quality balances and brings to perfection the one preceding".[30]

The section falls easily into two sub-divisions:

ATTITUDE TOWARD GROWING KNOWLEDGE (v 5[a])

ASPECTS OF GROWING KNOWLEDGE   (vv5[b]-7)

EXPOSITION

"For this very reason, make every effort to supplement your faith with virtue, and virtue with knowledge, and knowledge with

---

[29]   ESV Translates *aretē* at verse 3 as "excellence" and twice at verse 5 as "virtue".

[30]   Cited by M. Green, *2 Peter and Jude*, p80, presumably from J.A. Bengel, *Gnomon Novi Testamenti, 1773, (no reference given)*.

self-control, and self-control with steadfastness, and steadfastness with godliness, and godliness with brotherly affection, and brotherly affection with love" (1:5-7).

ATTITUDE

Peter makes it clear to his readers that their attitude to growth in Christian grace and knowledge should be neither indifferent neglect, nor complacent passivity, nor uninformed activity but, rather, reasoned, zealous and sacrificial effort. The terms in which Peter writes are quite explicit.

"For this very reason", *kai auto touto de,* recalls the entire foregoing argument. It is because Christ's divine power has provided everything we need for life and godliness both in his person, who calls us through his own glory and excellence, and in his promises, which make us partakers in the divine nature and escape sinful corruption, that we must actively exert effort to grow in grace. The lavish nature of the gift provides motivation to respond. God's gracious condescension to us calls for strong aspirations after him. Growth arises from God's great love to us in Christ.

"Make every effort" The verbal participle **"make"**, *pareisenegkantes,* combining a number of prepositions, implies: "to bring into a relationship alongside what has already been done", in that sense, "to apply". The noun **"effort"** *spoudēn,* is strong, meaning "earnestness", "zeal", "haste". Peter seems fond of the word and uses it also at 1:10, 15 and 3:14 in a verbal form. The joint nuance connotes ready, energetic effort, bringing all one's powers to bear on a situation in a speedy resolved response. Growth is driven by an applied zeal.

"Supplement" or "add" is *epichorēgēsate.* The Greek *chorēgos,* literally "chorus-master", was the person responsible for providing the chorus, an expensive commodity of singers for the necessary background in

Greek dramatic productions. In effect, it usually meant a rich patron staging the whole production at his own expense, acting as a liberal benefactor of the arts. Hence, the verb means "to furnish or provide (at one's own expense)", "to give, grant", "to support", "to lavishly supply". The term, then, implies a lavish supply and a costly support.

The verb *epichorēgeō* recalls the same bountiful action, where the different but equally strong verb *dōreomai* is used at verses 3 and 4 to describe how Christ "granted" both everything needed for life and godliness as well as his very great and precious promises of salvation. *Epichorēgeō* also describes the "rich entrance" believers will receive as they enter heaven, mentioned at verse 11. Its use there, as at verse 5, forms a sort of *inclusio*, encapsulating the entire section. Growth is set within a context of lavish supply.

In recalling the bountiful gifts of Christ's person and promises bestowing salvation and in anticipating their lavish welcome to glory, Peter's readers are to respond in kind to the prospect of growing in grace. Growth requires a response rich in supply, costly in support and sacrificial in attitude. Its source is divine, its motivation powerful and its outworking inspiring.

ASPECT

Peter notes, in a sorites format, some important aspects of this growth. While, as we have noted, it would be extreme to find fixed interrelationships within these aspects, some general pattern seems naturally discernible. "Faith" marks the foundation of the list, "love" its climax. "Virtue" and "knowledge" couple together as complementary aspects of Christian behaviour and mind. "Self-control" and "steadfastness" feature as dual quality within and without the Christian's life. "Brotherly affection" and "love" mark the Christian's attitude to others. "Godliness" is embedded between these last two groupings as illustrating a general piety of character and life-style.

"Faith" *pistei* is foundational. It is markedly Christian in emphasis and seems here as at verse 1 to indicate the believer's personal trust in Christ rather than a body of doctrine. It could imply not only "faith" per se but "faithfulness", though in this latter sense it is inevitably related in context to a faithfulness of commitment to God through Jesus Christ. As "faith" or "faithfulness" it occurs in other ethical lists within the New Testament (Ga. 5:22; 1 Ti. 4:12; 6:11; 2 Ti. 2:22; Tit. 2:2; Re. 2:19) and elsewhere as such in other early Christian literature. In New Testament thought, **"faith"** is both living and productive (Ja. 2:20; Ga. 5:6), which particularly suits its foundational quality. It is not the loyalty of pagan cults within Hellenism but essentially Christ-related in terms of a basis for the gospel and for the Christian life. Faith is basic. It is total dependance on Christ for salvation. Faith includes that personal step of trusting Christ as Saviour, having repented of sin, which begins the Christian life.

D. Guthrie, thus, rightly notes here its foundational nature: "These other virtues are unattainable until the step of faith has been taken".[31]

"Virtue" "excellence" or "goodness" *aretē* is consequential, the result of faith in the behaviour and life-style of the Christian. *Aretē* is a philosophical term meaning "virtue", "moral excellence", goodness in that sense. A knife's goodness is in its ability to cut, a racehorse's goodness in its swiftness of foot. *Aretē* crowns the perfection of qualities in life. This philosophical sense, tied, of course, in Greek writers to *human* perfection means that the word occurs little in the New Testament (Ph. 4:8;1 Pe. 2:9; 2 Pe. 1:3; 5 [*twice*]). Peter uses the

---

31   D. Guthrie, *New Testament Theology*, p600.

word in his first letter to describe the "excellencies" (*aretas*) of God, who has called his people out of darkness into his marvellous light (1 Pe. 2:9) and subsequently urges them to live good lives among the pagans (1 Pe. 2:12), having already required them to be holy, as God who has called them is holy (1 Pe. 1:15, 16). Peter obviously wants them in their lives as believers to display the *aretē* of God's holiness communicated to them in salvation. In his second letter, already at 2 Peter 1:3, Peter has referred to Christ's **"glory"**, his divine splendour and his **"excellence"** or "goodness" (*aretē*), his human perfection, as the source of his readers' calling and, here, at verse 5 he urges them to add this communicated **"virtue"**, "excellence" or "goodness" to their faith. Peter obviously wants his readers to display Christlikeness in their Christian behaviour. Holiness and Christlikeness in terms of communicated **"virtue"** "excellence" or "goodness" are resultant effects of God's saving calling of them in Christ, a communicated **"virtue"** to them in grace, consequential to their faith (cf. Ep. 1:4). Remarkably, Christ's "excellence" and "goodness" are communicated to believers in salvation.

Simon J. Kistemaker puts it well: "Of the seven virtues that are directly related to faith, Peter mentions goodness first. It relates to one of God's characteristics (see v.3). Because it is a divine attribute, we ought to reflect this virtue in our lives. Our daily conduct should be a demonstration of moral excellence. Faith and excellence support one another".[32]

"Knowledge" is helpful. The word also occurs elsewhere in New Testament lists at 2 Corinthians 6:6; 8:7. **"Knowledge"** here at verses 5 and 6 is *gnōsis* as it is at the close of the letter at 3:18. The more intensive form *epignōsis* is used at 1:2, 3, 8 and both as a noun and verbally twice at 2:20-21. The distinction has been drawn that *epignōsis* means "coming to knowledge", a 'given' knowledge

---

[32]   S. J. Kistemaker, *James, Epistles of John, Peter, and Jude*, p251.

describing the initial act of faith, whereas *gnōsis* means, "continuing in knowledge", a 'gained' knowledge describing growth in faith. This is helpful. While the distinction is helpful, it can be somewhat too extreme, since in coming to faith and growing in faith, there is both a 'given' and 'gained' aspect. This "**knowledge**", in either form, is relational as well as cognitive. It is not simply knowing facts but, through the knowledge of facts, knowing a person, that is, Christ. Indeed, we have already suggested in our exegesis that knowledge is the key theme of Peter's second letter: Chapter 1- true knowledge; Chapter 2 – false knowledge; Chapter 3 – practical knowledge. It could also be that Peter's stress on "**knowledge**" has reference to an incipient Gnosticism. But we will deal with this later when examining the false teachers. Here, at verses 5 and 6, "**knowledge**", in reaching to the mind, forms a helpful link with "goodness", on the one hand, which is behavioural and with the other graces that follow on the other hand. These trace out the progression of Christian character in detail. Our growing knowledge of Christ, relationally obtained through the revelation of Scripture leading to the initial personal step of faith, will help develop Christian character in a progressive and detailed way.

Thomas R. Schreiner notes: "True knowledge is rooted in God's grace. Bauckham separates too neatly *epignōsis* from *gnōsis*, saying that the former relates to conversion and the latter relates to progress in discernment for Christian living. There is some truth in this characterization, but it should be noted that progress in all these moral virtues is necessary for one's heavenly inheritance, and hence progress in knowledge is necessary, ultimately, for eternal life".[33]

"**Self-control**" *egkrateia* is inner. *Egkrateia* is literally "might within", "in-power" and is normally translated "**self-control**". Both in Greek philosophy and in Hellenistic Judaism it stresses personal control

---

[33]   T.R. Schreiner, *1, 2 Peter, Jude*, pp299-300.

over excessive pleasure and accentuates human ability to do so. It pertained not only to food, drink and sexual desire but also to all aspects of living. Socrates maintained, in this regard, that no one willingly rejects the best course once he sees it[34]. Aristotle, however, disagreed, spoke much of *akrasia* "lack of control" and offered no solution to the problem of human wickedness[35]. Philo cites self-control as the opposite of desire *(hēdonē)* and encourages restraint[36]. Josephus, similarly, praises self-control[37].

While **"self-control"** is frequent in Hellenistic writings, it is rare enough in the New Testament. However, its New Testament citations point to the answer, which Greek philosophy and Hellenistic Judaism failed to give. In the New Testament, apart from here, it occurs at Acts 24:25, where Paul addresses the Roman procurator Felix and his partner Drusilla, at Galatians 5:23 as listed among the fruit of the Spirit and in verbal form at 1Corinthians 9:25[NIV]: "Everyone who competes in the games goes into strict training *(egkrateuetai)*", the allusion to athletic training emphasizing the self-discipline the Christian must adopt in adding "self-control" to his faith. In all of these, the implication is that the "self" has already been changed through conversion to Christ and the "control" is that of the mastery of the Spirit over the believer's life, to which he now submits. Like all these aspects of growth, we are to work out this salvation that God has already worked in us (Ph. 2:12-13). M. Green sums it up admirably:

> That answer is to be found in the Christian way
> of life. For Christian self-control is submission to

---

34   Socrates: Plato, *Protagoras 352 C,* cited M. Green, *2 Peter and Jude,* p78.

35   Nicomachaean Ethics vii.3. cited M. Green, *2 Peter and Jude,* p78.

36   *De Specialibus legibus (The Special Laws) I.* 149-150, cited Peter H. Davids, *The Letters Of 2 Peter And Jude,* p180.

37   Josephus, *The Jewish War 2.120 [about the Essenes]; 4.373,* cited Peter H. Davids, *The Letters Of 2 Peter And Jude,* p180.

the control of the indwelling Christ; and by this means mature virtue (what Aristotle wistfully called 'divine virtue which is beyond man') does become a possibility for men.[38]

"Self-control" for the believer is Christ and his word controlling inner desires and intentions.

"Steadfastness" *hupomonē* is outer. It is made up of two Greek words: *hupo* "under" and *monē* "remaining". *Hupomonē* is "remaining under", hence translated, "steadfastness", "perseverance", "endurance". If **"self-control"** is the Christian dealing with the eruption of evil from within, **"steadfastness"** is the Christian combating adversity from without.

It occurs in Greek literature as a commendable human quality and often figures in a military context as courage and fortitude in battle. Aristotle contrasts **"self-control"** with **"steadfastness"** maintaining that the former is concerned with pleasures, the latter with sorrows;[39] hence the Greek philosophical schools of Epicureanism and Stoicism (cf. Ac. 17:18). The "stiff upper lip" syndrome is a modern heritage not of Christianity but rather of Stoicism. A more divinely orientated view of **"steadfastness"** is characterized in Judaism, as for example in the book of Job, where the quality is related to trust in God and in his providential purposes.

"Steadfastness" occurs in this latter sense widely in the New Testament as a desirable fruit of believers, being frequently found in the context of ethical lists (Ro. 5:3, 4; 8:25; Col. 1:11; 1 Th. 1:3; 1 Ti. 6:11; 2 Ti. 3:10; Tit. 2:2; He. 12:1; Ja. 1:3, 4; 5:11; 1 Pe. 2:20; Re. 2:2, 3, 19). This arises from the teaching of Jesus, where to "abide" in him and in his words produces fixity of character or perseverance,

---

38   M. Green, *2 Peter and Jude*, p78.
39   Aristotle, *Magna Moralia ii.6.34*, Cited M. Green *2 Peter and Jude*, p78.

a mark of true saving faith, which endures to the end (Jn. 15:1-8; Mt. 10:22; 24:13). Peter would particularly urge this quality on his readers, since he himself had lacked it and, now towards the end of his life, was perhaps reminiscing regretfully about it, since the false teachers he was combating certainly showed nothing of this perseverance (Jn. 21:15-25; 2 Pe. 1:14; 2:2, 20-22). Douglas J. Moo summarizes it well:

> Trials come in many forms and face believers at every turn: illness, the desertion of friends, financial pressures, death. The New Testament writers frequently refer to the constant pressure these difficulties put on Christians in this life; thus they are equally insistent on the need to cultivate endurance.[40]

"**Steadfastness**" for the believer is Christ and his word quelling outer pressures and adversities. God through Christ perseveres in the believer in salvation, which in turn, leads to steadfastness and perseverance in the believer's life, as he abides in Christ and his word.

"**Godliness**" *eusebeia* is a summary. Peter gathers up the foregoing qualities and galvanizes them together in a vertical axis before God. *Eusebeia* combines two Greek words: *eu* meaning "good" and *sebeia* meaning "fear" or "reverence". Hence, the word is translated "piety" "religion" "godliness" implying fear of God in the biblical sense. In Greek thought, it described that reverential attitude to the gods and man generally known as religion or piety, including where culturally applicable, such things as ancestry or morality, and in addition stressed the meticulous approach of the religious adherent to whatever principles, attitudes, actions, or rites were regarded as appropriate to his belief. Probably because of its general,

---

40   D. J. Moo *2 Peter, Jude*, p46.

polytheistic and humanistic content, *eusebeia* is relatively rare in biblical literature.

Where it does occur, however, the term embraces the highest aspects of biblical religion. It comes eventually to connote that practical life-style on the part of the believer through fear of God, which shows that his *eusebeia* is a matter of living a life that is like God and thus pleasing to God, "**godliness**" in that sense. *Eusebeia* occurs only nine times in the LXX (Greek Old Testament) but is frequently found in 4 Maccabees (47 times), Philo and Josephus. In the New Testament, it occurs once in Acts (3:12), 10 times in the Pastoral Letters (1 Ti. 2:2; 3:16; 4:7, 8; 6:3, 5, 6, 11; 2 Ti. 3:5; Tit. 1:1) and four times in 2 Peter (1:3, 6, 7; 3:11).

The uses in the Pastorals indicate living the kind of life that pleases God. Peter's use of the form is particularly instructful. He refers to it in a speech in Acts, making it clear that the healing of the lame man ought not to be attributed to "our own power or piety" (Ac. 3:12) but rather to God. While he does not use the actual term in his first letter, he certainly urges his readers toward godliness both in attitude and behaviour (1 Pe. 1:14-15; 2:11,12). In this second letter, he has already used it to describe the provision for "life and godliness", which the divine power has given to his readers (1:3). Later in this letter, he goes on to require them to live "holy and godly lives" in the light of Christ's return (3:11,12 NIV). Here at 1:6,7 Peter gathers up the preceding qualities and urges his readers to add to their faith a practical "godliness" which both reflects God's character and pleases God's person. Peter's *eusebeia* is obviously neither vague, nor formal but practical and personal. Above all, it is God-oriented. Simon J. Kistemaker, again, brings this out well when he comments:

> A Christian practices godliness when he is fully
> conscious of God's presence in every circumstance,

so that his life is guided by the motto of the Genevan
Reformer John Calvin: *Coram Deo* (in the presence
of God).[41]

"**Brotherly affection**" *philadelphia* is climactic and unique. While
it would be too restrictive to limit the Greek words for "love"
in watertight categories – *storgē* "affection", *philia* "family", *erōs*
"physical", *agapē* uniquely "Christian", some of these emphases
persist in usage in the New Testament[42]. "**Brotherly affection**" is
unique in that it is only in the New Testament associated with the
church. It is thus used beyond the kinship bonds of the family and
extended intentionally for relationships of believers to one another
within the Christian church[43]. The New Testament really does
expect Christians to regard one another as "family", familiarity
with which fact in Christian usage has too often bred contempt but
which we need so much in reality to revive.

Peter uses *philadelphia* strikingly in association with *agapē* in his
first letter at 1:22: "Having purified your souls by your obedience
to the truth for a sincere brotherly love, *(philadelphian)* love one
another *(agapēsate)* earnestly from a pure heart" and, also, in a list
of Christian virtues at 1 Peter 3:8: "Finally, all of you, have unity
of mind, sympathy, brotherly love, *(philadelphoi)*, a tender heart,
and a humble mind." Both exhortations stress the necessity of this
attitude for Christian living and flow naturally from Jesus' teaching
in summarizing the Law and the Prophets as love for God and for
one's neighbour (Mt. 22:34-40) and especially his teaching about
family relationships among believers (Mk. 3:31-35). The pronounced
way in which the rest of the New Testament makes demands on
Christians for "brotherly-love" simply underlines the significance

---

[41]   S. J. Kistemaker, *James, Epistles of John, Peter, and Jude,* p252.

[42]   C.S. Lewis, *The Four Loves*; cf. D.A. Carson, *Exegetical Fallacies,* Grand
       Rapids, Baker 1984, especially for *agapē* and *phileō*.

[43]   P.H. Davids, *The Letters Of 2 Peter And Jude,* pp182-183.

of all this (1 Jn. 4:20-21; He. 13:1; 1 Th. 4:9; Ro. 12:10). M. Green stresses well the very practical nature of "**brotherly affection**" when he writes:

> But this gift has to be worked at. Love for the brethren entails bearing one another's burdens, and so fulfilling the law of Christ; it means guarding that Spirit-given unity from destruction by gossip, prejudice, narrowness, and the refusal to accept a brother Christian for what he is in Christ.[44]

"**Love**" *agapē* is climactic and final. While it is recognized that there is no hard distinction between the various Greek words for love, especially *philadelphia* and *agapē* as used within the New Testament, nevertheless the context of usage does represent varying tones of emphases.

Agapē finds its root meaning within the teaching of Jesus where, based upon God's selfless and unique love for mankind, it is to be reflected in the lives of believers, as a communicable attribute from God. Jesus makes it clear that *agapē* for the Christian as love for God is the first and greatest command and it is to be carried out with great intensity. Love for others is the inevitable result and ranks as a second similar requirement from God (Mt. 22:37-40 cf. De. 6:5 and Le. 19:18). This "**love**" has little to do with feelings. It is not merely a fondness or liking motivated by the object of attraction, but rather personal action and will and is to be expressed even toward one's enemies "But I say to you, 'Love your enemies and pray for those who persecute you'" (Mt. 5:44). It is rooted in God's love, must be evident in the believer's attitude and is the hallmark of the believer's covenantal relationship with God (Jn. 3:16; 1 Jn. 3:16; 4:16, 20-21).

Agapē is frequent in New Testament ethical lists (2 Co. 6:6; Ga.

---

44   M. Green, *2 Peter and Jude*, p79.

5:22; Ep. 4:2; 1Ti. 4:12; 6:11; 2 Ti.2:22; 3:10; Tit. 2:2) and yet more frequent in the New Testament in general. Significantly, especially in Paul, it has a primacy among Christian virtues and is portrayed as the climax of these. It excels knowledge (1 Co. 8:1), is superior to the transient gifts of tongues and prophecy and takes pride of place even amid the abiding triad of faith hope and love (1 Co. 13:1-3). Love controls and binds other Christian virtues together in perfect unity (Col. 3:12-14) and is seen as the goal of Christian instruction (1 Ti.1:5).

Peter has already distinguished *philadelphia* from *agapē* in his first letter (1 Pe.1:22). There he characterizes *agapē* as requiring that Christians must love "earnestly", *ektenōs*, an athletic word typifying effort and focus, and "from a pure heart", *ek kardias,* an inner transformation from the evils, which Jesus claimed, arises from that quarter. *Agapē* for Peter means intensity and sincerity. In his second letter, the very placement of *agapē* after *philadelphia* at the close of the list marks an obvious climax (2 Pe. 1:7). Peter along with Paul stresses the primacy of *agapē* as the crowning Christian virtue and substantiates with Paul its inner and true nature.

Calvin distinguishes *agapē* from *philadelphia* by suggesting that the latter "is mutual affection among the children of God", while the former "extends wider, because it embraces all mankind".[45]

Again, M. Green summarizes aptly, and excellently.

> This word *agapē* is one which Christians to all
> intents and purposes coined, to denote the attitude
> which God has shown himself to have to us, and
> requires from us towards himself. In friendship
> (*philia*) the partners seek mutual solace; in sexual
> love (*erōs*) mutual satisfaction. In both cases these

---

[45]   J. Calvin, *Commentaries on II Peter*, p373.

feelings are aroused because of what the loved one
is. With *agapē* it is the reverse. God's *agapē* is evoked
not by what we are, but by what he is. It has its
origin in the agent, not in the object. It is not that
we are lovable, but that he is love. This *agapē* might
be defined as a deliberate desire for the highest good
of the one loved, which shows itself in sacrificial
action for that person's good. That is what God did
for us (Jn.3:16). That is what he wants us to do (1
Jn.3:16). That is what he is prepared to achieve in us
(Rom.5:5). Thus the Spirit of the God who is love is
freely given to us, in order to reproduce in us that
same quality. For men will never believe that God
is love unless they see it in the lives of his professed
followers.[46]

APPLICATION

The importance of the teaching of Peter's list can hardly be
overstated. Ethical instruction of the believer rooted in the Old
Testament finds its fulfilment in Jesus both in his person, his work
and in his teaching. What Peter says arises from the fundamentals
of Jesus' instruction that by their fruits true believers are known
and that continuing in Jesus and in his words produces much fruit
and much fruit gives proof of discipleship (Mt. 5:43-47; 7:15-20;
Jn. 15:1-8).

Peter's list, too, accords with the whole gamut of apostolic lists of
ethical instruction: the fruit of the Spirit (Ga. 5:16-26), the new self,
renewed in its Creator's image and clothed in appropriate Christian
dress (Col. 3:1-14), the sanctifying effects of Christian suffering (Ro.
5:1-5), trials (Ja. 1:2-5) and discipline (He. 12:7-11).

---

[46]   M. Green, *2 Peter and Jude*, p80.

According to Peter, the growth and increase of these 'listed virtues' brings about effectiveness and productivity in Christian life and witness, while the absence of them robs the Christian of the same. They assure the believer of his election and calling and sound the trumpet fan-fare for his move from grace to glory (2 Pe. 1:8-11).

The Christian church, then, needs to learn that its primary function in sanctification is growth in holiness. This requires stringent effort in terms of committed and continued practical godly living. The sanctification of the church is brought about neither by secondary experience, "letting go and letting God" nor by a continuum of crises, though God does work through our sufferings and trials. We must make and take time to be holy. This is not introspective selfish subjectivism and neglect of evangelism. It is the only true way towards Christian mission and effective outreach. If our own vineyard is not well kept, then the Lord's vineyard will suffer. We must take heed to ourselves as well as to the doctrine if we are to experience salvation for ourselves and for our hearers. The glorious truth is, if we practice what we preach and live what we profess, then many will see it, fear and trust in the Lord. The absence of growth in godly living produces the opposite effect. We must walk the walk as well as talk the talk. The persistent, practical pursuit of personal godliness and the development of Christian character – and there are no instant methods – through the right use of ordinary means, the word and prayer, is how the church grows in grace and in the knowledge of our Lord and Saviour Jesus Christ. Only this will bring true glory to him both now and forever. We need to take the apostle Peter seriously.

Chapter 6

TRUE KNOWLEDGE

FRUITFUL

2 PETER 1:8, 9

INTRODUCTION

Peter has presented the growing knowledge involved in salvation as a ladder in the literary format of *prokopē* (progress) or *sōreitēs* (a heap), the one Christian virtue leading on to the next in meaningful progression and increasing development (vv. 5-7). He now underlines the importance of this growth by describing its results. Referring back specifically to the list of Christian virtues just mentioned, Peter points out the salutary effects for Christian living, if the progression is followed and implemented, and, at the same time, indicates the detrimental effect of the absence or neglect of these virtues. This growth is not an optional extra for the Christian. Arising from the very nature of saving faith, it is portrayed as an absolute necessity for progress in the Christian life. Without it, faith is useless, in fact, dead. Peter points out the results of this growth or the lack of it in detail:

1. First, the results of this growing knowledge are *positively* stated, on a background illustration of the property market, its effectiveness, productivity or otherwise (verse 8).

2. Secondly, the results are *negatively* stated, on a background illustration of the human body, its functionality or dysfunction (verse 9).

EXPOSITION

POSITIVE

"For if these qualities are yours and are increasing, they keep you from being ineffective or unfruitful in the knowledge of our Lord Jesus Christ" (1:8).

"For if these qualities are yours" It is appropriate to take "**these qualities**", literally, *tauta*, "things", as referring to the immediate antecedent namely, the list of Christian virtues mentioned in verses 5 to 7. "**Yours**", the present participle, *huparchonta*, has a particularly significant nuance of meaning. It stresses abiding ownership of something in such a way that what is possessed is wholly at the owner's disposal, that is, absolute possession. The word was used as a noun in the papyri, with the meaning "property" and, hence, belongs to the realm of the property market[47]. Salvation, then, is the inalienable possession of the believer and totally at his disposal to develop. That development, too, is not only the believer's privilege but also his responsibility.

This fits in well with the entire nature of covenant salvation

---

[47] D. Lucas & C. Green, *The Message of 2 Peter & Jude*, p61 citing J.N.D. Kelly, *A Commentary On The Epistles Of Peter and Of Jude*, p307.

both in Old and New Testaments. Salvation was given by grace in the Old Testament as a relationship with God for the believer and his children, of which a tangible symbol was the inheritance of "the land". In his first letter, Peter expresses this celebration in terms of an inheritance bequeathed to the child of God, who is birthed for it by the God and Father of our Lord Jesus Christ. It is an inheritance kept inviolably for him, just as he is kept for it (1 Pe. 1:3-5). Here, in his second letter, the "property" of grace is also sovereignly gifted to the believer, which as his own, he must not only enjoy but use and develop. He must possess his possessions and make them his very own (Obad. 17). The acquisition is by gift not by works. However, he must work out the salvation that God has worked in him with fear and trembling (Ph. 2:12-13).

"And are increasing" It seems better to take "increase" as a separate, if related, action to **"yours"**, since both are present participles not dependent on one another, rather than as the NIV translates "possess these qualities in increasing measure". **"Increase"** *pleonazonta* means that the possessions grow in such a way as to prove more than enough, indeed, overflowing, with the additional thought of superabundance. In property language, this means that the acquisitions increase to mammoth proportions not only in terms of ownership but also financially – a sort of multi-million consortium of property. This emphasizes the responsibility of the believer to develop his faith. Peter has already used the strong expression "make every effort", the noun *spouden* (v 5) to express the focused intention of the Christian in that aspect of growth and, later in the letter, he uses the very same expression as a verb to urge Christians to godly living in the light of Christ's return (3:14 cf. 1:10;). There can be no idea here of sanctification being a lackadaisical attitude of resting on one's own oars or even on God's, important as a basic foundation is, that is, of simply "letting go and letting God", or of seeing growth as a miraculous 'instant' secondary experience of grace or dependent on a cycle of crises in the Christian life, though that does happen (cf.

Ro. 5:1-5; Ja. 1:2-8; 1 Pe. 1:6-9). Rather, the steady, constant process of continually adding to one's faith through prayerful application of the word in daily Christian living produces the virtuous, godly character. That is the kind of increase implicit here. In property language, it involves wise speculation and accumulation, in terms of ethical character rather than earthly goods. The possession of Christian grace and graces must increase in this way.

"They keep you from being ineffective or unfruitful" In this positive context, the use here of *litotes*-a double negative to stress a positive-enhances the imagery. We need eventually to turn the negative over and appreciate the positive thrust of meaning. The metaphor continues in the business world but also includes the world of nature. This accentuates the vividness of the expression.

"Ineffective" *argous* also means "idle", "useless". The other few usages of the word in the New Testament well illustrate its meaning. In the parable of the workers in the vineyard, Christ twice uses this term to describe those he calls to work as "standing idle in the market-place" (Mt. 20:3 [*argous*], 6 [*argoi*]). James describes faith without works as "useless" (Ja. 2:20 [*argē*]). The cultivation of these virtues for the believer keeps him from being idle and useless in his Christian life. Such a process, on the other hand, makes him industrious and effective in his faith.

"Unfruitful" *akarpous.* James speaks of faith without works as "useless" (Ja. 2:20), just as Paul writes of faith "working through love" (Ga. 5:6). *Akarpous* means "fruitless", "unproductive" and recalls the world of nature. In the parable of the sower, Christ concludes that the worries of this life and the deceitfulness of wealth and desires for other things choke this seed and make it "unfruitful" (Mk. 4:19). Jude depicts godless men, as "autumn trees, without fruit and uprooted-twice dead" (Jude 12 [NIV]). Adding these virtuous qualities to the believer's faith keeps him from being fruitless and unproductive. Positively speaking, cultivating Christian character, makes faith as Peter urges, fruitful and productive. Faith needs to yield a harvest both in Christian character and living.

Jesus claimed that fruit of this kind differentiated the false from the true teacher and was proof of genuine discipleship (Mt. 7:15-20; Jn. 15:7-8). One of the most forceful descriptions in the New Testament, which turns the coin over and illustrates the forcefulness of Peter's litotes, comes from Paul's prayer for the Colossian believers: "And we pray this in order that you may live a life worthy of the Lord and may please him in every way: bearing fruit in every good work, growing in the knowledge of God" (Col. 1:10 NIV). The phrase, **"in the knowledge of our Lord Jesus Christ"**, as a whole, can be taken in two ways. Taking **"in"** *eis* in the more general sense of "in respect of", "with reference to", it can mean that the cultivation of Christian virtues is the fulfilment and proof of the **"knowledge"** of Christ evident in conversion. Taking **"in"** *eis* in the sense of "into" or "resulting in", it means that the development of these Christian virtues enrich our saving knowledge of Christ. Both are not mutually exclusive but the latter seems more in keeping with what Peter is saying.

Again, with regard to the phrase, **"in the knowledge of our Lord Jesus Christ"**, **"knowledge"**, here the intense form *epignōsis*, relates this teaching to the main theme of Peter's letter (1:2, 3, cf. 6, 8; 2:20-22; cf. 3:18). Cultivation of Christian character, in this way, is basic to growth in grace and knowledge of our Lord Jesus Christ (3:18). It is, too, specifically this cultivation of Christian character that lies at the heart of Christian growth and sanctification. Whatever other rightful pursuits involve the believer: study of God's word, prayer; service within the church, witness and outreach, the practice of good works, kind deeds and hospitality, the cultivation of Christian character by adding these virtues to faith is not an optional extra but a basic necessity and fundamental to all these other Christian exercises. Positively put, speculating, and accumulating the graces inherent in salvation makes the believer effective and fruitful at the very heart of his Christian life, his covenant relationship with God through Christ his Saviour. It affects the very core of his character and behaviour. The repetition of growth in knowledge at 3:18 marks a positive closing *inclusio* of this theme at the end of the letter.

NEGATIVE

"For whoever lacks these qualities is so short-sighted that he is blind, having forgotten that he was cleansed from his former sins" (1:9).

"For whoever lacks these qualities is so short-sighted that he is blind" Peter's change from the specific "you" implicit in the verb at verse 8 to the more general "anyone" here at verse 9 may well be significant. He is not necessarily condemning his readers on this score, but warning them of the dangers of lacking growth in Christian virtue. The context of verse 9 is quite obviously that of the human body in terms of its function or dysfunction, ability or disability. This imagery will have a controlling influence over interpretation, just as the "property-market" imagery of verse 8 predominates there.

This illustration of bodily disability, since here at verse 9 the force of the argument is primarily negative indicating lack of Christian virtues, is emphasized by the use of the idea of blindness. There are many references to blindness, *tuphlos*, "**blind**", in the metaphorical sense of spiritual blindness throughout the teaching of both Jesus and the apostles, (Mt. 15:14; 23:17, 24; Lu.6:39; Jn. 9:39-41; 12:40; Ro. 2:19; 2 Co. 4:4; 1 Jn. 2:9; Re. 3:17 cf. He.6:4; 10:32 for spiritual enlightenment or the lack of it). This idea of spiritual blindness is clearly the meaning here. Those lacking Christian virtue and increase of it suffer from spiritual blindness. There are similarities, too, in the seriousness of this condition of spiritual blindness between the deficient believer and the totally blind unbeliever: superficiality, confusion, purposelessness and imminent personal danger characterize both. And, of course, the lack of Christian virtue and its growth is as serious a condition in the spiritual realm as being blind or short-sighted is in the physical realm.

"**Short-sighted**" is the participle *muōpazōn* from which our English "myopia". Myopia means being short or near-sighted, so that while objects near at hand are clearly seen, distant objects are hazy and indistinct. A problem, here, is that the original puts the adjective "**blind**" before the participle "**short-sighted**" and on the understanding that a blind person cannot be short-sighted as well as blind, some translations have reversed the order putting "**short-sighted**" before "**blind**". Some of these translations imply, in the light of the participial form of *muōpazōn*, that the short-sighted condition has led to blindness. e.g. (NIV; ESV; NKJV, cf. AV).

As to meaning, there are various options:

1. That "**short-sighted**" stands independently and implies, along with spiritual blindness, a condition of seeing things near at hand clearly but things distant indistinctly as, for example, being engrossed in temporal to the exclusion of spiritual matters, being too "earthly minded as to be any heavenly use" or so generally deficient in Christian wisdom as to lack overall purpose and direction.

2. That "**short-sighted**" in its participial function, with a meaning is similar to option one, leads to being "**blind**" and the order, "**blind, short-sighted**" is expletive and explanatory of such blindness.

3. That **"short-sighted"** *muōpazōn*, involving blinking or closing the eyes in a squinting fashion, implies intentionally closing one's eyes to spiritual truth and that this interpretation is supported by the following phrase **"having forgotten"** *lēthēn labōn*, literally, "having received or taken forgetfulness", which is also said to be intentional. The problem with this view is that the squinting is with a view to seeing the object more clearly not closing one's eyes to it.

It is, perhaps, unnecessary to be restricted to one particular viewpoint, as Peter is generally referring to spiritual disability and possibly varying his imagery to suit slightly differing results of the lack of Christian virtue. Lack of development in Christian virtue evinces spiritual blindness in that the true purpose of salvation is obscured. Growth in character becomes secondary, unimportant and, to a degree, irrelevant. It also makes a person short-sighted in that vision is stunted. The person lacks true foresight, insight, and wisdom. He loses the 'bigger picture'. It restricts his vision. Absence of growth in grace presents disability in terms of spiritual sight on both scores. It both prevents and distorts that sight. The two are invariably linked and equally culpable. Such disability leaves the professing believer, paradoxically, both blind and near-sighted!

"Having forgotten that he was cleansed from his former sins"
"Having forgotten" *lēthēn labōn* is, as noted above, literally "having received or taken forgetfulness". In physical terms, it implies amnesia and may have the sad modern connotation of Alzheimer's disease, which gives a pitiful illustration of confusion and bewilderment, often exasperated by the patient's own awareness of the condition. As far as intentionality is concerned, this rather depends as to whether we take *labōn* as "received" or "taken", where the latter, implying intentionality, is linguistically possible, a kind of self-induced spiritual amnesia.

While many commentaries link "**cleansed**" directly with baptism, others simply maintain the link solely with forgiveness. The latter is preferable, since baptism is not mentioned in the context. The implication here seems to be that the professing Christian's behaviour lacking growth and development in Christian virtue portrays him as a believer, who has forgotten the significance of his cleansing from past sins and his initiation into Christianity. His lack of Christian growth not only belies his faith but depicts him as unaware and, perhaps, indifferent to the whole matter. He lives, spiritually speaking, in a little world of his own, far removed from the redemption from sin professedly experienced.

The overall picture here that Peter paints is painfully clear. Lack of the presence of and growth in these qualities, which he has been describing, means that the professing believer is presenting all the signs of spiritual disability: blindness, short-sightedness and amnesia, a condition which, with so many links with that of the unbeliever, places a serious question mark over his personal calling and election, indeed, over his being regenerate at all! Christopher Green incisively comments:

> Perhaps the simplest solution is to take the words in their original order, with their normal meaning, and ask what it is that each disability prevents. Someone who is blind cannot see at all, someone who is short-sighted cannot see what lies ahead in the distance, and someone who has forgotten cannot remember what lies behind him. This fits the problem of the false teachers and the peril of their victims.[48]

What a sad picture of unproductive and fruitless professing Christians who do not grow in grace!

---

[48]   D. Lucas & C. Green, *The Message of 2 Peter & Jude*, p62.

APPLICATION

The positive benefits of adding these Christian virtues to one's faith are vividly portrayed on the background of the property metaphor here. Effectiveness and productivity are maximized and the Christian "business" is seen to prosper and advance. Similarly, the negative defects of the lack of growth in these graces are painfully obvious in the schema of a dysfunctional and disabled spiritual "body". Blindness, short-sightedness, and amnesia portray a sad picture of what ought to be Christian well-being. The saddest of all is that the Christian church has neither taken sufficiently seriously the contrast spiritually between the two conditions nor the reasons leading to them. Christians sadly tend to be hyperactive in zeal and outreach, without the corresponding introspective soul-culture necessary to a healthy and balanced diet of Christian growth. They will, too, put every sophisticated and self-motivated activity before growth in Christian character.

The words of an "old-fashioned" Christian praise need to be experienced again, if this situation is to be remedied:

> Take time to be holy, speak oft with thy Lord;
> Abide in Him always, and feed on his Word.
> Make friends of God's children, help those who
> are weak;
> Forgetting in nothing His blessing to seek.
>
> Take time to be holy, the world rushes on;
> Spend much time in secret with Jesus alone –
> By looking to Jesus, like Him thou shalt be!
> Thy friends, in thy conduct, His likeness shall see.
>
> Take time to be holy, let Him be thy guide;
> And run not before Him, whatever betide;

In joy or in sorrow still follow thy Lord,
And, looking to Jesus, still trust in His Word.

Take time to be holy, be calm in thy soul;
Each thought and each temper beneath His control;
Thus led by His Spirit to fountains of love,
Thou soon shall be fitted for service above.[49]

---

[49]   William Dunn Longstaff (1822-94).

Chapter 7

ASSURED

2 PETER 1:10, 11

INTRODUCTION

Peter now gathers up all he has been saying thus far in a conclusive confirmatory note. His readers are to take action to ensure that they are truly Christians. The subject of these two verses is assurance of salvation. Peter wants them to be sure they are really saved. His desire is that they know that they know Christ. This aspect of true knowledge is its assured nature. This will bring contentment rather than complacency to his readers and will provide a further impetus for growth in grace in their lives. In that way, it will contribute to the main reason for Peter's writing his second letter to them (3:1, 2 cf. 3:18).

Other New Testament writers have the same perspective in view. John writes his gospel so that his readers might believe that Jesus is the Christ, the Son of God, and that by believing they might have life in his name (Jn. 20:31). John writes his first letter to those who believe in the name of the Son of God, so that they might know that they have eternal life (1 Jn. 5:13). With all the troubles in the Corinthian church, Paul in his first letter urges self-examination before participation in the Lord's Supper (1 Co. 11:27-28). At the end of his second letter to the same church, he is equally adamant about the necessity of self-examination: "Examine yourselves, to see whether you are in the faith. Test yourselves. Or do you not realize this about yourselves, that Jesus Christ is in you? – unless indeed you fail to meet the test!" (2 Co. 13:5). The writer to the Hebrews is concerned about his readers having a superficial foundation of salvation, a flawed or impaired repentance and faith (He.5:11–6:12) and urges them to discover for themselves the certainty of God's saving promise, a promise confirmed by an oath (He.6:13–7:22).

Peter deals here with the same subject of assurance of salvation. First, he describes the nature of assurance (v10[a]), then its incomparable benefits both for this life and the next (vv10[b]-11).

EXPOSITION

NATURE

**"Therefore, brothers, be all the more diligent
to make your calling and election sure" (1:10[a]).**

"Therefore, brothers" Assurance of salvation involves human effort on the part of the believer. The slogan of Christian passivity, "Let go and let God" may, to some extent, underlie justification. It certainly is not the watchword for either sanctification or assurance of salvation. For these, the Christian's effort is responsibly required. **"Therefore"** gathers up the foregoing, both that immediately preceding and, indeed, all that Peter has written thus far. It embraces not only the thrust of possessing growth qualities of Christian character in increasing measure (v8), the effort of adding to one's faith the required virtues (vv5-7) but even the basic acquisition and implementation of those great and precious promises from which these graces in salvation ultimately spring (vv3-4). "**Therefore**" is a grand summary.

"**Be all the more diligent**" includes the verb *spoudasate*. The equivalent noun *spoudē* "eagerness", "earnestness", "diligence" is used in verse 5, where Peter urges his readers to "make every effort" to add to their faith the Christian virtues he mentions. The same zeal that is required for growth in grace is necessary for gaining assurance of salvation for, of course, the two are interrelated – "By this my Father is glorified, that you bear much fruit and so prove to be my disciples" (Jn. 15:8 cf. Mt. 7:16-20). Human effort on the Christian's part is required. The infinitive "**to make**" *poieisthai* in the reflexive mood, "to make oneself" is emphatic and implies not only human but personal effort. Being sure of one's salvation is something intensely personal. Others cannot do this for us. The individual believer alone can and must do it personally.

"**Your calling and election**" Assurance of salvation remarkably implies a divine source. The amazing thing is that Christians are required to make themselves sure of something over which they have no ultimate control, their salvation by sovereign grace! "**Calling and election**" *klēsin kai eklogēn*, are closely related both in language and meaning. If there is any distinction, it is that God elects man in eternity (Ep. 1:4) but also calls him in time (Ro. 8:30).

Jesus, Paul and Peter all explain the nature, order and purpose of calling and election in a similar way (Jn. 15:16; Ro. 8:29, 30; Ep. 1:4, 5; 1 Pe. 1:1-2, 9,15). The nature is sovereign. Election and calling are and remain God's redemptive acts. The order is rational. Election precedes and gives rise to calling. The purpose is gracious. Holiness and purity are the results in the believer's life. Here, Peter inverts the order: calling and election, obviously for a particular purpose. He wants his readers to trace behind their calling, which has brought them to faith, the source of God's electing grace, and to view the increased growth and supplemental virtues to faith as proof of their calling and election. Peter was not saying that purely human attempts at growth in grace completed salvation and qualified a believer for heaven. He was simply recalling what Jesus had taught and the apostles continued to teach, that fruit was proof of genuine faith and proof of a work of sovereign grace.

"**Sure**" Assurance of salvation invites practical demonstration. "**Sure**" *bebaian* in Greek literature has a legal connotation and has a ring of confirmatory evidence, namely, definitely sure. This is also evident, to a degree, in New Testament usage, for example, of the prophetic word (2 Pe. 1:19), of faith (2 Co. 1:7), of promise (Ro. 4:16), of confidence (He. 3:6,14), of an anchor of the soul (He. 6:19), of a covenant or last will and testament (He. 9:17). Here, as regards "**sure**", relating to calling and election, the legal force might be seen in demonstrable evidence as confirmation of salvation. Peter thus recalls the list of growing Christian virtues already noted (vv5-7) as evidence of assurance. In a similar fashion, John in his first letter, mentions a moral test of obedience to Christ's commands (1 Jn. 2:3), a social test of loving Christian brothers (1 Jn. 3:14) and a doctrinal test of believing in Christ with the consequent result of no longer continuing in sin (1 Jn. 5:1,18) all as an exercise in helping towards assurance of salvation. The Christian can humbly yet confidently point to certain aspects of character formation and growth in his life as evidence of salvation. This brings him assurance of grace and salvation in a demonstrable way.

Calvin puts it well:

> He (Peter) draws this conclusion, that it is one proof
> that we have been really elected, and not in vain

called by the Lord, if a good conscience and integrity of life correspond with our profession of faith.[50]

BENEFITS

"for if you practise these qualities you will never fall. For in this way there will be richly provided for you an entrance into the eternal kingdom of our Lord and Saviour Jesus Christ" (1:10^b, 11).

"For if you practise these qualities you will never fall" One benefit of assurance of grace and salvation is spiritual security. **"These qualities"**, *tauta* cf. vv8 and 9, like "therefore" could refer back to the exercise of supplementing faith with Christian virtue, and to its source in the great and precious promises of salvation as well as to the present project of making calling and election sure. The verb *ptaisēte* as "fall" has led to serious misunderstanding. First, taking the word as a synonym for "sin", in the sense of "never sin", it has led to the concept of "sinless perfection" which is biblically indefensible (1 Jn. 1:8). Secondly, the possibility of falling "from" grace rather than "within" grace is the suggested implication and this also lacks biblical warrant (Jn. 10:28-29; Ro. 8:29-30; Ph. 1:6).

The verb *ptaiō* yields various meanings: "to stumble" "to trip", "to fall", "to stumble so as to fall", "to be ruined", "to be lost". **"Fall"** here could have the sense of "stumble" or "fall" without meaning to be completely or finally lost. The racehorse stumbles or falls in progress but it does not necessarily abort completely either the purpose of the race or its nature as a racehorse. This seems to be the sense here. Such is consistent with other New Testament usage. James mentions that we all, as Christians stumble *(ptaiomen)* in many ways, but the man who does not stumble *(ptaiei)* in speech evinces maturity, for he controls his entire body (Ja.3:2). Paul suggests that

---

50   J. Calvin, *Commentaries on II Peter*, p376 (Addition mine).

while Israel was "broken off" to facilitate Gentiles entering the kingdom (Ro.11:17, 19-20), they did not "stumble *(eptaisan)* so as to fall *(pesōsin)* beyond recovery?" (Ro.11:11 ^NIV). Jude concludes his letter by praising God who is able both to keep his people from falling *(aptaistous)* and to present them before his glorious presence without fault and with great joy and does so on a strongly exultant note (Jude 24). Peter's words seem to have a similar sense here. **"Fall"** here means to "stumble" or "come to grief/ruin" *within* grace not *from* grace. The true believer cannot fall from grace. It is a denial of his eternal security.

One of the benefits of assurance for the believer, then, as he pursues these qualities of living is a security and preservation during his earthly pilgrimage. He does not come to ruin, fall into gross error or stumble into grievous doubt, despair or fear without recovery. Negatively, this is his experience. Positively, Peter next shows the joyous context of his prospect as he enters his heavenly home. Here and hereafter, he is safe in the arms of Jesus.

"For in this way there will be richly provided for you" The other benefit of assurance of grace and salvation Peter notes is a rich reward for the believer in heaven. The lavish nature of this entrance here is emphatic. **"Richly"** translates *plousiōs* the word normally used for material wealth and possessions. The word group is used in the New Testament both literally of temporal riches and metaphorically also of spiritual wealth. It has the latter connotation here as heaven comes into view. This idea of heavenly riches is emphasized by an expression Peter has earlier used in verse 5 associated with *spoudē* "eagerness", "earnestness", or "effort". This is similar usage to what we have seen also in the case used at verses 5 and 10 and mentioned previously. **"There will be provided for you"** is literally "there will be 'chorused' for you": *epichorēgēthēsetai*. As we have noted earlier, in Greek drama, the *chorēgos* was the "chorus-master". This person was usually a person who, as a patron of the arts, provided at his own expense the whole dramatic production, protagonists or main actors and the chorus as well – a large team of choral narrators – to present the theme. The expression "chorused" used here and in verse 5, also in verbal form, implies a rich and lavish provision, no expense being spared. At verse 5, it describes the Christian's attitude of adding to or supplementing his faith. Here, at verse 11, it describes the lavish **"entrance"** or "welcome" the Christian receives as he moves from grace to glory, from earthly security to heavenly reward. The use of the word at verse 5 and 11 forms an *inclusio* encapsulating the entire section. The believer enjoys spiritual riches both here and hereafter.

"An entrance into the eternal kingdom of our Lord and Saviour Jesus Christ" You would naturally think that this expression: **"eternal kingdom"** was frequent in the New Testament. In fact, it is not. It is used here in these terms and almost nowhere else, other than some slight reference to it in Christian literature almost as an allusion or quotation from Peter's letter here. However, unique as it is, its theme is enduring. It recalls the richness of the believer's relationship with Christ as king, begun here on earth, now continuing, growing, and reaching fulfilment in heaven. It echoes Jesus' words: "Come, you who are blessed by my Father, inherit the kingdom prepared for you from the foundation of the world" (Mt. 25:34). It forms a fitting conclusion to Peter's advice on assurance, the benefits in this life of a secure and preserved salvation and of a lavish and rich reward in the life to come.

John MacArthur sums it up well:

> Assurance of one's having entered into **the eternal kingdom** is the experience of the Christian who practices what Peter has listed. That was great encouragement to the apostle's weary readers. No believer needs to live with doubt regarding salvation, but he may have assurance **abundantly**

supplied in the present. A rich heavenly reward in the future may also be implied (cf. 2 Tim. 4:8; Heb. 4:9; 12:28; 1 Peter 5:4; Rev. 2:10; 22:12).

The Lord will reward His children based on their faithful pursuit of righteousness (see again 1 Cor. 3:11-14; 2 Cor. 5:10). Assurance in this life and riches in heaven are the benefits of spiritual diligence and fruitfulness.[51]

APPLICATION

Assurance of grace and salvation is not an optional extra for the Christian but a basic necessity. It is not simply a required additional interest for him, it is something intensely personal that he and he only can and must do for himself. That is why this command here in Peter's letter, comes so meaningfully from Peter himself.

Peter is the true and classic "backslider" and he writes to us from that perspective. Once Peter walked on the water by faith, then he stumbled and fell into it. At one time Christ commends him for his startling and divinely revealed confession of faith, then immediately Christ berates him for being a tool and mouthpiece of Satan. Proudly he claims that he will never forsake Jesus, yet shamefully declaims all knowledge of his Master before a servant girl. Confidently he rises to become leader as fisher of men. Depressingly he goes back to fishing for fish, drawing others after him. Who, like Peter, could give us the answer to the constant backsliding that dogs so much of our own Christian experience? We need to heed his advice.

By now, as he writes, Peter's glorious zenith as "an apostle to the Jews" (Ga. 2:8 [NIV]) is almost passed. He goes on to tell us next in

---

[51]   John MacArthur, *2 Peter and Jude,* p45, (Emphasis his).

his letter that Christ has revealed to him that the close of his life is near. He gives this advice not only as a man who knew depressing backsliding in his life as well as the solution to it, but as a believer about to face his Master and Judge. But for himself, he is assured – not, as so often in the past, by self but by God – that the trumpets will all sound and he will enter his glorious reward. Of that too, he is assured, both in terms of an earthly and a heavenly assurance.

It is not so for all "professing" believers. Some who profess and profess to have done mighty works in Christ's name will hear those awful words: "I never knew you. Away from me, you evildoers!" (Mt.7:23 [NIV]). Some who have the right foundation but have built a flawed superstructure on it – wood, hay, straw rather than gold, silver, precious stones – will be saved as a man escaping through the flames with nothing to show for it (1 Co. 3:10-15). Some like Hymenaeus and Alexander, who rejected faith and a good conscience, and made shipwreck of their faith will sadly move in this direction (1 Ti.1:19-20). The term backslider is often wrongly used today of those who have never truly come to faith in the first instance.

The answer to all this is not found in secondary Christian experience or hyper Christian activity or zealous Christian witness, important and valuable as all of these might or might not be, but by the "right use of ordinary means", of the word and prayer – above all, as Peter advises: adding lavishly to our faith Christian virtue, in cultivating and developing personal biblical godliness, in growing practically in grace and making our calling and election sure. Only then, will we receive this lavish reward. John Albert Bengel writes and writes well: "You may be able to enter, not as having escaped from a shipwreck, or from fire, but as it were in triumph".[52]

May God grant that ultimate experience to us all.

---

[52]   J.A. Bengel, *Gnomon of the New Testament*, vol. 5, p90 cited in S.J. Kistemaker, *James, Epistles of John, Peter, and Jude*, p257.

Chapter 8

REMEMBERED

2 PETER 1:12-15

INTRODUCTION

Peter writes of this true knowledge, the leading theme of Second Peter Chapter 1, as saving (vv3, 4), growing (vv5-7), fruitful (vv8, 9), assured (vv10, 11) and, now, as remembered (vv12-15). In fact, remembrance is the means whereby all the benefits of true knowledge of God come to Peter's readers. God used the faculty of memory to communicate the blessings of salvation both in Old and New Testaments. The last words of Jacob, Moses and David are prominent examples of this as is the ordinance of the Passover. In the New Testament, Jesus, Paul and Peter often look back and recall, while the Lord's Supper itself is structured in these terms. Thus, the Sabbath is not only a weekly remembrance of God as Creator (Ex. 20:8-11) but also of God as Redeemer (Ex. 20:2; De. 5:6), who brought his people out of Egypt by a mighty hand and outstretched arm and, as a weekly reminder, specifically focuses on recalling God's redemption of his people from their slavery in Egypt (De.

5:15). The Passover is an annual reminder of this redemptive event (De. 16:1-3). The New Testament counterpart, the Lord's Supper, reflects a similarly redemptive memorial aspect (Lu. 22:19) and, consistently, the apostles employ remembrance to communicate the meaning of the gospel, even to those who have received, accepted and experienced it (1 Co. 15:1; 2 Pe. 1:12; Jude 5; cf. 2 Pe. 3:1-2).

This emphasis together with writings described as "Testaments" penned during the intertestamental period ascribing glory to great men after their decease as well as apocryphal works such as the Gospel of Peter, the Acts of Peter and the Apocalypse of Peter has led some scholars to regard Second Peter as belonging to the same literary genre: a "Testament of Peter". They contend that it was written pseudonymously to honour Peter after his death and, hence, is certainly not of Petrine authorship.

However, just as the theory of First Peter as a baptismal homily is defective, so the idea of Second Peter as a "testament" is similarly indefensible, largely on the grounds that, in both cases, the letters do not satisfy the criteria of any examples we have of those literary genres. There is simply insufficient evidence to prove that 1 and 2 Peter belong to such forms of literature, even if there may be indications of these ideas within the letters.

Peter presents this "remembrance" section (vv12-15) in three quite distinct ways:

> First, in verse 12, Peter reminds his readers forcefully of these things, possibly on the background of recalling some words of Christ himself to Peter, with a view to bringing about his readers' stability, a stability he readily recognizes they already have, but which still requires the emphasis of his reminder.

Secondly, in verses 13 and 14, Peter refreshes his readers' memory, an activity he clearly regards as appropriate, probably again on the background of Christ's words to himself, this time with a view to their submission to Christ, in the light of his own imminent death.

Thirdly, in verse 15, Peter makes a determined effort to ensure that, even after his death, his readers will themselves always be able to recall these things, with a view to their continuing stimulation toward Christian growth and godliness, a process of recall drawing on the entire spectrum of Scripture for its inspiration.

All of this anticipates the continuing theme of remembrance of Scripture both immediately afterwards here at 1:16-21 and later again at 3:1-2f. as a major feature of Second Peter, where Chapter 2 forms a kind of important contrasting interlude to this theme. We will continue to note this vital and expanding discussion on Scripture relative to knowledge within the letter, as we investigate Peter's emphasis on the purpose of this remembrance, and review it further at Chapter 3:

REMINDER	(v12)
REFRESHMENT	(vv13-14)
RECALL	(v15)

EXPOSITION

"Therefore I intend always to remind you of these qualities, though you know them and are established in the truth that you have. I think it

right, as long as I am in this body, to stir you up by way of reminder, since I know that the putting off of my body will be soon, as our Lord Jesus Christ made clear to me. And I will make every effort so that after my departure you may be able at any time to recall these things" (1:12-15).

REMINDER

"Therefore I intend always to remind you of these qualities" The forcefulness of Peter's approach is emphasized. There is a double future here, which expresses his determined attempt to remind them. Literally, it reads: "so I will always be about to remind you", for the verb *mellēsō* basically means, "to be about to do something" and is also here in the future tense. **"These qualities"** *toutōn*, is a comprehensive, repetitive, descriptive particle of Peter's. In verses 8 and 9, it refers to the increasing supplements to faith Peter advises and it occurs again at verse 15 both gathering up the features to be remembered and anticipating advice given by the writer in the rest of his letter.

"Though you know them and are established in the truth that you have" Peter's reminder is notwithstanding his readers' knowledge of these things. His intention to remind them is all the more forceful on this background. Paul and Jude are of the same mind (1 Co. 15:1; Jude 5). The apostles are not teaching novel truths but what is already known, received and experienced. This, in itself, points up the importance of reminder in the process of evangelistic and instructional practice. Paul's words to Timothy are apposite here: "Keep reminding them of these things" (2 Ti. 2:14 NIV).

Peter's reminder stresses the depth of his readers' acceptance of these things. He gladly congratulates them in his reminder. Peter's readers **"know"** *eidotas* with intensity the qualities of which he has been writing. Already and throughout his letter, there is this stress on knowledge of these things both in terms of *epignōsis* and *gnōsis* (1:2, 3, 5, 6, 8; 2:20, 21; 3:18). He reminds them of something they have come to know and increasingly know. It is not just cognitive but rather relational and experiential, knowledge of both head and heart. They are also **"established"** *estērigmenous*. There is nothing superficial about his readers' knowledge; they are rooted and grounded in these things. There is a stability and maturity about them. They are established **"in the truth that you have"**. Theirs is a defined "truth" *alētheia*, which in Christ has led them to God and freed them from sin (cf. Jn. 14:6; Jn. 8:32). It is also a present truth **"you have"** *parousē*. They do not simply profess but possess these things.

The keynote here is stability and that, in Peter's own memory, recalls a troubled period of his life, when he was anything but stable, those days between his confession and restoration, when Christ pointedly advised him:

> "Simon, Simon, behold, Satan demanded to have you, that he might sift you like wheat, but I have prayed for you that your faith may not fail. And when you have turned again, strengthen *(stērison)* your brothers" (Lu.22:31-32).

The memory of those words never seems to have left Peter, particularly the commission to strengthen or establish other brothers. His own harrowing experience left him in no doubt as to the necessity of stability in Christ and thus drives him to remind others of its necessity. So, in his first letter, in a closing benediction he affirmed that God, after his readers have suffered a little while, will restore, and make them strong *(stērixei)* (1 Pe. 5:10). Later, at the close of his second letter, he warns his readers not to be carried away by the error of lawless men and fall from their secure position (*stērigmou*) but rather grow in the grace and knowledge of our Lord and Saviour Jesus Christ (2 Pe. 3:17,18). Peter's fixation, born of his own frustrating experience, was to establish others in their faith, so that they would not go through the suffering and shame, which he had brought upon himself. His reminder is obsessively and personally passionate. We do well to take it to heart.

M. Green notes well the significant recurrence of the term, "established" "strengthen", which comes from the same Greek root:

> And there may be something poignant in his use of the word *established* to describe his hesitant and wavering readers. For that is the word which Jesus used of him on one memorable occasion when, although so fickle, he was sure that *he* was established in the truth and could not possibly apostasize (see Lk.22:32). It seems to have become a favourite word of this turbulent man who now really was established. He uses it in his final prayer at the end of 1 Peter (5:10), and a similar word occurs in a significant context in 2 Peter 3:17.[53]

Reminder is a first and necessary exercise in remembrance of scriptural knowledge.

REFRESHMENT

"I think it right . . . to stir you up by way of reminder" Peter's attitude here relates to the appropriateness of his reminder. He regards his action as *dikaion*: right, just, and proper. The particular way in which he describes remembrance here is, **"to stir you up by way of reminder"**. The verb is, *diegeirein*. It means literally to "awaken" or "arouse" a person from sleep and is used like this in

---

[53]   M. Green, *2 Peter and Jude*, pp87-88 (Emphasis his).

the New Testament. Here, the sense is metaphorical and "refresh" is perhaps too weak a term, as the idea is to "stir" a person quite strongly. Peter uses the word again in this letter at 3:1, where the sense is obviously again figurative. This idea, though, calls to mind Peter and the sleeping disciples in Gethsemane (Mt. 26:36-46; Mk. 14:32-42; Lu.22:39-46). Peter thinks it entirely appropriate for him to stir their memory about these things, to the point of rousing them from spiritual slumber. It is a stirring and arousing refreshment.

"as long as I am in this body, . . . since I know that the putting off of my body will be soon, as our Lord Jesus Christ made clear to me." Peter is conscious, as he refreshes their minds, that his is a frail and creaturely body. There is no word for body in the original. Rather, *skēnōma*, a tent, is twice used (vv13,14), but this does emphasize Peter's frailty. The expression is not evidence of a Greek despising of the bodily as opposed to the spirit condition, but taken, as Calvin points out, in the normal biblical sense of "an implied contrast between a fading tabernacle and a perpetual habitation, which Paul explains in 2 Cor. v.1".[54]

There is also a degree of urgency about Peter's words, for he mentions that he will soon strike this tent and put it aside **"as our Lord Jesus Christ made clear to me"**. "Soon" (*tachinē*) (v14) could also incorporate the idea of "sudden" or "swift", as the word does at 2:1, but this is not crucial as to its meaning. Where and when the Lord Jesus had made this clear to Peter has been a matter of some debate. Was it a special revelation given to Peter like those given to Paul, but of which we have no evidence? Certainly, apocryphal works such as the Acts of Peter with its Quo Vadis (Where are you going to?) legend portray it as something of a mystery. Perhaps a better source, though certainly still allowing for an unknown special revelation, would be again to recall words of Jesus to Peter?

---

54   J. Calvin, *Commentaries on II Peter*, p380.

101

Jesus, according to a conversation with Peter recorded at John13:36-38, replies to Peter's question: "'Lord, where are you going?'" and hints at Peter's going the same way as he, Jesus, would in the future but not at that present point of time: "Jesus answered him, 'Where I am going you cannot follow me now, but you will follow afterwards'". This conversation may well be substantiated by Jesus' later remarks to Peter on the occasion of his restoration by the then risen Christ:

> "'Truly, truly, I say to you, when you were young, you used to dress yourself and walk wherever you wanted, but when you are old, you will stretch out your hands, and another will dress you and carry you where you do not want to go.' (This he said to show by what kind of death he was to glorify God.) And after saying this he said to him, 'Follow me'" (Jn. 21:18,19).

It has been objected that this describes the *manner* of Peter's death rather than its *timing*, as "**soon**" in the text before us implies. However, *tachinē* as noted means "swift" or "sudden", which would better suit this interpretation. Nevertheless, the general theme is Peter's death and Jesus' words here seem the most likely source of Peter's "revelation". If this is the case, there is, again, behind Peter's motivation to remind and to refresh the memory of his readers the words of Jesus. This time, however, they come from a slightly later sequence in Peter's life and stress, if the preceding words of Jesus in restoring Peter mean anything, the need for Peter's total submission to his Lord as a continuing requirement of Christian living and service. Again, as Peter refreshes his readers' memories of these things, he recalls from his own quite devastating personal reminiscences and affirms the need for absolute submission to Christ as Lord. The feeding of lambs and sheep and the following of Christ as Lord are inextricably bound together in a bond of submission which drives Peter and should drive his readers too, to remember these things with passion, verve and total commitment, while they live in the tent of this body.

Christopher Green comments helpfully:

> Knowing that his death was imminent, Peter wanted to make the best use of the time left to him. Strikingly, he has no new teaching to impart to the Christians. Instead, he simply has to *refresh* their *memory*. He had told them certain things in a previous letter which he wishes to ensure they do not forget. His teaching in this letter will be preventative, to stop the new teaching from so flooding their minds with novelties and wonders that they lose their critical faculties and become victims of a brainwash.[55]

Refreshment that is robust and stirring is a second and helpful aid in developing remembrance of scriptural knowledge.

RECALL

"And I will make every effort" Peter here reverts to the strong expression he has previously used in encouraging his readers. The verb behind this expression is *spoudasō*. He has already used the noun *spoudēn* at verse 5 in urging his readers to add to their faith the Christian virtues he advises and at verse 10 he uses the verb *spoudasate* to require diligence of them in making their calling and election sure. The same eagerness he demands of his readers regarding their growth in grace and assurance of salvation, Peter himself uses in his passionate aim to ensure that they are left an adequate reminder of these things after his death.

---

[55]   D. Lucas & C. Green, *The Message Of 2 Peter & Jude,* p69 (Emphasis his).

"So that after my departure" The word Peter uses here to describe his **"departure"** or death is *exodon* literally *"exodus"*. Some have taken this as anticipating his following allusion to the Transfiguration (vv16-18), since Luke uses this same term in describing Jesus' conversation with Moses and Elijah on that occasion. This is certainly a possibility. Perhaps, more importantly, it describes Peter's attitude of mind, as a Christian toward his death. He has already used the imagery of "striking a tent" at verses 13 and 14 as Paul also does in 2 Corinthians 5:1, though not using this same word. Here, Peter describes death for the Christian as an *"exodus"*, a kind of deliverance from a somewhat inferior and enslaved condition to a superior one of the ultimate perfect freedom and total possession of the promised inheritance (1 Pe. 1:3-5 cf. Jn. 8:34-36). Paul also, toward the end of his life, views death in sacrificial metaphor as "being poured out like a drink offering" and in nautical language almost as 'casting off from moorings' (2 Ti. 4:6). All this imagery stresses the glorious expectation that death for the believer is something to be desired rather than dreaded.

"You may be able at any time to recall these things" Peter's hope also contexts his thinking here. With regard to reminding his readers of these things, the background appears to be Peter's memory of his unsure early days of faith when he needed stability and was so reminded by Christ (cf. v12). In respect of refreshing his readers' memory of the same, Peter seems conscious of Christ's requiring his absolute and continuing submission on that unforgettable occasion of his restoration (cf. vv13, 14). Here, as he teaches his readers to recall these matters in the future, the context is quite obviously after his death. His passion for their remembrance, in that sense, goes even beyond his urgency regarding the same while he is "in the tent of this body" (v13 NIV).

Peter's words in regard to recalling these things after his death are clearly future. As his intention to remind them was future, *mellēsō* (v12), so his efforts post-mortem respecting recall are future too, *spoudasō* (v15), which is future tense. The recall is also universal. They must be able to bring these things to mind "always", "**at any time**", *ekastote* (v15). Above all, the recall is personal. Peter's readers themselves must be able to recall these things. The verb "**may be able**" is *poieisthai*. The middle voice in this present infinitive is reflexive and emphasizes that the activity and responsibility of recall is laid firmly on the shoulders of Peter's readers themselves.

What mechanism, then, will Peter put in place, so that after his departure, his readers will be able to recall these things? Many answers have been suggested, including all of Peter's writings, the remainder of this present letter and even the apocryphal writings of Peter as well. But the answer to this important question is surely this, Scripture itself? Just as in reminding his readers and in refreshing their memory, Jesus' own words to Peter motivate, so in teaching his readers to recall these things after his death the entirety of Scripture is the necessary stimulation. That this is so arises from Peter's later words in this letter:

> "This is now the second letter that I am writing to you, beloved. In both of them I am stirring up your sincere mind by way of reminder, *(diegeirō humōn en hupomnēsei)* that you should remember the predictions of the holy prophets and the commandment of the Lord and Saviour through your apostles," (3:1, 2).

Certain important features stand out here:

1. The general reference here at 3:1, 2 to "reminder" and "remember" is the same theme as at 1:13-15.

2. The precise reference to stir you up by way of reminder at 1:13 and "stirring up your sincere mind by way of reminder" at 3:1, using the same verb *diegeirein* "to refresh", "to stir", "to arouse", "to awaken", substantiate the same theme.

3. The mention at 3:2 of "the predictions of the holy prophets and the commandment of the Lord and Saviour through your apostles" is highly suggestive of the importance of Scripture as the foundation of the church and amplifies a biblical context (cf. Lu. 24:25-27; 44-45; Ep. 2:20).

4. The later reference of Peter in this letter to Paul's letters as "the other Scriptures" (3:16) may well present a development of the biblical principle underlying 3:2.

5. The possibility, based on external evidence, that Mark was Peter's interpreter, writing down accurately but not in order things said and done by the Lord further broadens the scope of Peter's "biblical" influence (Eusebius Ecclesiastical History 3.39.15).

All of this tends to support the view that Peter had in mind the totality of Scripture when he passionately looked forward to making every effort to leave provision, after his death, for his readers to recall these things.

Martyn Lloyd-Jones dealing with this passage comments attractively and authoritatively:

> In other words, the discipline of the Christian life demands that never a day should pass but that we should remind ourselves of certain things. It is not enough to say we have Christ as our salvation; the moment we realise that, we must have Him every

day, we must stimulate the memory. That is the value of reading the Bible, that is the value of prayer and meditation; and I say that we are but tyros in the Christian life if we have not discovered that we are opposed by an evil system. We must forcibly remind ourselves daily of certain principles, otherwise they will merely remain vaguely in the realm of memory, and they will not be actively operating in our daily life . . .

. . . the business of the church and of preaching is not to present us with new and interesting ideas, it is rather to go on reminding us of certain fundamental and eternal truths.[56]

Recall of Scripture in a context of ultimate spiritual realities is a third means toward perfecting remembrance of scripture knowledge.

APPLICATION

Peter underlines the importance of remembrance for Christian living in a vivid and varied way. It is not living in the past he is commending but rather recall of the past so as to renew the present and revitalize the future. He does this too, from his own store of memories.

Peter recalls truths from his own bitter experience to stabilize believers in their Christian life and service. He refreshes their memories with lessons from his own past that they might completely and continually submit to Christ's lordship in both present and future. He makes every effort, too, to ensure that after he is dead and gone, they themselves will practice recall and so be stimulated in

---

[56]   D.M. Lloyd-Jones, *Expository Sermons on 2 Peter*, p57.

holy living. He does all this motivated by Scripture: whether Christ's own words, prophetic promises about him or apostolic confirmations concerning him. These are the stuff of which true Christian recall is made. Scripture is the right and proper means toward these ends.

We must recover Peter's teaching today. We need to be reminded by Scripture to seek and find stability in Christian experience, to be refreshed in our memories toward constant submission to Christ and to learn for ourselves the skill of biblical recall, true meditation, so as to be constantly stimulated to godliness. Then recall of the past will, thus, ensure renewal of the present and revitalization of the future.

Peter's traumatic background here echoes Christ's words to him in the Gospels. This forms the background which leads eventually to his instructions in Chapter 3 concerning the entirety of Scripture: "the predictions of the holy prophets and the commandment of Lord and Saviour through your apostles" (3:2). Recall of Scripture is the answer to so many of our needs as Christians. Second Peter is primarily about the knowledge of God through Scripture.

TRUE KNOWLEDGE

APOSTOLIC WITNESS

2 PETER 1:16-18

INTRODUCTION

Having instructed his readers in various aspects of true knowledge, Peter now encourages them by informing them of the foundation of that knowledge. The foundation is firm, true and dependable. If they are to take on board the advice that he has already given them, they must be assured of the veracity of these truths. If Peter's instructions are worth reminding his readers about not only during the remainder of his earthly ministry, which is drawing to a close, but also after his demise, they must have a firm foundation. That is the lesson he turns to now, as he concludes his directions to them about true knowledge (1:16-21).

The source of this knowledge falls naturally into two sections:

1. Apostolic witness (vv16-18).
2. Prophetic prediction (vv19-21).

The divisions are obviously scripturally orientated. Later in this letter, Peter wants his readers to recall "the predictions of the holy prophets and the commandment of the Lord and Saviour through your apostles" (3:2). This is also the pattern of the risen Jesus' instructions to his disciples in terms of Law, Prophets and Writings, the three main divisions of the Old Testament, given after his resurrection and prior to his ascension (Lu. 24:26, 27, 44,45). Paul, too, seems to have a scriptural source in mind, when he writes of the church as built on the foundation of the apostles and prophets, with Christ himself as the chief cornerstone (Ep. 2:20) and underscores the office of true apostles over against those claiming to be super-apostles (2 Co. 12:11-13). Both in evangelizing the outsider in his Gospel and assuring the believer in his first letter, John also reflects the importance of first-hand apostolic testimony (Jn. 20:30, 31; 21:24, 25; 1 Jn. 1:1-4), while the writer to the Hebrews stresses both prophetic and apostolic norms underlying Christ's great salvation (He. 1:1-2:4).

Peter, already on the day of Pentecost, in his speech to the Jewish Council and in his first letter to Christians facing persecution in Asia Minor, had stressed apostolic witness and prophetic prediction as the basis of a proclaimed salvation (Ac. 2:1-41; 4:1-22, cf. v30; 1 Pe. 1:10-12). The overall pattern of prophetic prediction and apostolic witness alongside Christ's person, words and works, obviously form the substratum of the biblical revelation of salvation. We have clearly here a scripturally orientated gospel, which is, for this reason, firmly and dependably grounded. Here, in verses 16 to 18, we examine one aspect of this source – apostolic witness. In the next chapter, we shall review the other side – prophetic fulfilment, verses 19-21. Both aspects together form a biblical gospel whose instruction and outworking is to be taken seriously.

EXPOSITION

APOSTOLIC WITNESS

"For we did not follow cleverly devised myths when we made known to you the power and coming of our Lord Jesus Christ, but we were eyewitnesses of his majesty. For when he received honour and glory from God the Father, and the voice was borne to him by the Majestic Glory, 'This is my beloved Son, with whom I am well pleased', we ourselves heard this very voice borne from heaven, for we were with him on the holy mountain" (1:16-18).

TRUE

The apostolic witness is true.

NEGATIVE

"For we did not follow cleverly devised myths". The true nature of this witness is first described negatively. **"Myths"** is *muthois*. In Greek literature, the term was used to describe legendary stories of Greek gods and heroic figures particularly regarding their participation in so-called miraculous events or their performance of extraordinary feats. These were not literally true, but were meant to convey a message that was instructful for the day. They had no basis in reality and usually abounded in fantasies. Hence, in that context, they had a wide range of meaning and might be translated "myths, "stories", "fables", "allegories", "legends".

Within biblical and related literature, the term is used pejoratively stressing a lack of historicity, being morally obtuse, childish and even nonsensical. There seems little relationship to Gnosticism here, however, and, if so, only to a very incipient form of Gnosticism. Paul uses the term in the same pejorative sense as expressive of human desires without reference to reality, man-centred and devoid of redemptive power. This is evident when he berates false teaching of his day as "old wives' tales" (1 Ti.4:7^{NIV}) or in other similarly disparaging terms (1 Ti.4:7 cf. 1:4; 2 Ti.4:4; Tit. 1:14). Philo uses this same verb "follow" and, as Peter does, employs the same sense of the term for unreality not truth quite widely in his writings. Peter here could be using the term "myth" in a polemical sense to counter the false teachers and their teaching, "stories they have made up" (2:3 ^{NIV}). He certainly seems to employ it in the same deprecatory sense as Paul does, namely, lacking historicity, facticity, moral or redemptive benefit.

"Cleverly devised" *sesophismenois*, means "slyly invented", "deceitfully concocted". It comes from the basic verb *sophizō*, "to make wise" and, as a term, implies false or feigned wisdom. This adjectival description of myth underlines the pejorative sense, in which the term is used here.

Apostolic witness rejects cleverly devised myths as false knowledge of the true gospel.

POSITIVE

"When we made known to you" The true nature of apostolic witness is then expressed positively. **"Made known"** is *egnōrisamen*. The verb is often used in the New Testament of imparting a new revelation or a divine mystery (Jn. 17:26; Ro. 16:26; Ep. 1:9; 3:3, 5,10 cf. Lu. 2:15; Jn. 15:15; Ac. 2:28; Ro. 9:22,23; 2 Co. 8:1; Col. 1:27; 4:7,9).

The change in this section from the first person singular "I"

(vv12-15) to first person plural "we" (cf. vv16-18) is also significant.
"**We**" certainly designates the apostles, Peter, James and John, if we
take the section as referring to the Transfiguration as most probably
seems the case, and possibly also implies those who evangelized
these readers as well (cf. "your apostles" at 3:2). In both cases, the
"apostolic" nature of the witness is stressed.

"The power and coming of our Lord Jesus Christ" "Power" is
dunamin and **"coming"** is *parousian*. The immediate context in
which this description occurs is that of the Transfiguration (vv17,
18). It is significant to note that each of the synoptic accounts is
prefaced by a statement of Jesus that there are those standing here
who will not taste death before they will see the kingdom of God
'come with power' (esp. Mk. 9:1 cf. Mt. 16:28; Lu.9:27). In the
light of Peter's frequent use of couplets in this letter, it has been
suggested that we take both words "**power**" and "**coming**" together,
grammatically a form known as *hendiadys*, thus meaning "powerful
coming", an interpretation certainly in keeping with other similar
New Testament descriptions of Jesus' ministry (Mt. 24:30; 28:18).
There is a strand of Old Testament messianic thought portraying the
Messiah as a "Coming One" and this thought seems to be reflected
in the pertinent question of the disciples of John the Baptist to Jesus
in the New Testament: "Are you the one who was to come, or should
we expect someone else?" (Lu.7:19 NIV cf. Ps. 118:26). Calvin takes
the phrase "**the power and coming**" as including "the substance
of the gospel" explicitly mentioning two things: "that Christ had
been manifested in the flesh, – and also that power was exhibited by
him",[57] a reference to the first coming and earthly ministry of Jesus
rather than specifically to Christ's return. However, the fact that the
word for "**coming**" is *parousia*, that, in Greek literature, it frequently
designates the visit of a royal or other high-ranking person and that,
though it can and does describe in the New Testament "presence"

---

[57]   J. Calvin, *Commentaries on II Peter*, p382.

pure and simple (2 Co. 10:10; Ph. 2:12), it almost becomes a technical term of Christ's Second Coming (Mt. 24:3, 27, 37, 39; 1 Co. 15:23; 1 Th. 2:19; 3:13; 4:15; 5:23; 2 Th. 2:1, 8; Ja. 5:7,8; 1 Jn. 2:28) and Peter uses it later in that very sense in this letter (3:4,12). This all makes it reasonable to suppose that included in the phrase "**the power and coming of our Lord Jesus Christ**" is the idea not only of a vivid description of the Transfiguration, which Peter is about to mention but the Transfiguration as a proleptic prophecy of Christ's return. But there is no need to choose alternatively between the First and Second Comings. "**The power and coming of our Lord Jesus Christ**" includes the totality of God's revelation of his Son and this is substantially what Peter and the apostles are proclaiming as true, authentic, good news not invented or concocted myths or fables. Calvin again puts it well:

> And we know how much labour men bestow on frivolous refinements, and only that they may have some amusement. Therefore no less seriously ought our minds to be applied to know the truth which is not fallacious, and the doctrine which is not nugatory, and which discovers to us the glory of the Son of God and our own salvation.[58]

Apostolic witness regards the power and coming of our Lord Jesus Christ as the only source of the true knowledge of the authentic gospel.

RELIABLE

The apostolic witness is reliable.

---

[58]   J. Calvin *Commentaries on II Peter*, p382.

EYE-WITNESS

"But we were eyewitnesses" The witness is reliable because it has first-hand eyewitness authenticity. **"Eyewitnesses"** is *epoptai*. The term is strong and embraces both awesome sight and gripped attention. It is an unusual word found only here as a noun in the New Testament, though Peter in his first letter uses the corresponding verb *epopteuō* to describe a pagan viewing of Christian good deeds and an unbelieving husband's appreciative gaze of his believing wife's fine Christian behaviour (1 Pe.2:12; 3:2). Later, also in his first letter, Peter in a similar way but using a different term, describes himself as a witness (*martus*) of the sufferings of Christ (1 Pe.5:1).

The word *epoptēs* was used for those who were not only spectators or general observers but also came in time, particularly in Greek mystery religions, to describe an initiate who was permitted to look into the divine mysteries and through such activity to become a participant in them. It may then refer, here in the context, to the three disciples, Peter, James and John, who were with Jesus on the mount of Transfiguration. What the three disciples saw was vividly described by the Evangelists: Matthew wrote: "his face shone like the sun, and his clothes became white as the light" (Mt. 17:2), Mark: "and his clothes became radiant, intensely white, as no one on the earth could bleach them (Mk. 9:3); Luke: "And as he was praying, the appearance of his face was altered, and his clothing became dazzling white" (Lu. 9:29). All three synoptic writers also mention the appearance of Moses and Elijah talking with Jesus. The distinct impression is given that all these people were not hallucinating but that this was real authentic vision to be taken seriously and authoritatively. It could, within the setting of the letter, also have polemical significance contrasting the apostles' first-hand witness within compared to the false teachers' claimed authenticity outside the circle of authoritative revelation. Again, in the very format of the Transfiguration, prophetic prediction (Moses and Elijah, Law and

Prophets) goes hand-in-hand with apostolic witness (Peter, James and John).

If this were the case, the "we" implicit in the verbs in verse 16 would have similar force to the "we" explicit in the pronoun in verse 18 emphasizing the authentic eyewitness nature of apostolic authority. As already noted, John underlines the same first-hand apostolic authority in both his Gospel and first letter (Jn. 1:14; 19:35; 1 Jn. 1:1-3; 4:14).

"Of his majesty" "Majesty", *megaleiotētos*, carrying overtones of "grandeur" and "sublimity" is again a very rare word in the New Testament. Its Old Testament usage at Jeremiah 40:9 (LXX) and Daniel 7:27 is not exclusively of God but could include human persons of high dignity. However, the other New Testament occurrences at Luke 9:43 of the greatness of God at Jesus' healing the boy with the evil spirit immediately after the Transfiguration, when all the disciples were helpless to do anything, and at Acts 19:27 of the "divine majesty" of the goddess Artemis points to divine rather than human majesty. "Here, as the next verse makes clear, it refers to the divine majesty which Jesus received from God".[59]

It is significant and in keeping with both the magnificence of the revelation and the depravity of the human mind that, even though the disciples were aware of the "majesty" of Jesus' part in the healing of the boy with the evil spirit, they "did not understand" (Lu.9:45), which presumably includes both the healing (vv42-43) and Jesus' words predicting his betrayal and subsequent death (v44). Regardless of God's majesty, the god of this world continued to blind the eyes of mankind to the glory of salvation in Christ and to the way in which that glory would ultimately come about through Jesus' suffering and

---

[59]   R.J. Bauckham, *Jude, 2 Peter*, p217.

death as Son of Man. But the apostolic vision of the Transfiguration was real, authentic and divine.

EAR–WITNESS

"For when he received honour and glory from God the Father". The witness is reliable because it is not only 'eyewitness' but 'ear-witness' as well. This contrasts the modern judicial view of authenticity where "hearsay" is regarded as of little or no value as compared with "eyewitness". In Scripture, the 'eyewitness' is accompanied and confirmed by the 'ear-witness', in this instance specifically the voice at the Transfiguration. Hence, **"honour and glory"** have been taken separately as referring to these twin aspects of witness. As Alford has put it: "honour in the voice which spoke to him; glory in the light which shone from him".[60]

"Honour and glory" as a word-pair appears 13 times in the New Testament, always in the letters and Revelation, sometimes varied in order and with additional attributes (Ro. 2:7, 10; 1 Ti. 1:17; He. 2:7, 9; 2 Pe. 1:17; Re. 4:9, 11; 5:12, 13; 7:12; 21:26 cf. the parallel expression in Hebrews 3:3). This, together with Peter's preference for couplets, may suggest that they are to be taken together. But unlike the earlier **"power and coming"**, there is hardly the same necessity and Alford's analysis seems reasonable. God as **"Father"** occurs in the trinitarian format in First Peter (1 Pe. 1:2,3) as also here in the setting of the Transfiguration. D. Guthrie comments that therein "This glory of Christ is inseparably linked with the glory of God".[61]

"And the voice was borne to him by the Majestic Glory" This turn of phrase is peculiar and specific. It emphasizes the divine authority of the voice. That the voice **"was borne"** (*enechtheisēs*) to

---

[60]   H. Alford, *The Greek Testament,* 1880, cited by M. Green, *2 Peter and Jude,* p94.

[61]   D. Guthrie, *New Testament Theology,* p91.

him by the "**Majestic Glory**" (*megaloprepous doxēs*) indicates this. "**Majestic**" a different word for that used at verse 16 for "majesty", *megaloprepeia*, was frequently used of God and his works in the LXX (Greek Old Testament), though only here in the New Testament and the entire phrase "**Majestic Glory**" is really a *periphrasis* or substitute descriptive word for God himself. It may equate, in that sense, with the use of the "cloud" in the synoptic accounts of the Transfiguration (cf. Ex. 16:10; Nu.14:10; Eze.1:4). It is obviously emphatic of divine authority. God himself was in the voice.

"**This is my beloved Son, with whom I am well pleased**" Peter's account of the Transfiguration most resembles that of Matthew within the Synoptics, though there are differences (Mt. 17:1-13 cf. Mk. 9:2-13; Lu. 9:28-36). The Transfiguration has been regarded by some as a post-resurrection occurrence but the grounds supporting this are insufficient. The words: "**This is my beloved Son**" are generally referred to Psalm 2:7 and those "**with whom I am well pleased**" to Isaiah 42:1, combining the idea of Jesus both as Messianic King and Suffering Servant respectively. Both underline the authority of Christ's personal work. There may be some grounds for taking "**beloved**" *agapētos* as a separate messianic title with some backward reference to Abraham's "sacrifice" of Isaac (Ge. 22:2), though the "beloved" nature of the Son is invariably linked with God's choice of him as Messiah. These words are heard also at Jesus' baptism, with the addition of the phrase, "listen to him" at the Transfiguration. Peter omits the words "listen to him" and manifests other differences from the Synoptics perhaps because his purpose in recording the same is different. The entire substance of the words of the voice with this Old Testament background reflect the authority of God's Word and his authentication in terms of 'ear-witness' of Jesus. This is the point Peter is making.

"**We ourselves heard this very voice borne from heaven, for we were with him on the holy mountain.**" Again, this emphasizes the authority of the voice from heaven as authoritative 'ear-witness'. "**We**" *hēmeis* is emphatic being a separate word and not merely included in the verb as in verse 16. The repetition of "**borne**", *enechtheisan*, as at verse 17 pronounces the divine source and communication of the voice. The actual presence of the disciples with Christ on the "**holy mountain**" serves again emphatically. The epithet "**holy**", *hagiō*, has been taken as evidence of lateness, a sort of early Catholicism, and so a challenge to Petrine authorship. However, it is perfectly possible to regard "holy" not as implying any sense of veneration but rather designating the mountain as "set apart" for God's use consistent with other usage of the word in Scripture (cf. Ex. 3:5). There are more grounds for linking "**holy mountain**" with "my holy hill" of Psalm 2:6 in the context. The holiness of the mountain simply serves to complete the sense of awe connected with the authenticity of the 'ear-witness'.

Christopher Green summarizes well the dependability of this apostolic testimony both of eye and ear when he writes:

> The authority of the apostles is being defended precisely on the issue of whether they spoke about God accurately and authoritatively; hence Peter's emphasis that they both saw and heard. He said the same of the Jewish council; the apostles 'cannot help speaking about what we have seen and heard'. Today we have to accept that same double authority. It is not simply their testimony to a series of encounters with Jesus that is important and decisive. They claim to have the right to give the only true interpretation, the unique meaning, of those events, because they heard that interpretation from the mouth of God himself. The Bible is not the subjective record of a

religious quest that we can supplement or challenge with our own experiences. God has spoken.[62]

APPLICATION

The church needs to recover the authority of the word of God and it needs to recover it in a biblical way. One of the sad things in the history of the church is the way in which liberal criticism has attacked and undermined the authority of the Bible. Even sadder is the way the new evangelicalism has so often side-lined and ignored that authority. Jesus was particular as he opened up each section of the Old Testament, Law, Prophets and Writings and expounded in them all those things relating to himself. The apostles were equally focused on confirming both the Old Testament and Jesus' testimony. They did this in a quite self-conscious way. Not only did they confidently assert their own authority as apostles, but in addition, they detailed the implications of prophetic prediction and our Lord's teaching in their writings as well. It is remarkable the number of places in the New Testament where this self-conscious apostolic authority surfaces.

We need to receive the testimony of the apostles in this way. We must take it as seriously and authoritatively as they took it. This is the main reason why the "history" of the Canon is not a sequence of Church Councils setting their imprimatur on the entire New Testament but largely confirming what was already a given fact – the inspiration of apostolic writings – and merely determining those books of questionable apostolic authority. It was because of the self-authenticating nature of apostolic writing. We need to examine that authentication in detail and take it to heart afresh. The apostles were the mouth-pieces of God.

---

[62]   D. Lucas & C. Green, *The Message Of 2 Peter & Jude*, p79.

We need also to preach the word in this way. We must be conscious of the underlying storyline of revelation within Scripture. "The new (Testament) is in the old concealed, the old is in the new (Testament) revealed".[63] When this marks our proclamation, it gives intrinsic biblical authority to our message sourced in its author, the Holy Spirit.

The reformers were troubled in their era by claims of extra-biblical revelation, dreamers and visioners. The dreamers and visioners have not all gone away. That is why the Westminster Fathers were quite clear about the perimeters of a given revelation: "which maketh the Holy Scripture to be most necessary; those former ways of God's revealing His will unto His people being now ceased".[64]

If we are to see what Paul saw at Thessalonica: ". . . our gospel came to you not only in word, but also in power and in the Holy Spirit and with full conviction" (1 Th. 1:5), then we must heed what Peter and all the apostles taught about the true and authoritative nature of apostolic witness. We must both receive the gospel and proclaim it in this way.

The writer to the Hebrews' urgent warning and John's warm and personal introduction to his first letter fittingly corroborate Peter's apostolic witness about the majestic voice at the Transfiguration:

"Therefore we must pay much closer attention to what we have heard, lest we drift away from it. For since the message declared by angels proved to be reliable and every transgression or disobedience received a just retribution, how shall we escape if we neglect such a great salvation? It was declared at first by the Lord, and it was attested to us by those who heard, while God also bore witness by

---

[63]   *Saint Augustine Quotes* (A-Z Quotes.com).

[64]   *Westminster Confession of Faith*, Glasgow 1958, (Free Presbyterian Publications), Chapter 1 Subsection 1.

signs and wonders and various miracles and by gifts of the Holy
Spirit distributed according to his will" (He. 2:1-4);

"That which was from the beginning, which we have heard,
which we have seen with our eyes, which we looked upon and have
touched with our hands, concerning the word of life – the life was
made manifest, and we have seen it, and testify to it and proclaim
to you the eternal life, which was with the Father and was made
manifest to us – that which we have seen and heard we proclaim also
to you, so that you too may have fellowship with us; and indeed our
fellowship is with the Father and with his Son Jesus Christ. And we
are writing these things so that our joy may be complete" (1Jn.1:1-4).
The apostolic witness is both true and reliable. It is also authoritative,
for it is written Scripture.

Chapter 10

TRUE KNOWLEDGE

PROPHETIC PREDICTION

2 PETER 1:19-21

INTRODUCTION

Peter has already sourced the true knowledge of salvation in apostolic witness (vv16-18). He now bases that knowledge on prophetic prediction (vv19-21). Peter has previously underlined the importance of prophetic witness for the gospel and its mission. He quotes liberally from the Old Testament when preaching on the Day of Pentecost (Ac. 2:17-21 – Jl. 2:28-32; Ac. 2:25-28 – Ps. 16:8-11; Ac. 2:34,35 – Ps. 110:1), alludes to its importance again, citing it in his defence before the Jerusalem crowd and the Jewish Sanhedrin on the occasion of healing the cripple (Ac. 3:17-26; v.25 – Ge. 22:18; v.26 – Eze. 3:19; Ac. 4:11 – Ps.118:22) and mentions prophetic authority even in the home of the Gentile Cornelius (Ac. 10:43). The whole of the Old Testament is obviously prophetic, as far as Peter is concerned. In his first letter, he is equally adamant about the significance of the prophets: they spoke of the saving grace that was to come to Peter's readers; they focused intently in their predictions on the details to which the Spirit of Christ in them pointed regarding both the sufferings of Christ and his subsequent glories and, in all of this, they were conscious that what they predicted was not for themselves but for a later generation, that of Peter's readership, a prediction that was the very envy of angelic enquiry (1 Pe. 1:10-12).

It is natural, then, when we come to Peter's second letter, to anticipate a further mention of the prophets, especially in the context of explaining the source of salvation's true knowledge, and this is emphatically so. Peter underlines the importance of prophetic prediction in the boldest of terms. Indeed, the structure of that presentation of prophetic prediction recalls the format of his words about apostolic witness being both through, 'eye-witness', and, paradoxically, also, through 'ear-witness'. Peter does this in these verses in a similar double format:

1. AUTHORITY OF PROPHETIC PREDICTION: LIGHT IN THE DARKNESS (v19)
2. ORIGIN OF PROPHETIC PREDICTION: VOICE IN THE SILENCE (vv 20, 21)[65]

EXPOSITION

PROPHETIC PREDICTION

"And we have something more sure, the prophetic word, to which you will do well to pay attention as to a lamp shining in a dark place, until the day dawns and the morning star rises in your hearts, knowing this first of all, that no prophecy of Scripture comes from someone's own interpretation. For no prophecy was ever

---

[65] See D. Lucas & C. Green, *The Message of 2 Peter & Jude*, pp81, 83.

produced by the will of man, but men spoke from God as they were carried along by the Holy Spirit" (1:19-21).

AUTHORITY: LIGHT IN DARKNESS

Peter first affirms the authority of prophetic prediction and teases out the implications by showing how it brings the light of the true knowledge of salvation in the darkness of man's sin. Prophetic prediction pierces the darkness with the true light of the gospel.

"And we have something more sure, the prophetic word" is *kai echomen bebaioteron ton prophētikon logon*. This has been taken in two ways, as illustrated in the different translations, namely that the Old Testament is confirmed by the apostolic teaching, as in the NIV translation: "And we have the word of the prophets made more certain" or that the apostolic teaching is confirmed by the Old Testament, as in the ESV translation: "And we have something more sure, the prophetic word". Some preliminary considerations are necessary before reaching a determination.

"And we" is naturally set over against **"to which you will do well to pay attention"**. The "we" certainly implies the apostles but could possibly, in this context, also include Peter's readers in their capacity of understanding and knowledge of the prophets.

"Prophetic word" *prophētikon logon*, has been interpreted in a number of ways: (1) Old Testament messianic prophecy. (2) The whole Old Testament understood as messianic prophecy. (3) Specific Old Testament prophecies as, for example, Psalm 2:6, 7; Isaiah 42:1 (cf. 2 Pe.1:17). (4) Old Testament and New Testament prophecies generally. (5) 2 Peter 1:20-2:19. (6) The Transfiguration itself as a prophecy of the Parousia or Second Coming of Christ.[66]

---

[66]   See R. J. Bauckham, *Jude, 2 Peter*, p224.

In the light of general New Testament usage and specifically of Peter's use as noted in introduction, "**prophetic word**", though including some of the other suggestions, seems best taken as in sense (2) above: the whole Old Testament understood as messianic prophecy.

"**More sure**" is *bebaioteron*. *Bebaios* means, literally, "strong" as of the root of a tree or plant and figuratively, "reliable", "dependable", "certain" as of hope (2 Co. 1:7), promise (Ro. 4:16), confidence (He.3:6,14), will (He.9:17) and previously in Peter, calling and election (2 Pe.1:10). At 2 Peter 1:19, Bauer, Arndt and Gingrich translate: "we possess the prophetic word as something altogether reliable",[67] where the comparative form is obviously taken in a superlative sense, as is possible in Greek.

The sense that the apostolic teaching is confirmed by the Old Testament as in ESV: "we have something more sure, the prophetic word" is clear because:

i.   The strength of prophecy is universally used as a final argument in the New Testament, something particularly evident in the Gospels; Acts, Romans 15, 1 Peter 2, Hebrews and Revelation.

ii. The Jews normally rated this special revelation of the voice, (*Bath Qol*) literally "the daughter of the voice", as secondary to written prophetic revelation and as only relevant where written revelation was not extant or had ceased.

iii. This term is more grammatically consistent, maintaining both the syntax of the sentence and the comparative, or if regarded as necessary, the superlative sense of *bebaioteron*.

---

[67]   W. Bauer, W.F. Arndt, F.W. Gingrich, *A Greek-English Lexicon*, p137.

My own preference is for this latter interpretation as in the ESV. This, in my view, does not necessarily rule out the implication that the apostolic witness of the Transfiguration confirms Old Testament prediction, but rather that this very fact emphasizes the fundamental and prior authority of Old Testament revelation. This, above all, is surely the point that Peter is making. Calvin's comments are, as ever, most helpful:

> But it appears at first sight strange, that the word of the prophets should be said to be more sure or firmer than the voice which came from the holy mouth of God himself; for, first, the authority of God's word is the same from the beginning; and, secondly, it was more confirmed than previously by the coming of Christ. But the solution of this knot is not difficult: for here the Apostle had a regard to his own nation, who were acquainted with the prophets, and their doctrine was received without any dispute. As, then, it was not doubted by the Jews but that all the things which the prophets had taught, came from the Lord, it is no wonder that Peter said that their word was more sure.[68]

"To which you will do well to pay attention" The wisdom of heeding Old Testament Scripture, on the grounds of its authority as revelation is underlined by Peter here, as is evident in the entire context. One disregards Scripture's authority at one's peril.

"As to a lamp shining in a dark place" **"Lamp"** or "light", here *luchnō*, is an apt metaphor used elsewhere in the Bible for Scripture itself (Ps. 119:105, 130 cf. Ps. 43:3; Pr. 6:23) or for those who teach it (Jn. 5:35). **"Dark"**, *auchmērō*, is a rare and strong word meaning,

---

68   J. Calvin, *Commentaries on II Peter*, p385.

initially, "dry" and developing the sense of "thirsty, sunburnt and so squalid" or even "the squalor and gloom of a dungeon".[69] The NEB translates it as "murky". It contrasts with *lampros* "bright" and approximates to *alamprēs* "without light". It, thus, connotes a situation of deep gloom and darkness. This vivid imagery emphasizes the authority of Scripture revelation as penetrating deep darkness and introducing bright light. Compare: "The unfolding of your words gives light; it gives understanding to the simple" (Ps. 119:130[NIV], cf. Jn. 1:5). What an apt metaphor for the authority and priority of the prophetic word of the Old Testament and, indeed, of all Scripture.

"Until the day dawns and the morning star rises" "Day" may refer to the great Old Testament expectation of judgement, the day of the Lord, which confronts those who oppose God and are punished, but also, to a degree, of salvation, which comes to those who love and obey God and are vindicated and delivered (Is. 13:6, 9; cf. Is. 40:1-11; Eze. 13:5; 30:3; cf. Eze.16:59-63; 37:24-28; Jl. 1:15; 2:1, 11, 31; 3:14; Am. 5:18, 20; Obad. 15; Zep.1:7, 14; Mal. 4:5). This **"day"** is presented in the New Testament with a similar purpose of judgement and salvation, the consummation of God's will (cf. Ac. 2:20, 21; 2 Co. 1:14; 1 Th. 5:2; 2 Th. 2:2), for it is the day of Christ who appeared as Lord and final Judge (2 Co. 1:14; Ph. 1:6, 10; 2:16). For Peter, that day is a day, when the present world order ceases and a new order is established (2 Pe.3:10, 12, 13).

"The morning star rises" "Morning star" is *phōsphoros*, literally, "light-bringer". The term was used to describe the planet Venus on which the first rays of the sun were visible, heralding the dawn. It was also used in Greek literature for royal and divine persons. The epithet **"rises"** *anateilē*, may well introduce a messianic note in view of the usage of **"star"** in a biblical connotation as referring to Christ's

---

69   J.W.C. Wand (p161), E.H. Plumptre (p174) cited respectively in D. Lucas & C. Green, *The Message Of 2 Peter & Jude*, p82 n45.

coming (Nu.24:17; Mal. 4:2; Lu.1:78, 79; Ep. 5:14; Re. 2:28; 22:16).
Again, the enlightening messianic prophetic Scripture persists.

"In your hearts" particularly in the context of Christ's return as a
public, objective and universal event is striking. This glorious impact
of Scripture in the heart might not only be seen as enlightenment
at conversion (2 Co. 4:6) but also as the continuing work of
sanctification through the word, where the believer is more and more
conformed to the image of Christ (2 Co. 3:18 cf. Ro. 8:29; 1 Co.
13:12; Ph. 3:20, 21; 1 Jn. 3:2) or generally of biblical enlightenment
of the mind. Peter is here surveying the entire range of Scripture's
impact upon the life in salvation, from nature through grace to glory.
The word of God is an enlightening and transforming agency, a
converting and a sanctifying ordinance. The prospect of the **"day"**
will focus the believer's attention on the work of grace through the
word, but that is a life-long experience from conversion in grace to
consummation in glory.

Peter thus shows the superiority of prophetic prediction as a
prior means of revelation, its saving quality as an enlightening and
transforming force and its relevance throughout the entire work of
grace. From start to finish, Scripture is supreme as a saving revelation.
It is a reliable, dependable, certain, confirmed and a confirming
means of grace. Michael Green sums up well the authority of this
prophetic prediction, light in the darkness, when he writes:

> Whatever the precise details, the main emphasis
> is manifest: we are on pilgrimage throughout
> our lives in this dark world. God has graciously
> provided us with a lamp, the Scriptures. If we pay
> attention to them for reproof, warning, guidance
> and encouragement we shall walk safely. If we
> neglect them, we shall be engulfed by darkness.

The whole course of our lives ought to be governed
by the Word of God.[70]

ORIGIN: VOICE IN SILENCE

Peter secondly emphasizes that the origin of prophetic prediction
comes not ultimately from a human source but from God himself.
It is God who, in Scripture, speaks into the silence caused in man's
heart through sin. Prophetic prediction penetrates man's deaf ears
with the life-giving word of the gospel.

"Knowing this first of all" is *touto prōton ginōskontes*. It underlines
the priority of Peter's remarks. If his readers "do well to pay
attention" to the prophetic word, Peter now gives the reason for such
an admonition. Heeding the written revelation of Old Testament
Scripture is of first-rate importance, because of its authority in the
light of its origin.

**"That no prophecy of Scripture comes from someone's own
interpretation"** The origin rather than simply the interpretation
of prophecy seems to be the basic issue here. **"Own"** is used in the
Old Testament, Philo, other Jewish literature, and in the Church
Fathers largely in reference to the author not to the recipient of the
revelation. **"Comes from"** *ginetai*, present in tense and general in
meaning translates as: "is", "arises", "comes about", "derives (from)",
which suits this sense and would only with difficulty be forced to
mean "belongs to", "comes under the scope of", "is the object of one's
own interpretation" as required by the other sense. **"Interpretation"**
epiluseōs could also be translated "revealment", "setting forth",
"prompting", "inspiration".

Peter was dealing, in the event, not with the matter of
interpretation per se but authentication and, in the flow of his

---

[70]   M. Green, *2 Peter and Jude*, p100.

reasoning, even taking into consideration the misconstruction of the false teachers, he was emphasizing the origin of the prophetic word as not exclusively the prophet's **"own"** preserve but both the prophecy and its interpretation as coming ultimately from God. This was the answer to the false teachers and their teaching that Peter goes on to address in Chapter 2 of this letter. The vividness of the imagery of this term **"interpretation"**, *epiluseōs*, as an "interpretative unfolding", an "untying" an "explanation" of things beyond human understanding by the Spirit, who in the first instance gave the word of prophecy, makes this passage one of the highlights of the Bible's teaching on inspiration and an immense encouragement to our understanding on that score.

Peter confirms the origin of prophecy, first of all, negatively and then positively.

NEGATIVE

"For no prophecy was ever produced by the will of man" This statement is emphatically negative and contextually meaningful. **"No"** translates two Greek words *ou*, "not" and *pote* "ever". There is no circumstance or time where **"prophecy"**, *prophēteia*, might ever be deemed as sourced exclusively in man. **"Produced"** translates *ēnechthē*, which is the aorist passive from the verb *pherō*, "I carry" or "I bear". The sense is that prophecy is never "carried" or "borne" from man. Its source is never human. The intriguing thing is that a combined form of the same verb is used twice at verses 17 and 18, *enechtheisēs, enechtheisan*, to describe the voice being borne or carried to Jesus at the Transfiguration. The same verbal form which describes positively the divine coming of the voice in apostolic witness, is used negatively to deny any human source of prophetic prediction. Scripture, conversely, elsewhere forcefully speaks of the human not the divine origin of false prophecy (Je. 23:16; Eze. 13:23).

POSITIVE

"But men spoke from God as they were carried along by the Holy Spirit" The positive side is equally powerful and is accentuated both by passive verbal forms and the order of the sentence. **"Men spoke from God".** What a remarkable summary of the glorious divine/ human balance in biblical inspiration! It was indubitably **"men"** who spoke. Of this there was not a doubt: consciously, thoughtfully and vocally is the natural inference of these words. There is nothing here of "the Montanist claim, that they were like a lyre struck by the plectrum of the Holy Spirit" or of the mechanical view of inspiration in Philo, a Jewish contemporary, who wrote of "a compulsive divine possession which turned men into a *theophoros*, a 'God-bearer'" or of the utterances of Bacchic frenzies also cited by Philo, but rather that the prophets "are carried along in the path of God's will by their own glad and willing consent."[71] **"From God"** At the same time it was equally obvious that God was the source of prophecy. The phrase is emphatic and means that they spoke what was "derived from God" or "controlled by God" with, perhaps, the emphasis on the former.[72] The original Greek might be paraphrased: "but carried along by the Holy Spirit, men spoke from God", which further elucidates the meaning and emphasizes yet again, the divine rather than the human origin of prophecy. As in the former negative case already mentioned, elsewhere, positively, Scripture also speaks of the divine rather than the human origin of true prophecy, (2 S. 23:2 cf. Ac. 28:25, He. 3:7; 10:15).

B.B. Warfield described this process of inspiration as "concursus", that is, both human beings and God being fully involved in the

---

71   M. Green *2 Peter and Jude*, p103 n1.

72   C.D.F. Moule *Idiom-book* p73 cited S.J. Kistemaker, *James, Epistles of John, Peter, and Jude*, p275, also cf. Justin, *1 Apol.37*: "the things taught through the prophets from God *(apo tou theou)* . . ." cited by R.J. Bauckham, *Jude, 2 Peter*, p233.

process of inspiration,[73] while S. Voorwinde helpfully comments on this subject:

> Thus he draws our attention to a profound mystery. The words of Scripture are divine words, and yet they are also the words of human writers. We cannot explain this antimony. All we can do is observe the evidence there is for it.[74]

"Were carried along" is *pheromenoi* again from *pherō*, "I carry"; "I bear". This time the verbal form is a present participle in Greek, which underlines the continual activity of the Holy Spirit in carrying these men along in this process. While the verb is used generally, it is quite significantly used as a nautical term for a sailing ship carried along by the wind in its sails (cf. Ac. 27:15,17). This together with the earlier mentioned verbal form *epiluseōs* (v20) as of untying a knot or elucidating and explaining a mystery provides two fascinating metaphors with which to conclude this purple passage on the doctrine of biblical inspiration. God's Spirit blows the prophetic prediction from departure to destination, untying the inexplicable on course – both inspiration and interpretation are involved as to its origin. T.R. Schreiner comments well on this: "Evangelical theology rightly infers from this that the Scriptures are authoritative, infallible, and inerrant, for God's words must be true".[75] Prophetic prediction brings light into darkness and sound into deafness. And it is God who speaks.

Peter has now shown that both apostolic witness and prophetic

---

[73]   B.B. Warfield, *The Inspiration and Authority of the Bible*, Philadelphia: Presbyterian & Reformed, 1948, pp83-96 as cited by T.R. Schreiner, *1, 2 Peter, Jude*, p324.

[74]   S. Voorwinde, *"Old Testament Quotation in Peter's Epistles"*, *Vox Reformata* 49, 1987, pp3-16 as cited by T.R. Schreiner, *1, 2 Peter, Jude*, p324.

[75]   T.R. Schreiner, *1, 2 Peter, Jude*, p324.

prediction underlie Scripture and give abundant reason for his reader to heed his advice. Christopher Green brings us up to speed with regard to Peter's views on revelation and inspiration and anticipates continuance of this theme in the remainder of his letter:

> Quite clearly, Peter puts on an equally divine and authoritative footing the message of the New Testament apostles and the message of the Old Testament prophets (cf. 3:2,16). God spoke to both groups, giving them his once-for-all and irrevocable explanation of his actions. So certain is Peter of this parallel that he will even call Paul's letters by the awesome word *graphē*, 'Scripture' (3:16; cf. 1:20). How dare we think we can replace that?[76]

APPLICATION

The authority of Scripture is not only based on apostolic witness but on prophetic prediction as well. The reverential way in which Jesus and the apostles viewed the Old Testament makes this clear. Whether by quotation or allusion, the prophetic word as the storyline of the Old Testament was, for them, the final court of appeal – a "more sure" authority than anything. "It is written", "Scripture says", "The Holy Spirit speaks" or simply the quotation or allusion alone with no introductory words at all, implied that God was speaking and underline this reverence and respect for Scripture.

Charles Wesley's hymn recalls all this so well:

> Come, Holy Ghost, our hearts inspire;
> Let us Thine influence prove,

---

[76]   D. Lucas & C. Green, *The Message Of 2 Peter & Jude*, p84.

Source of the old prophetic fire,
Fountain of life and love.

Come, Holy Ghost, for moved by Thee
The prophets wrote and spoke;
Unlock the truth, Thyself the key;
Unseal the sacred book.[77]

We lose all this at our peril. Our hearts no longer burn, our understanding lacks lustre and becomes banal, and our preaching is flat and lacks edge of motivation when we fail to appreciate the "prophetic fire". God's family is built not only on the foundation of the apostles but also on that of the prophets as well. With this clearly in view, Scripture will lead to a fresh dimension of discovering Jesus as chief cornerstone once again. To the law and to the testimony! If they do not speak according to this word, they have no light of dawn (Is. 8:20). We need to recover both apostolic witness and prophetic prediction (and its fulfilment) in perfect tandem, if we would truly see Jesus. True knowledge of him and growth in him are based on Scripture, Scripture alone, *Scriptura Sola*. God's word *is* truth (Jn.17:17).

---

[77]   The Church Hymnary revised edition, Presbyterian Church in Ireland, Oxford 1997, Hymn 196.

Chapter 11

FALSE TEACHERS

2 PETER 2:1-3

INTRODUCTION

In Chapter 1 of his second letter Peter outlines the features of true knowledge of God. In Chapter 2, by way of contrast, he describes false knowledge of God. Chapter 2 begins with an introductory summary of false teachers (2:1-3), continues with a reasoned excursus from the Old Testament explaining God's judgement on these false teachers but his deliverance and vindication, amid this judgement, of the righteous (2:4-10[a]) and closes with a detailed description of the false teachers, their damaging influence and the nature of God's judgement on them (2:10[b]-22).

There are strong similarities in thought, language and expression between Chapter 2 of Second Peter and Jude verses 4-16. This has led to extensive discussion as to the priority of these two letters, some holding Second Peter as earlier than Jude and some vice-versa. Hence, some maintain that Jude is dependent on Second Peter and some that Second Peter is dependent on Jude. In this, the majority opinion favours the latter. A third option is that both Second Peter and Jude are both from an independent source. Of course, there may be no corresponding dependence between Second Peter and Jude at all, or, indeed, of an independent source. But the similarities would suggest to many that correspondence is likely. These similarities do not necessarily impinge on the integrity or authenticity of either writing. The problem remains basically unsolved and note will be made, where correspondence seems to be relevant to our present study.

The introductory section (2:1-3) flows readily from the previous chapter. Indeed, the structure is chiasmic, that is, an X–like format, with some degree of inverse correspondence between the first and the last features:

A$_1$. Apostles (1:16-18)
B$_1$. Old Testament prophets (1:19-21)
B$_2$. Old Testament false prophets (2:1^a)
A$_2$. False teachers (2:1^b-3),

with possibly an *inclusio* feature opening and closing the sequence, from "follow cleverly devised myths" (1:16) to "will follow" (2:2) and "false words" (2:3). This points up the contrast between the apostles and the false teachers.

This introductory section includes, as does the whole of Chapter 2, a correlation between the doctrinal heresies and immoral behaviour of the false teachers, a feature of note both in Old Testament false prophets and other New Testament false teachers, the harmful effects on the false teachers themselves, on the church and, indeed, on the truth itself, all of this accompanied throughout by the inevitable judgement of God, which falls on the perpetrators of this false knowledge.

While these features occur throughout the entire chapter, some specific format is discernible in this introductory section:

DESTRUCTIVE HERESIES	(2:1)
IMMORAL BEHAVIOUR	(2:2, 3ᵃ)
DIVINE JUDGEMENT	(2:3ᵇ)

EXPOSITION

> "But false prophets also arose among the people, just as there will be false teachers among you, who will secretly bring in destructive heresies, even denying the Master who bought them, bringing upon themselves swift destruction. And many will follow their sensuality, and because of them the way of truth will be blasphemed. And in their greed they will exploit you with false words. Their condemnation from long ago is not idle, and their destruction is not asleep" (2:1-3).

DESTRUCTIVE HERESIES

Peter describes the destructive heresies propagated by the false teachers.

"But false prophets also arose among the people, just as there will be false teachers among you" Peter refers to the false teachers and others in the future tense in verses 1-3: **"will bring in"**, **"will follow"**, **"will be blasphemed"**, **"will exploit"**, and, then, in the remainder of the chapter reverts to the present tense. Paul does the same in a similar context at 1 Timothy 4:1f. Some suggest that this happens here because Second Peter is pseudonymous and the writer's mask falls off. But this is not necessarily the case. A reasonable explanation for the tense change is simply that Peter sees these things as fulfilling prophecies of Jesus and of the Old Testament regarding false prophets and false teachers (De. 13:1-5; Mt. 24:23-28).

"False prophets", *pseudoprophētai* were present in Old Testament days and it was an offence punishable by death (De. 13:1-5; 18:20; cf. [Is. 28:7, cf. 17b-18; Je. 23:14; Ez. 13:1-23; Zep. 3:4f]). The idea of "false", both in the case of false prophets and false teachers is probably in regard both to their personal claims and the substance of their teaching. In the Old Testament, false prophets differed from true prophets because: (1) They did not speak with divine authority (De.18:20; Je.14:14; 23:21, 32; Eze. 13:2-7). (2) Their message was frequently one of peace and security in contrast to the prophecies of future judgement of the true prophets (Je. 4:10; 6:14; 14:13, 15; 23:17; 27:9, 16-18; Eze. 13:10-16; Mi. 3:5, 11). (3) They were condemned to punishment by God (Je. 14:15; 23:15; 28:16-17 cf. De. 18:20).[78]

"False teachers" is *pseudodidaskaloi*. The change of title from prophets to teachers is swift and significant. The emergence of false prophets and teachers is widely predicted in the New Testament. Jesus, Paul, John and Jude all warn of the same (Mt. 24:11-15, 20-24; Ac. 20:29-30; Ga. 1:6-9; Ph. 3:2; 2 Th. 2:1-3; 1 Ti. 1:3-7; 1 Jn. 2:18-19; Re. 16:13-14; 19:20; 20:10; Jude 3-4). Many different views and heresies populate the pages of the New Testament: Judaisers, Libertines, Antinomians, False Christs, Antichrists, Nicolaitans and perhaps even incipient Gnostics. The usual term is **"false prophets"**. Perhaps, then, the term **"false teachers"** is used here because, while those of whom Peter writes did not claim the "office" of prophet, they aspired to that next in importance, namely, **"teacher"** (Ac. 13:1; Ro. 12:6-8; 1 Co. 12:28, 29; Ep. 4:11). Mayor interestingly identifies some of the characteristics of Old Testament false prophets as strikingly resembling the features of those whom Peter berates:

---

[78] See R. J. Bauckham, *Jude, 2 Peter*, p238.

"Their teaching was flattery; their ambitions were financial; their lives were dissolute; their conscience was dulled, and their aim was deception (see Is. 28:7; Je. 23:14; Ezk. 13:3; Zc. 13:4)".[79] This illustrates in both Old and New Testaments the link between false teaching and immoral behaviour, which is noteworthy later in this introductory section and throughout Chapter 2.

"Who will secretly bring in destructive heresies" "Who will secretly bring in" translates *hoitines pareisaxousin*. There is no word for **"secretly"** in the original but this is clearly the nuance of the verb in context. The same verbal form is used at Galatians 2:4, where Paul mentions "false brothers secretly brought in" and a similar verbal form is used at Jude 4, where "certain people have crept in unnoticed". The difference between Peter's situation and Jude's seems to be that in the case of the former the false teachers arose from *within* the church, in the latter they came in from *outside*. The sense of the verb *pareisagō* is clearly to "smuggle in", "insinuate", "infiltrate" in a guileful manner.

"Destructive" *apōleias*. This confirms the sense of the verb above. *Apōleia* means "destruction", "utter ruin" even "damnation" in the full biblical sense of divine condemnation (Mt. 7:13; Jn. 17:12; Ac. 8:20; Ro. 9:22; Ph. 1:28; 3:19 He. 10:39; Re. 17:8,11). Of the 18 times the term is used in the New Testament, Peter uses it five times in his second letter, three times in this present section – a remarkable emphasis – and twice in the following chapter (2 Pe.3:7, 16). The form is a Hebraism literally "heresies of destruction" which accentuates the meaning. These heresies are, indeed, "damnable" [AV], for they send people to hell. Their object is to damn not save, to curse not bless.

"Heresies" *haireseis*. From a basic verbal form of "to choose", the term designates a "private choice", "opinion", and "variant". In the

---

[79]   J. B. Mayor, *The Second Epistle of St. Peter and the Epistle of St. Jude*, (1907). noted in M. Green, *2 Peter and Jude*, p105.

New Testament, it is used, not necessarily pejoratively of a "party" or "sect" as, for example, Pharisees, Sadducees, even of Christians (Ac. 5:17; 15:5; 24:5, 14; 26:5; 28:22) or of a "faction" with a certain degree of divisiveness (1 Co. 11:19; Ga. 5:20) or of "a person who stirs up division" (Tit. 3:10). Here, it clearly carries sinister overtones, certainly so far as Christianity is concerned. And, while the classic understanding of "**heresy**" as false teaching arises more distinctively in terminology later with Ignatius circ. 110 A.D., the term used here means clearly more than faction or factiousness. Little detail of doctrinal aberrance is given in our letter, but Peter is condemning "*false teachers*" and it is natural to presume that they inculcated *false teaching*. This is even evident in his later term "**false words**" (v3). The substance of their teaching, clearly self-willed, is also false, for it denies both the work of Christ and the truth itself. Donald Guthrie suggests, comparing these false teachers with those of Jude's letter, that those Peter condemns possibly "made a special point of denying the redemptive work of Christ" as well as also inferring from 2 Peter 3:5 [RSV] that "their doctrine of God was defective".[80] Some have seen the plural *haireseis* as unusual and harking back to a claimed *agraphon* or unwritten saying of Jesus! "There shall be schisms and heresies",[81] and the plural may well imply a number of heretical views. But whatever the resolution, it seems reasonable to take "heresies" not simply as descriptive of the false teachers' erroneous lifestyle but of their teaching as well. Calvin's observation is, as usual, insightful:

> He calls them *opinions of perdition*, or destructive
> opinions, that every one, solicitous for his salvation,
> might dread such opinions as the most noxious
> pests. As to the word *opinions* or heresies, it has
> not, without reason, been always deemed infamous
> and hateful by the children of God; for the bond of

---

[80]   D. Guthrie, *New Testament Introduction*, p853.
[81]   See P. H. Davids, *The Letters Of 2 Peter And Jude,* p220, for introduction to discussion.

holy unity is the simple truth. As soon as we depart
from that, nothing remains but dreadful discord.[82]

"Even denying the Master who bought them" The language
and tone are similar to Jude 4, with certain notable differences.
The parallel phrase is: "and deny our only Master and Lord, Jesus
Christ". Peter sharpens the focus of these destructive heresies in
vivid imagery. **"Even"** well translates *kai* with which the phrase
begins. It accentuates the criminal intent and extent of the heresies.
"Denying" *arnoumenoi* is strong, meaning "to refuse", "to be
unwilling", "to firmly say no" and, as a present participle, denotes a
habitual pattern of refusal in rejecting divine authority (cf. v10; Jude
8). **"Master"** renders *despotēn*, an unusual but strong term. The word
designates earthly masters of slaves in some references (1 Ti.6:1-2;
Tit. 2:9; 1 Pe. 2:18) but is also used of God and possibly also of
Christ (Lu. 2:29; Ac. 4:24; 2 Ti.2:21; Jude 4; Re. 6:10). It stresses the
absolute power of the master over the slave and the unquestioning
obedience due in response, not only in the context of slavery but
also as creature to creator, subject to ruler, disciple to teacher. **"Who
bought them"** climaxes the false teachers' reaction in their rebel
stance. It also, by way of complementary contrast, illustrates the
sovereign master's gracious care and redemptive control over his
slave. **"Bought"** *agorasanta* means "to purchase", "to redeem out of
the market-place (*agora*)". In the Old Testament, the idea was used
of the redemption of Israel from Egypt, not only rescuing them
from a state of bondage but also liberating them "to be his people"
(2 S. 7:23, cf. 1 Pe. 4:2).[83] In the New Testament, the term occurs
twenty-five times for a simple commercial transaction but also for
the effect of the death of Christ (1 Co. 6:20; 7:23; Re. 5:9; 14:3).
For other 'purchasing' verbs see Mark 10:45; Acts 20:28; Romans

---

[82]   J. Calvin, *Commentaries on II Peter*, p393, (Emphasis and translation his).
[83]   M. Green, *2 Peter and Jude*, p106, (for further implications).

6:17-18; 1 Timothy 2:6; 1 Peter 1:18.[84] It means, of course, the false teachers deny Christ's power to redeem from sin.

The glory of this vivid description of Christ's work accentuates the criminality of the false teachers' rebellion. They strike at the very heart of the work of grace in their insolent denial of Christ as sovereign Master. It is, of course, a denial *de facto* by the way they live but also *de jure* by the fabricated words they teach. That shows the despicable as well as the destructive nature of their heresies. M. Green catches the glowing heights and the lowering depths of this expression when he writes:

> This fascinating phrase shows us something of what the cross meant to our author, for *bought* emphasizes both the seriousness of man's plight and the costliness of Christ's rescue (cf. Mk. 10:45; 1 Tim. 2:6; Rev. 5:9).[85]

These words, however, have become a crux of interpretation from a theological point of view. Two problems emerge, and both are related: Does this mean that Christians can apostatize in the sense of falling from grace? And do these words "**the Master who bought them**" imply unlimited or universal rather than limited or particular atonement?

Much has been written and spoken to resolve these issues. Henry Alford confidently states, "No assertion of universal redemption can be plainer than this".[86] John Owen argued that the "buying"

---

[84]   D. Lucas & C. Green, *The Message Of 2 Peter & Jude*, p88, n14.

[85]   M. Green, *2 Peter and Jude*, p106, (Emphasis his).

[86]   Henry Alford, *Alford's Greek Testament: An Exegetical and Critical Commentary*, 5th Ed., 4 vols. (1875; Grand Rapids: Guardian, 1976), vol.4, pt. 2, p402, cited S. J. Kistemaker, *James, Epistles of John, Peter, and Jude*, p282 n7.

by Christ was nonsoteriological in this text, so that Peter did not even have spiritual salvation in mind. T.R. Schreiner comments: "The interpretation suffers from special pleading since redemption is invariably soteriological".[87] Wayne Grudem suggests a reference back to Deuteronomy 32:6 ("bought"[NIV] Footnote), so that the Master is the saving God, that Christ's specific work of redemption is not in view here and that, by inference, the "**them**" harks back to "the people" namely Israel, in verse one, making the theological dispute irrelevant to this particular text.[88]

There is not space in a work like this for a full detailed discussion on this theme. The matter also arises again at 2:17-22. Some comments of Thomas R. Schreiner seem appropriate at this point and are worthy of thoughtful consideration:

> I would suggest that Peter used phenomenological language. In other words, he described the false teachers as believers because they made a profession of faith and gave every appearance initially of being genuine believers. Peter did not refer to those who had been outside the community of faith but to those who were part of the church and perhaps even leaders among God's people. Their denial of Jesus Christ reveals that they did not truly belong to God, even though they professed faith. Peter said that they were bought by Jesus Christ, in the sense that they gave every indication initially of genuine faith. In every church there are members who

---

[87]　J. Owen, *The Death of Death in the Death of Christ* (1851; reprint, Carlisle, Pa.: Banner of Truth, 1995), 250-52, cited in T.R. Schreiner, *1, 2 Peter, Jude,* p330 and n17.

[88]　W. Grudem, *Systematic Theology* (Leicester: IVP; Grand Rapids: Zondervan, 1994), p615, cited in D. Lucas & C. Green, *The Message Of 2 Peter & Jude,* p89, and n16, 17.

appear to be believers and who should be accepted as believers according to the judgment of charity. As time elapses and difficulties arise, it becomes apparent that they are wolves in the flock (Acts 20:29-30), that though they called on Jesus as Lord their disobedience shows that he *never* knew them (Matt 7:21-23), that they are like the seed sown on rocky or thorny ground that initially bears fruit but dries up and dies when hard times come (Matt. 13:20-22).[89]

This seems to be an excellent and adequate summation.

"Bringing upon themselves swift destruction" Peter rounds off his resumé on destructive heresies by indicating God's judgement upon the false teachers. This note of divine judgement is, of course, the sole subject in this introductory section as in verse 3[b], but it also occurs here. This is consistent with the note of judgement throughout Chapter 2. While, at times, this note of judgement occurs in a continuous section, it frequently is as an on-going theme that breaks regularly into the whole discourse on false teachers, somewhat like a recurrent refrain in a symphony. Divine judgement, as we will further see, will also entail self-inflicted pain on the false teachers even prior to an eschatological climax of God's final judgement.

"Swift" is *tachinēn*. It means both "soon" in the sense of "imminent", "at hand" and "sudden" in the sense of "unexpected" "unforeseen". Both meanings may well be included as in the use of the word for Peter's death at 1:14. Here, perhaps, if any, **"swift"** in the second sense is preferable because of the suddenness and inevitability of divine judgement. One could, perhaps, project an *inclusio* in the occurrence of *tachinos* between 1:14 and 2:1, but the structure makes

---

89   T.R. Schreiner, 1, 2 Peter, Jude, pp331-332 (Emphasis his).

this less likely. Certainly, divine judgement comes both in the context of death and at Christ's return (cf. Jn. 12:48; 2 Th. 1:7-10). A more likely *inclusio*, though it may simply be emphatic repetition, is the word "**destruction**" *apōleia*, which Peter has just used in the genitive as a Hebraism to describe "**heresies**" at 2:1 and is repeated at 2:3. Damning heresies inevitably bring damning judgement.

The heresies are not only divisive but destructive. They oppose both what God says and what God does. Hence, the character of God and the work of Christ are the focus of their opposition. They creep in stealthily and undermine insidiously, for their object is the destruction of God's truth and, since God's word is truth, these heresies are a virus to Scripture itself. The virus must be cleansed and countered forthwith, if true knowledge of God is to continue. It is a deadly virus.

Immoral Behaviour

Peter specifies the immoral behaviour that accompanies these destructive heresies.

"**And many will follow their sensuality**" Immorality is first mentioned in quite emphatic and vivid terms. The baleful influence of the heresies is widespread. "**Many**", *polloi*, recalls the majority, as Jesus emphasizes, who opt for the broad road leading to destruction, and the many false prophets who lead many astray (Mt. 7:13-14 cf. 24:10-12). Peter here seems quite fond of the specific verb for "**follow**" *exakolouthēsousin*, for he uses it at 1:16; 2:2, 15 and it is found nowhere else in the New Testament. This verb accentuates the lurid attractiveness of the false teaching. Alexander Nisbet comments: "It is not strange to see the most dangerous heretics have many followers; every error being a friend to some lust".[90] Above all, the immorality is categorized as "**sensuality**" *aselgeiais*. The term is a strong one

---

[90]   A. Nisbet, *1&2 Peter*, p247.

meaning reckless and hardened immorality. Basically, starting from the idea of "sensual" indulgence, it moves quickly in the direction of "sexual" promiscuity and approximates to ideas of "lascivious", "voluptuous", "perverse", "pernicious" behaviour (Ro. 13:13; 2 Co. 12:21; Ga. 5:19; Ep. 4:19; probably 1 Pe. 4:3; Jude 4 cf. *Wisdom* 14:26). Here, like heresies, it is plural and allows of varying forms. This section being introductory, Peter uses it later in the chapter to describe the "**sensual**" lifestyle of these lawless men (2:7) and the "**sensual**" desire of their sinful human nature (2:18). Jude uses it of those who change the grace of God into licence for "immorality" [NIV] (Jude 4) and later cites by way of illustration the inhabitants of Sodom and Gomorrah and the surrounding towns (Jude 7). "Shameful ways" [NIV] and "sensuality" [ESV] are fair translations but are vividly complemented by the context, which make the meaning much more explicit. It is a more than lurid and aberrant immorality. Some, like T. Fornberg and T.A. Miller suggest respectively, that the term, in context, may refer to doctrinal deviation rather than sexual immorality and not to literal sexual immorality.[91] But this is improbable. While doctrinal deviation was doubtless present, it was accompanied by these flagrant excesses as well. This is the whole point of the inextricable mess the false teachers create, which Peter emphasizes. T.R. Schreiner rightly assesses: "What attracts people to these false teachers is that they advocate a licentious lifestyle, and therefore many people are only too glad to follow their example".[92] It is not beyond the bounds of possibility also, that the false teachers' scepticism about Christ's return and, hence, future judgement might drive the licentious, uninhibited lifestyle.

"And because of them the way of truth will be blasphemed"
The idea of the godly life being a "**way**" was rooted deep in the Old Testament, where lifestyle or behaviour was predominant. In

---

91   See T.R. Schreiner, *1, 2 Peter, Jude*, p332, n22.
92   T.R. Schreiner, *1, 2 Peter, Jude*, p332, cf. J. Calvin, *Commentaries on II Peter*, p394, n1 (Ed.).

rabbinic texts, Jewish teaching is termed *halakah* or "walk", a way of life. This spills over into the New Testament, where in Acts the early Christian movement was designated "the Way" (Ac. 9:2; 19:9, 23; 22:4; 24:14, 22). Peter later in this chapter, writes of "the right way" (v15) and "the way of righteousness" (v21), which the false teachers abandoned. Here, **"the way of truth"**, *hē hodos tēs alētheias*, seems to come directly from Psalm 119:30 (LXX 118:30). As such, it combines both the Hebrew concept of "truth" as dependable, reliable, covenantally sure and the Greek idea of "truth" as accurate, correct, right. **"The way of truth"** is both ethical and cognitive. That perfectly illustrates the inextricable link between immoral behaviour and false teaching and not only exemplifies a great offence against Jesus' teaching, who predicted the same of the false prophets (Mt. 7:15-23), but also the outright denial perpetrated by the false teachers against Jesus' person, who alone is the truth (Jn. 14:6).

"Blasphemed" is a literal translation and may seem somewhat strong. Some would suggest "slander", "maligned", and "brought into disrepute". It is rightly translated **"blaspheme"** in 2:10, 11 and 12, as Peter continues his diatribe against the false teachers' behaviour. This harks back to Isaiah 52:5 "And all day long my name is constantly blasphemed" [NIV]. Paul quotes this, writing to the Romans (Ro. 2:24). Peter is equally concerned that his readers should cause no offence to non-believers and voices that concern in his first letter (cf. 1 Pe. 2:11, 12, 20; 3:15-16; 4:14-15). In view of the seriousness of the false teachers' offence, **"blasphemed"** is hardly an understatement but accurately describes the result arising from the false teachers' activities. The sin is against the truth itself – that is blasphemous!

"And in their greed" In the false teachers' lifestyle, immorality is supplemented by **"greed"**. **"Greed"** *pleonexia* "connotes an uncontrolled, covetous desire for money and wealth".[93] It is identified

---

93   J. MacArthur, *2 Peter & Jude*, p78.

with idolatry and, hence, the source of many ills (Col. 3:5). Paul associates greed with immorality in a striking way (1 Co. 5:10; 6:10 Ep. 5:3) and is particularly conscious of the problem it causes for religious leaders, mentioning it negatively in qualifications for elders (1 Ti.3:3; 6:3-10; Tit. 1:7). Peter alludes to this greed writing to elders in his first letter "not greedy for money, but eager to serve" (1 Pe. 5:2 NIV) and mentions it later here at 2:14-15 of the false teachers as "experts in greed" NIV alluding to Balaam son of Beor, "who loved the wages of wickedness" NIV. Greed spawns many ills not only in Christian leaders but generally in the church. It does relate to finance, for many worship money instead of God. But greed and covetousness, both within and without the church, are not limited to finance but attack in many other insidious and vicious ways, which need to be guarded against.

"They will exploit you" While G.H. Clark rightly cautions that "this passage should not be narrowly restricted to money",[94] nevertheless the content is strongly suggestive of financial misuse. **"Exploit"** translates *emporeusontai*. The verb *emporeuomai* has a commercial background and means "to buy and sell", "to traffic in", "and to realize gain from". It is used in a non-pejorative sense at James 4:13, where the idea of exorbitant gain it is not necessarily implied, but, here, it has sinister overtones and is rightly rendered **"exploit"**. Paul uses it of false teachers "who have been robbed of the truth and who think that godliness is a means to financial gain" (1 Ti.6:5^NIV) and associated this idea of profiteering with false instruction: "Unlike so many, we do not peddle the word of God for profit" (2 Co. 2:17^NIV). In a context where **"bought"** (v1) is used to depict redemption, Peter H. Davids insightfully comments: "Thus the metaphor is that of their using falsehood to make merchandise of believers whom the

---

[94] G. H. Clark, *2 Peter: A Short Commentary* (Phillipsburg: Presbyterian and Reformed, 1975) p40, cited by D. Lucas & C. Green, *The Message Of 2 Peter & Jude*, p91.

Lord has bought; they are, so to speak, operating a business selling someone else's property".[95]

"With false words" is *plastois logois*. The metaphor of exploitation is rounded off in this expression. *Plastois* comes from *plassō* "I form" and has obvious etymological links with our English word "plastic" which, to a degree, fabricates other substances such as wood, metal, and china. The words of the false teachers are set to deceive by way of fabricating the truth.

The phrase does seem a natural *inclusio* contrasting the description given at 1:16 where the apostles are said not to have followed "cleverly devised myths", *sesophismenois muthois*, and, since *plastein logois* is a classical expression in Greek for deceitful speech, the continuation of this vivid language climaxes Peter's description of the deceitful effects of this false teaching.

Simon J. Kistemaker puts the link between doctrinal heresy and immoral behaviour succinctly when he writes:

> Teaching and conduct go together. What the false teachers taught, they also practiced, with the inevitable result that Christians who followed them brought the Christian way of life into disrepute.[96]

The heresies are inextricably linked with immoral behaviour. They promote sensuality and greed, as they revive our fallen nature. They devalue and debase Scripture, as they fabricate the truth. They ruin the attractiveness of the gospel for the unbeliever. This process must be stopped.

---

[95]   P. H. Davids, *The Letters Of 2 Peter And Jude*, p224.
[96]   S.J. Kistemaker, *James, Epistles of John, Peter, and Jude*, p283.

DIVINE JUDGEMENT

Peter pronounces upon the false teachers a divine judgement, which is inevitable and impending. **"Their condemnation from long ago is not idle, and their destruction is not asleep"** Peter's language again is vivid and terrifying. Some take these words as an introduction to the following section rather than a conclusion of the foregoing, but the latter seems preferable as Peter in Chapter 2 frequently interjects divine judgement but as frequently after he has forcefully made a point of its just appropriateness as before. This format is clearly parallelism, where the verbs and nouns of both two sentences correlate. The language is fearfully gripping, for **"condemnation"** and **"destruction"** are personified.

"Their condemnation from long ago is not idle" The inevitability of divine judgement is first stressed. **"Condemnation"** *krima*, a legal term, brings us into a court-room setting. Condemnation is **"from long ago"**. *ekpalai*. This suggests a sentence that has been long time pronounced, but its execution has simply been delayed. **"Is not idle"** *ouk argei* connotes the unavoidable nature of due process, in spite of appearances to the contrary. Compare 3:4: "For ever since the fathers fell asleep, all things are continuing as they were from the beginning of creation". Peter, in his first letter, has already warned of the inevitability of divine judgement, not only for the family of God but for outsiders as well (1 Pe. 4:17). Jude couches this fearful prospect in similar terms: "For certain people . . . who long ago were designated for this condemnation" (Jude 4). So here, Peter claims that judgement is, as it were, already hanging over their heads. They are like men on death row, awaiting execution.

"And their destruction is not asleep" The impending nature of doom is next stressed. **"Destruction"** *apōleia* is for the third time emphatically mentioned in this introductory section. The personification is put fearfully: **"is not asleep"** *nustazei*. The heathen

Baal may justifiably be taunted as being asleep, by the prophet Elijah on Mount Carmel, (1 K. 18:27), but it is an affront so to describe the God of Israel with whom the psalmist reverentially pleads to "awake" to judgement (Ps. 44:23), for he neither slumbers (*nustaxei*) nor sleeps (Ps. 120:4 LXX – Ps. 121:4). And the nations whom he stirs to effect his judgement will neither slumber (*nustaxousin*) nor sleep (Is. 5:27 LXX – Is. 5:27). All of these Old Testament images may be in Peter's mind, for the only New Testament occurrence of this word is of the drowsy bridesmaids at Matthew 25:5, where again the context is suggestive. Peter had just described the fate of the false teachers as "swift" *tachinēn*(v1). Here, he emphasizes the point dramatically.

Calvin comments graphically:

> Unless then one is so mad as to sell the salvation of his soul to false teachers, let him close up every avenue that may lead to their wicked inventions. For the same purpose as before he repeats again, that their destruction delayed not, that is, that he might frighten the good from their society. For since they were given up to a sudden destruction, every one who connected himself with them, must have perished with them.[97]

They are, in truth, "damnable" heresies, meriting our condemnation and God's judgement.

APPLICATION

False teachers and false teaching are not taken seriously enough by today's church. True, we do not want to indulge in inquisitorial

---

[97]   J. Calvin, *Commentaries on II Peter*, p395.

witch-hunts or to look for specks in others' eyes while ignoring the beams in our own, but we have become far too tolerant of every wind or whim of doctrine. This is largely the influence of postmodernism on our thinking. The fact that not only does "anything go" but that it "should go" is axiomatic. Everyone doing what is right in one's own eyes is never regarded as a criticism of society, even if it is in the church. But the idea of one's inalienable rights being pursued to whatever ridiculous lengths are desirable is ridiculously abysmal. This has had harmful effects outside the church but has been disastrous within. Not only has it harmed kingdom work but incessantly blurs what the kingdom itself is and what kingdom work is about. Ideas like "regulative principle" are sadly regarded as among obscure absurdities of a forgotten generation. What the Bible has to say about even a Christian subject becomes largely irrelevant.

Peter here brings us back to earth with a bang. His warning about false teachers, their teaching and their lifestyle is a sobering reminder of what we need today. Above all, it does not just bring back warnings about the false prophets of the Old and the false teachers of the New Testament, it brings us back to Jesus himself and to his solemn and riveting remarks on the subject.

Jesus reminds us of the *intentional* deception of false prophets and teachers. He specifies their attractive and hypocritical garb, their fruitless, godless lifestyle, their boastful religious profession and activities, their total lack of saving grace – "I never knew you" (Mt. 7:23) – and their ultimate condemnation and damnation. That puts a very different picture on the naive toleration so fashionable today. As ever, we need to "test the spirits" (1 Jn. 4:1). The warning is justifiably biblical. The connection between false teachers and immoral living brings upon them God's judgement. God's truth in Scripture is not only precise and accurate, it is moral and practical.

Chapter 12

FALSE KNOWLEDGE

EXAMPLES

2 PETER 2:4-10ᴬ

INTRODUCTION

Having briefly introduced his readers to the false teachers, and their teaching, Peter now discloses details of God's judgement on them as ungodly and, amid this judgement, promises vindication and deliverance for those who are righteous. The format of what Peter says is drawn on the background of God's condemnation in three specific episodes from the Old Testament – the Angels, the Flood and Sodom and Gomorrah – and woven into this story of judgement is God's preservation of Noah and Lot. The structure is presented in terms of a conditional argument from the greater to the lesser. If God did not spare judgement on these three occasions in the past, he will not spare the false teachers from judgement in the future. T.R. Schreiner has helpfully tabulated the argument as follows:

If God judged the angels
(v4), and if he judged the
flood generation (v5),

> while at the same time
> sparing Noah (v5),

and if he judged Sodom
and Gomorrah, (v6),

> while at the same time
> preserving Lot (vv7-8),

then it follows that the Lord will preserve the godly
in the midst of their trials (drawing this conclusion
from the examples of Noah and Lot), and it also
follows that the Lord will punish the ungodly on
the day of judgment (drawing this conclusion from
the three examples of the angels, the flood, and
Sodom and Gomorrah).[98]

There is, one long conditional sentence beginning with "For
if" (*ei gar*) at verse 4, the *protasis* – helpfully emphasized in some
translations by the repetition of "if" (not in the original but
understood) at verses 5, 6, 7, and concluding with "then" (not in
the original but understood) at verses 9, 10ᵃ, the *apodosis*.

The parallels in language, format, and presentation with Jude
(verses 5-7) are as significant as are the differences. Both Peter and
Jude have two illustrations in common – the judgement on Angels
and that on Sodom and Gomorrah. Peter introduces the judgement
on the Flood generation as a third, while Jude gives the example of
the Israelites wandering in the desert. Hence, Peter's order is more
chronologically in line with the Old Testament than that of Jude.
Peter also introduces a theme absent in Jude, namely, the preservation

---

[98]   T.R. Schreiner, *1, 2 Peter, Jude*, p335.

of the righteous, obviously as encouragement to his readers in the light of the threat of the false teachers. In Second Peter, it is a threat that seems to come from *within* the Christian community, whereas in Jude, the false teachers seem to come from *outside* the church. Jude's account is, in some ways, more detailed and more explicitly reflective of traditional Judaism than that of Peter. Some have taken this as evidence for the priority of Jude and that Second Peter was dependent on Jude not vice-versa, as noted earlier in Chapter 1. The question of priority, however, does not materially affect the essential meaning of either Second Peter or Jude.

ANGELS	(2:4)
FLOOD	(2:5)
SODOM AND GOMORRAH	(2:6-8)
CONCLUSION	(2:9-10ᵃ)

EXPOSITION

> **For if God did not spare angels when they sinned, but cast them into hell and committed them to chains of gloomy darkness to be kept until the judgement; if he did not spare the ancient world, but preserved Noah, a herald of righteousness, with seven others, when he brought a flood upon the world of the ungodly; if by turning the cities of Sodom and Gomorrah to ashes he condemned them to extinction, making them an example of what is going to happen to the ungodly; and if he rescued righteous Lot, greatly distressed by the sensual conduct of the wicked (for as that righteous man lived among them day after day, he was tormenting his righteous soul over their lawless deeds that he saw and heard); then the**

**Lord knows how to rescue the godly from trials,
and to keep the unrighteous under punishment
until the day of judgement, and especially those
who indulge in the lust of defiling passion and
despise authority (vv4-10ᵃ).**

ANGELS (2:4)

The first example relative to the false teachers is the judgement of
the angels, whose sin is noted and whose condemnation is inevitable,
horrific and future.

"For if God did not spare angels when they sinned" The general
point is clear. The details expand the meaning. If God did not spare
angels in their privileged position, he will not spare false teachers who
are only men. **"God"** and **"angels"** are juxtaposed in the original: *ho
theos aggelōn,* which stresses the contrast. **"Angels"** lacks the definite
article as compared with **"God"**. This gives the nuance "even angels",
emphasizing the angels as a category of beings higher than mankind,
yet subject to God's judgement. C. Bigg comments on the lack of the
definite article: "the absence . . . gives the sense of 'even angels'".[99]

"When they sinned" is the aorist active participle "sinning" or
"having sinned" *hamartēsantōn.* It denotes single action in the past
and gives the reason for God's judgement even of angels. The details
of the angels' sin is not noted. Scripture only mentions the sin of
angels tangentially, so great care must be taken to avoid dogmatism
on the matter. Some have cited Scripture such as Genesis 6:1-4;
Isaiah 14:12-17, Ezekiel 28:11-19; Luke 10:18; Revelation 12:7-9;
20:1-3, 7-10, as well as texts mentioning elect and fallen angels,

---

[99]   C. Bigg, *A Critical and Exegetical Commentary on the Epistles of St. Peter
and St Jude, New International Critical Commentary,* (Edinburgh: T. and
T. Clark, 1901, Repr. 1978), p274 cited by D. Lucas & C. Green, *The
Message Of 2 Peter & Jude,* p96, n6.

principalities and powers, demons and demonology, conjecturing a pre-temporal fate of Satan and his minions consummated in eternal condemnation. However, alternative interpretation for some of these texts are given, which questions this "theology" and may indicate more the outworking of Satanic and fallen angelic activity in human situations rather than direct allusions to Satan and his angels themselves. Hence, the "sons of God" of Genesis 6:1-4 may refer to the human descendants of Seth, the "Lucifer" of Isaiah 14:12-17 to the king of Babylon and the lament of Ezekiel, 28:11-19 specifically to the king of Tyre. This is not to say that Satan and his angels and their ultimate condemnation is not a biblical concept, for it is. Scripture does give evidence of this, but its gaps and silence warns against unjustifiable elaboration.

Jewish tradition has greatly developed the theme of angels sinning in this dangerously elaborate way, and particularly evident in its treatment of Genesis 6:1-4. References to this tradition are found in 1 Enoch, Baruch, the Gospel of Peter, the Apocalypse of Peter and Jubilees. Specifically, with regard to Genesis 6:1-4 in some of this literature, the "sons of God" are regarded as angels who copulate with women and the "Nephilim", the "giants" are the result. Hence in this, sexual immorality is added to the angels' sin of disobedience to God. However, such interpretation may be speculative rather than accurate and conclusion drawn from the same could well be questionable. Some have regarded similarities in language, thought and allusions to be so prominent that they discern this Jewish tradition behind references in 1 and 2 Peter and Jude (cf. 1 Pe. 3:19, 20; 4:6; 2 Pe.2:4; Jude 6) and include this in their reckoning of background, dependence and priority in relation to 2 Peter and Jude. But these background sources are largely pseudepigraphous, extra-canonical and non-biblical, and this need not necessarily be the case.

Whether or not Peter knew this Jewish tradition, how far it influenced him, if it did, and what bearing this has in the relationship of 2 Peter to Jude is not the subject for exhaustive discussion in a commentary like this. What is important for us to determine on this background is whether we can gain further information on the nature of the angels' sin. Peter writes in his first letter about Christ preaching "to the spirits in prison, because they formerly did not obey, when God's patience waited in the days of Noah, while the ark was being prepared" (1 Pe. 3:19, 20), but the recipients of this preaching are not specified definitively as angels. Peter also alludes in his first letter to the gospel being preached "even to those who are dead" (1 Pe. 4:6), but that seems even less relevant to our present investigation. More relevant is the later description in Peter's second letter at 2:10. "and especially those who indulge in the lust of defiling passion and despise authority" and the parallel to 2:4 which we are presently considering at Jude 6: "And the angels who did not stay within their own position of authority, but left their proper dwelling, he has kept in eternal chains under gloomy darkness until the judgement of the great day". These latter two references are much more specific.

In the light of this, the most that can be said about the angels' sin is that it did seem to include disobedience to and rebellion against God. As to anything further, it would seem to be unwise to be dogmatic. The very lack of definition of the nature of the sin on Peter's part at this point simply emphasizes that, to a degree, that aspect of the subject was irrelevant. What was relevant was the point he is making throughout this section, that if God did not spare angels, 'heavenly beings', but judged them, he would certainly not spare the false teachers but judge them too.

"But cast them into hell and committed them to chains of gloomy darkness". This fact of the judgement is fearfully emphasized in detail, though the specific details are difficult to define. **"Cast them into hell"** is the word *tartarōsas*, aorist active participle from the verb *tartaroō* 'I hold captive in Tartarus'. Tartarus in Greek mythology was lower than hell and reserved for the worst and most rebellious offenders among both men and gods, like the so-called god Tantalus. This is the only occurrence of the verb in the Bible, though the noun "*tartarus*" is used as a place of divine punishment at 1 Enoch 20:2 and elsewhere in Jewish Greek literature (LXX Jb. 40:15; 41:23; Pr. 30:16; *Sib. Or.*[100] 4:186; Philo, *Mos.*[101] 2:433; *Praem.*[102] 152). This does not necessarily presuppose Peter's knowledge of Greek mythology, for *Tartarus* would have been a known and accepted synonym for "hell" or "the underworld" in his day. Michael Green's comment is insightful, even if, as some claim, there was not the same necessity for Peter's use here as for Paul's: "Just as Paul could quote an apt verse of the pagan poet Aratus (Acts 17:28), so could Peter make use of this Homeric imagery".[103] Jesus' use of the term Gehenna, the name of Jerusalem's rubbish dump where fires continually burned, for the inextinguishable torments of eternal anguish is also comparable (Mt. 5:22, 29-30; 10:28; 18:9; 23:15, 33; Mk. 9:43, 45, 47; Lu. 12:5). The language is again vivid and its meaning fearful.

"And committed them to chains of gloomy darkness"

"**Committed**" *paredōken* is strong and, as at Acts 8:3 and 12:4, means to "hand over for imprisonment". "**To chains of gloomy darkness**" presents a variant reading, which is exceedingly difficult of resolution. "**Chains**" translates *seirais* meaning "chains", "cords", or "bands". Jude uses a different term *desmois* for a similar sentiment in regard to the rebel angels: "he has kept in eternal chains (*desmois*) under gloomy darkness until the judgement on the great day" (Jude 6). The variant here at 2 Peter 2:4 for *seirais* is *sirois*, from which our English "silo", which means "pits" or "dungeons". Manuscript evidence is evenly divided, though perhaps somewhat the better for "dungeons", while kindred pseudepigraphous literature favours

---

[100]   *Sibylline Oracles* (Pseudepigrapha).

[101]   Philo, *De Vita Mosis* (Jewish Writer).

[102]   Philo, *De Praemiis et Poeniis* (Jewish Writer).

[103]   M. Green, *2 Peter and Jude*, p110.

"chains" with a hint of "dungeons" in the idea of "valleys" in 1 Enoch. As to the more difficult reading or possibility of scribal error or change, it can be argued both ways. We have opted for "chains" on the grounds of wider usage. This is a perfect example where variant readings make little difference to the overall meaning. C. Green comments judiciously: "In reality it matters little, because the creatures are out of harm's way under God's lock and key. 'It would be hazardous to dogmatize with undue definiteness on the strength of this passing allusion, as to the condition of these inhabitants of the unseen world', is Plumptre's wise comment".[104] Whatever the resolution, the plight of the rebel angels is fearful and horrendous. They are kept as prisoners in dungeons for judgement.

"To be kept until the judgement". This makes the main point and does so graphically. The ultimate fate of the false teachers like the rebel angels is future. For that, they are being **"kept"** and that reservation is for the final judgement at the last day (cf. 2:9; 3:7; Jude 6). **"Until the judgement"** translates *eis krisin. eis* "into", "towards", here denotes both purpose and future inevitability. There is no escaping the final day of judgement. It is God's purpose and comes inevitably to all. There is a fearful parallel with the fate of the devil who, though now bound, is being kept for eternal judgement hereafter (Re. 20:10). If God deals so with the angels' sin of pride and rebellion, he will most certainly deal with that of the false teachers who molest Peter's readers. The fate of the false teachers is exceedingly grave. Frederick S. Leahy's comment in a work dealing with the whole theme of biblical demonology is both balanced and theologically sound. It is apposite here:

A consideration of 1 Tim. 5:21 with its reference
to the 'elect angels' and of 2 Pet. 2:4 and Jude 6

---

[104] E. H. Plumptre, *St. Peter and St. Jude, Cambridge Bible for Schools and Colleges* (Cambridge: Cambridge University Press, 1879), p179, cited by D. Lucas & C. Green, *The Message Of 2 Peter & Jude*, p97, n10.

which speak of 'the angels that sinned' and 'the angels which kept not their first estate', will show that angels as well as men are predestinated and foreordained, a realm in which it is dangerous to speculate. We are to confess what we believe because it has been revealed. Where there are gaps in the revelation, or in our understanding of the revelation, we must never try to fill them by a process of logic. It must suffice us to state that only a part of the angelic host was placed on probation, or created with the possibility of sinning, and that number did wilfully sin; whereas the perseverance of the elect angels was guaranteed by God's decree of election.[105]

The main point here is, that, if the angels suffer and will suffer such fearful judgement, so also will the false teachers. What an ultimate and awful tragedy.

FLOOD (2:5)

The second example relative to the false teachers is that of the Flood which deluged a world characterized by godlessness and disobedience, but from which Noah and his family were saved.

"If he did not spare" The overall contrast from greater to lesser continues. The verb *epheisato* is identical to that of verse 4 though the particle *ei* "if" is absent. The conditional sense is rightly taken as understood, being part of the entire syntax from verse 4 to verse 10.

"The ancient world," *archaiou kosmou*. This begins another contrast within a contrast from the greater to the lesser. There is a contrast between the larger and godless nature of the world and the smaller

---

[105]   F.S. Leahy, *Satan Cast Out*, A Study in Biblical Demonology, pp13-14.

and righteous character of Noah and his family. Peter appears to see the world in three-time sequences: first, there is the **"ancient"** world here mentioned as also at 3:5, 6; secondly, there is the present world (cf. 3:7) and, thirdly, the new world after the judgement (cf. 3:13). R.J. Bauckham insightfully notes that while **"world"** *kosmos* here means primarily the inhabitants of the world, it "also emphasizes the universal scope of the Flood and invites comparison with the coming eschatological judgment, the second such universal judgment (cf. 3:6-7)".[106] The largeness of the entire world is clearly in view. The Flood is not local but worldwide. The world is exceedingly sinful too.

"But preserved Noah, a herald of righteousness, with seven others", This brings us to the positive side of Peter's argument, namely, God's preservation of the righteous, a feature omitted in the case of the angels (v4). **"With seven others"** recalls the description at 1 Peter 3:20: "in which a few, that is, eight persons, were brought safely through water". Some suggest that here the literal description "Noah the eighth" refers either to the peculiar use of "eighth" in early Christian literature as typifying the day of resurrection or a day of new creation or that Noah was the eighth in line from Adam. However, it is much more likely to refer as at 1 Peter 3:20 to Noah his wife, his three sons and their wives and stress the fewness of those preserved compared to the large number condemned. What an amazing encouragement to Peter's readers, who rejected false teaching and followed apostolic instruction.

"A herald of righteousness" Noah is not mentioned in the Old Testament as preaching righteousness, though there is a reference to this in the post-apostolic writings. It may, of course, simply mean that Noah's godly lifestyle addressed the godlessness of his generation. The writer to the Hebrews notes how Noah's building of the ark was a mark of his faith and "condemned the world", as he became heir

---

[106] R. J. Bauckham, *Jude, 2 Peter*, p250.

to the righteousness that comes by faith (He. 11:7). Additionally, the phrase could imply that he was vocal as well as active. The sight of a man building a boat in the desert would provoke both ridicule and questions that Noah may well have answered. Calvin strikes the balance well when he writes: "But I rather think that he is called the preacher of righteousness, because he laboured to restore a degenerated world to a sound mind, and this not only by his teaching and godly exhortations, but also by his anxious toil in building the ark for the term of one hundred and twenty years".[107] Praise God for both the preaching and the example of preachers of righteousness.

"**When he brought a flood**" The idea of largeness resumes. "**Brought**" *epaxas* recalls "bringing upon themselves swift destruction" at verse 1, where the verb is the same and the false teachers are multiple, just as are the false prophets in the Old Testament. *epagein* means "to bring something upon someone", mostly something bad. "**Flood**" is *kataklusmon*, from which our English "cataclysmic", and is emphatic in meaning. The language closely recalls that of Genesis 6:17 particularly in the LXX (6:18), where the universality of the Flood is noted: "I am going to bring floodwaters (*ton kataklusmon, hudōr*) on the earth to destroy all life under the heavens, every creature that has the breath of life in it. Everything on earth will perish" NIV. The totality of the destruction is stressed.

"**Upon the world of the ungodly**" "**World**" *kosmos* is repeated in the original and, as a universal term, it relates to the extensiveness of the world's inhabitants. Those inhabitants are described as "ungodly" *asebōn*. This begins the second premise of the contrast. The world is not only large, it is also godless. The term "ungodly" is highly significant particularly in this letter. *Asebēs* means, literally, "without fear" and is best understood not in the secular but rather in the biblical sense, which depicts society as corrupt, full of violence and

---

107   J. Calvin, *Commentaries on II Peter*, p398.

rebellion against God and lacking in reverence for his commands, all of which results in an evil way of life. The term occurs frequently especially in the Wisdom books of the Old Testament. Perhaps the best Old Testament description is in the climactic summary at Genesis 6:5,11:

"The LORD saw that the wickedness of man was great in the earth, and that every intention of the thoughts of his heart was only evil continually . . . Now the earth was corrupt in God's sight, and the earth was filled with violence". Jesus alludes to such a situation as characterizing the days at the coming of "the Son of Man" (Mt. 24:37-39). Excess in godlessness is described by the term. Peter also uses it to contrast "godliness" *eusebeia,* which he frequently mentions in this letter (1:3, 6-7; 2:9; 3:11). It also contrasts with "righteousness" *dikaiosunē* as in the context here. The "world" is extensively large and excessively godless. Noah and his family were, on the other hand, notably few and markedly righteous. The contrast is pointed.

Simon Kistemaker stresses the dual teaching of preservation and judgement here appropriately:

> If God did not spare the ancient world in the days of Noah, how much less can he be expected to spare the false teachers in Peter's day? Yet as God protected believing Noah and his household, so he will spare believers who remain true to the teaching of Scripture. In other words, Peter's message is designed to exhort and encourage the readers of his epistle.[108]

This exhortation and encouragement would be of immense comfort to Peter's readers.

---

[108] S. J. Kistemaker, *James, Epistles of John, Peter, and Jude,* p288.

SODOM AND GOMORRAH (2:6-8)

The third example relative to the false teachers is that of Sodom and Gomorrah and the destruction of these cities along with the preservation of Lot, as of Noah previously from the Flood. Significantly, Peter gives here the order of judgement by water first in the Flood and then judgement by fire in the destruction of the cities, an order that he later repeats in his letter (cf. 3:5-7).

The differences here between Peter and Jude are also noteworthy. Jude gives the sins of the inhabitants of these cities in detail, stresses the "eternal" nature of their punishment and omits all reference to the deliverance of the righteous. Peter mentions the sins in less detail and highlights the preservation of the righteous in Lot's escape, while categorically affirming the condemnation of the unrighteous. Peter's presentation here contrasts the wickedness of the cities' behaviour with the righteousness of Lot's lifestyle, a feature that underlines the inner frustrations and difficulties of the righteous as they live among a wicked and perverse generation. This letter is obviously meant as a comfort and encouragement to his distressed readers as well as a severe warning against false teaching and godlessness in the light of God's judgement.

"if by turning the cities of Sodom and Gomorrah to ashes he condemned them to extinction, making them an example of what is going to happen to the ungodly"

Peter's language is aggressively vivid. **"the cities of Sodom and Gomorrah,"** in particular, often together with other "cities of the plain", in general, are expansively cited in the Old Testament as examples of sinfulness and rebellion (De. 29:23; 32:32-33; Ps. 107:34; Is. 1:9-10; 3:9; 13:19; Je. 23:14; 49:18; 50:40; Lam. 4:6; Eze. 16:46-58; Ho. 11:8; Am. 4:11; Zep. 2:9). Jesus coupled "the days of

Noah" and "the days of Lot" as exemplifying this situation just prior to the coming of the kingdom in final judgement (Lu. 17:26-29).

"If by turning the cities of Sodom and Gomorrah to ashes," **"Turning . . . to ashes"** translates *tephrōsas* and, the expression, while only used here in the Bible, is mentioned in Judaistic, post-Christian literature and by Dio Cassius in describing the eruption of Vesuvius in 79 A.D. when Pompeii and Herculaneum were buried in lava. The similar phrase **"condemned to extinction"** *katastrophēs katastrepsai* is found in the LXX account of the destruction of Sodom (Ge. 19:29). **"Example"** *hupodeigma* (cf. Jude's *deigma* at v7) is a better translation here than "pattern" or "model", which is in other places the case (cf. He. 8:5; 9:23), for this fits the context here (Jn. 13:15; He. 4:11; Ja. 5:10). The destruction of the cities serves as a shocking preview of the final judgement. **"Ungodly"** is the usual term, *asebēs*, literally "without fear". All Peter's language emphasizes the sinfulness and rebellion of the ungodly and the awful nature of the final judgement that will come upon them: As with Sodom and Gomorrah, so also with the false teachers – catastrophic destruction and judgement.

> **"and if he rescued righteous Lot, greatly distressed by the sensual conduct of the wicked (for as that righteous man lived among them day after day, he was tormenting his righteous soul over their lawless deeds that he saw and heard)"**

Peter contrasts Lot's righteousness with the unrighteousness of the Sodomites. Like Noah, **"a herald of righteousness"**, Peter describes Lot as **"righteous"** three times: **"righteous Lot"** (v7); **"that righteous man"** (v8ª); **"his righteous soul"** (v8ᵇ). That is not the impression given by a first reading of what Genesis says about Lot, even if he receives this kind of acclaim in extra-canonical sources. In Genesis, Lot appears to be greedy, choosing the better portion of land, the plain, over his senior Abraham, even at a time when this area was notoriously sinful (Ge. 13:10-13). He is represented as weak, morally depraved and compromising by sending out his own daughters to have sex with the Sodomites, who wanted rather to have sex with Lot's male guests (Ge. 19:6-8). Lot is lax and hesitant in having to be dragged out of Sodom (Ge. 19:16) and carelessly permissive in getting drunk and so allowing his daughters to have sex with him in a drunken stupor (Ge. 19:33, 35). Clearly, Lot had serious defects in character. Why, then, does Peter describe him quite emphatically as **"righteous"**?

"Righteous", *dikaios*, could here be used as describing Lot's status rather than his character, but this hardly suits Peter's strong terminology. **"Righteous"** could also be used vaguely as stressing the difference between Lot and his social context. In comparison with the majority of those around him he was "good" and "decent" in his lifestyle and this, perhaps, is nearer the mark. However, even in the Genesis' account, there seems to be another side to Lot. He did offer hospitality warmly to these strangers and, at least, attempted to give them protection under his roof from the mob. The offering his own daughters sexually to substitute for the sin of homosexuality is abhorrent and inexcusable. True, few of us have ever encountered such a life-threatening situation, yet Lot's behaviour was morally reprehensible (Ge. 19:1-11). Abraham does plead for the "righteous" to be spared from Sodom's destruction in the most emphatic of terms obviously thinking of Lot and his family and, quite clearly, God's mercy in sparing Lot from destruction relates to Abraham's prayer: "So it was that, when God destroyed the cities of the valley, God remembered Abraham and sent Lot out of the midst of the overthrow when he overthrew the cities in which Lot had lived" (Ge. 19:29 cf. 18:16-33). Abraham certainly categorized Lot among the "righteous". T.D. Alexander in a helpful article "Lot's Hospitality: A Clue to His Righteousness" concludes "The portrait of Lot as 'righteous' represents an accurate interpretation of the author's intention in Genesis 18-19".[109] Peter's remarks about Lot amplify this interpretation.

Peter's description of Lot, as of the Sodomites, is equally aggressively vivid. Lot was **"greatly distressed"** translates *kataponumenon*, which at Acts 7:24 describes the way the Egyptian ill-treated the Israelite in front of Moses. Lot was distressed by the **"sensual conduct of the wicked"**. **"Wicked"** is literally "careless" *athesmōn*. **"Sensual"** is *aselgeia*, a term which Peter uses in his first letter to describe the paganism in which his Christian readers "have spent enough time in the past doing what pagans chose to do – living in debauchery (*aselgeiais*), lust, drunkenness, orgies, carousing and detestable idolatry" (1 Pe. 4:3 [NIV]). Lot abhorred this lawless display of debauchery. As Lot **"(lived among them day after day, he was tormenting his righteous soul over their lawless (*anomois*) deeds that he saw and heard)"**. **"Tormenting"** is better active than passive and translates *basanizō*, which Mark used respectively for "torture" [NIV] and "straining at the oars" [NIV] (Mk. 5:7; 6:48). Lot, then, day by day and through his senses of sight and hearing by living in Sodom tortured himself with these lawless deeds he experienced around him. We wonder, then, why he had to be dragged out of Sodom. But therein lies the tragedy. Many a believer through voluntary but wrong decisions, where personal gain takes precedence over spiritual considerations, chooses to put himself in a place and among people where he is daily not only distressed but, indeed, tortures his conscience – he alone is responsible for being there – and yet finds it difficult to leave, for Satan makes sure of that. Only God's merciful preserving and delivering grace can resolve such a situation. How glorious is such grace. Clearly, Lot's greatest struggle was within. Calvin, as ever, puts it well:

---

[109] T. D. Alexander, *Journal of Biblical Literature*, 104 (1995):289-91 cited T. R. Schreiner, *1, 2 Peter, Jude*, p341n51

But Peter expresses more than before, that is, that just Lot underwent voluntary sorrows; as it is right that all the godly should feel no small grief when they see the world rushing into every kind of evil, so the more necessary it is that they should groan for their own sins. And Peter expressly mentioned this, lest when impiety everywhere prevails, we should be captivated and inebriated by the allurements of vices, and perish together with others, but that we might prefer this grief, blessed by the Lord, to all the pleasures of the world.[110]

Lot was no paragon of virtue, but Peter's epithet of 'righteous' was not inappropriate. Lot's offering of hospitality to and protection of the strangers, while the method of the latter was culpable, was practically well-intentioned. His resistance toward and refusal to join the violence and excesses of surrounding society, even if he had placed himself voluntarily in the area, was commendable. His daily tortured conscience testified to his abhorrence of the breaking of God's law. This is a prime feature in the description "righteous". His being rescued by divine providence and his not turning back were evidence of a righteousness through justification by divine grace in answer to Abraham's prayer that not only ten but even one 'righteous' might activate God's mercy. All of this would comfort and bless Peter's readers suffering the torture of false teaching with its associated immoral behaviour all around them. 'Righteous Lot', in that sense, was a faint spark of hope in the darkness engulfing them.

CONCLUSION (2:9-10ᵃ)

In verses 9 and 10ᵃ, Peter draws his conclusion from these three examples. In verse 9 he makes backward reference to the

---

[110] J. Calvin, *Commentaries on II Peter*, pp398–399.

Old Testament episodes, amplifying God's judgement on the unrighteous and his preservation of the godly. In verse 10^a, a hinge verse, he applies these lessons to the false teachers citing their sensual desires and rejection of authority as particularly pertinent. Most commentaries include verse 10^a in this foregoing section and verse 10^b with the following verses 11-22, which describe in lurid detail the defects of the false teachers and their teaching. In that sense, verse 10^a is a hinge verse concluding the previous section and introducing the subsequent theme. But obviously any division must not be allowed to disrupt the unitary sense of the letter.

> **"Then the Lord knows how to rescue the godly from trials, and to keep the unrighteous under punishment until the day of judgement, and especially those who indulge in the lust of defiling passion and despise authority".**

"Then the Lord knows how to rescue the godly from trials" This ends the long continuous Greek sentence beginning at verse 4: **"for if God did not spare angels"**. Verse 9 begins the concluding *apodosis*, of which verse 4 is the opening *protasis* of this long conditional sentence. Hence, the NIV understandably introduces verse 9 with the words (not in the original) "– if this is so, then", which in ESV translation is reduced to **"then"** (also not in the original). This grammatical nuance must be kept in view, if the sense of conclusion is to be appreciated.

"Rescue" is *ruesthai,* which is used of Lot in verse 9, just as **"preserved"** or "protected", *ephulaxen*, is used of Noah in verse 5. The differing situations of Noah and Lot need to be recalled to fully grasp the glorious versatility of God's preserving grace. The Flood was a universal and complete judgement with an entirely new beginning following it. The destruction of Sodom and Gomorrah was local and temporary bringing its own lesson of condemnation. The experiences of Noah and Lot were similar yet somewhat different.

M. Green puts it well: "Furthermore, the examples of Noah and Lot are instructive for showing *how* God delivers the godfearing (*eusebeis* as opposed to the *asebeis*, the ungodly) from tests. Neither had an immediate deliverance. Noah had to help himself by building an ark in obedience to God's instructions – despite the mirth of his neighbours: Lot had to endure long years of self-recrimination for his foolish decision to go and live in Sodom. Yet, at the time of his choosing, God delivered them both. God may allow us to face long years of waiting before he intervenes; he may use us to help ourselves out of the difficulty. But he well knows how to deliver the godly; he can be relied on".[111]

"From trials" "Trials" here translates *peirasmou,* which is singular. The Greek word can also be translated "temptation" and both "trial" and "temptation" are appropriate translations of this Greek word in the New Testament. The language is strongly reminiscent of the Lord's Prayer where both "deliver", "rescue" (*rusai*) and "temptation" (*peirasmon*) (Mt. 6:13) as here, are used. The context here probably favours "**trial**" and the generic plural "**trials**" is a reasonable rendering. However, the "inner" experience of both Noah and, certainly, of Lot does not exclude the notion of "temptation". So absolute dogmatism, here, precludes both depth and helpfulness in meaning. Some have thought the idea of the ultimate "**trial**" or "test", the final judgement, is also in view. Noticeably, the proposition is *ek* "out of" not *apo* "from". God delivers his people *out of* trials and temptations ultimately not necessarily *away from* them. The corollary is that, as Christians, we are to be in the world but not of it. Douglas Moo's comment is well worth considering. "Thus I think he includes in the 'trial' here all those challenges to faith that Christians experience in this world".[112]

---

[111] M. Green, *2 Peter and Jude,* p113-114 (Emphasis his).
[112] D.J. Moo, *2 Peter, Jude.* p106 (Emphasis his).

"And to keep the unrighteous under punishment until the day of judgement" While God wonderfully preserves the godly, he most surely condemns and punishes the unrighteous. This is the absolute and fearful affirmation here. The words **"keep . . . under punishment"** in the ESV translation render the Greek *kolazomenous tērein* and suggest a remanding or holding over for future punishment. Since *kolazomenous* is the present passive participle from the verb *kolazō* (I punish), some suggest that the future judgement impinges into this present life. Hence the NIV translates: "and to hold the unrighteous for the day of judgment, while continuing their punishment". Similarity of language and expression concerning the angels at verse 4 has been used to argue the case both ways and there is some scriptural evidence for the idea of divine punishment intruding into this life. However, grammatically speaking, present participles (and present passives in the New Testament are rare) are used in a future sense in the New Testament and, generally speaking, the context here favours a future nuance. Calvin comments: "The participle *kolazomenous*, though in the present tense, is yet to be thus explained, that they are reserved or kept to be punished, or, that they may be punished. For he bids us to rely on the expectation of the last judgment, so that in hope and patience we may fight till the end of life".[113]

"Especially those who indulge in the lust of defiling passion and despise authority" In this bridge verse, the foregoing lessons are pertinently applied by reference to the false teachers, with whom the chapter opens, and the two relevant defects characterizing them – fleshly sensuality and rejection of authority – form an introduction to the subsequent verses of the chapter which describe their defects in detail. The language of Jude 8 is similarly aggressive and vivid, though not necessarily to be completely identified with Peter's words here: "Yet in like manner these people also, relying on their dreams, defile the flesh, reject authority, and blaspheme the glorious ones".

---

[113]   J. Calvin, *Commentaries on II Peter*, p400.

"Indulge in the lust of defiling passion" The expression is strong and lurid. **"Indulge in"** is *poreuomenous* and its association with **"lust"**, "corruption", "pollution", *miasmou*, and with **"defiling passion"**, *sarkos en epithumia*, is translated "follow (i.e. indulge) their physical nature in desire that defiles".[114] It is hard to avoid the conclusion that there is reference to sexual immorality here.

"And despise authority" "Authority" *kuriotētos* has been variously interpreted:

1. As referring to angelic powers as in Ephesians 1:21, Colossians 1:16, in the parallel passage of Jude 6-8 and in the continuing context verses 10[b]-12.

2. Civil authorities, a view supported by Luther, Calvin and more recently by Bo Reicke.

3. A local church authority such as a presbyterate similar to the situation in 3 John and *1 Clement*, though this fits awkwardly with the next verse.

4. Apostolic authority, which though highly honoured may not suit Peter's explicit language here.

5. God's own authority or that of the Lord Jesus Christ in light of the references of "Lord", *kurios*, throughout the letter (2 Pe. 1:2, 8, 11, 14, 16; 2:9, 11, 20; 3:2, 8, 9, 10, 18).[115]

Perhaps the most likely in context is a combination of 1 and 5, any authority derivative from the divine triune God. Douglas

---

[114]   Arndt & Gingrich, *A Greek-English Lexicon,* p699.

[115]   See discussion in all the commentaries at 2 Peter 2:10[a], and especially helpful is the list in D. Lucas & C. Green, *The Message Of 2 Peter & Jude,* pp104-105.

Moo's insightful comment regarding authority *in principle* is helpful here: "It makes good sense, then, to see this second accusation as a specific example of the former. 'Despising authority', in other words, is a general charge to the effect that the false teachers are self-willed and rebellious. Peter is not thinking of any specific authority, he is thinking of the principle of authority".[116]

APPLICATION

Peter's three examples are vivid in expression, insightful in interpretation and helpful in application. The pride and rebellion of the angels is a sober reminder of the arrogance and rejection towards God that springs from a fallen nature. The picture of these celestial beings chained in dark dungeons awaiting not some meagre test or superficial trial but a judgement of final irreversible condemnation fills us with horror. Of course, a sceptical world not only makes light of such a fate but also rejects it with scorn. But we who are Christ's know better and should increase our efforts to see a lost world acknowledge this and be saved from such a disastrous end.

The apathy and disobedience of those of Noah's day is an added warning along the same lines. The increasing growth of sin on a worldwide scale met by a universal flood is adequate illustration of how God's punishment fits the crime of man's sin. The preservation of Noah and his family brings great comfort to believers, who appreciate God's delay in bringing his second universal judgement and moves us yet further to double our efforts to see a lost and fallen world saved.

The sheer sensuality and flagrant vice of Sodom and Gomorrah have definite echoes in our sophisticated twenty-first century society. The link between a depraved lifestyle and a rejection of God and

---

[116]   D. J. Moo, *2 Peter, Jude.* p108.

the standards and principles of his word reminds us starkly of the importance of sound teaching and its reception and the dangers of false teaching and its acceptance both within and without the church. Errant philosophy and misconstrued biblical truth bring in their wake an unhealthy, sick society. Indeed, the pernicious results of the false teachers and teaching in Chapter 2 are a constant foil to the healthy consequence arising from the sound teachers and teaching in Chapter 1. Lot's experience, in this case, brings not only hope but also an incentive to patience and trust in God, who will eventually adjust the scales and vindicate his justice in judgement.

However, the most intriguing feature of these examples alongside the certainty of divine judgement on the godless is the divine preservation of the righteous. This is graphically portrayed not only in the differing backgrounds but slightly varying aspects of "righteousness" in both Noah and Lot. Whether the believer stands confidently firm in the promises of God, though ridiculed by a sceptical world, as Noah did, or whether he remains somewhat under-confident with a tortured conscience in a setting in which he has responsibly but wrongly placed himself, as Lot did, the glory of God's providential grace is constant and deals with whatever flawed form of human nature it finds. All of this inspires confidence in that grace and promotes the desire to see our unbelieving friends share in it with us. The importance of Scripture in all of this should not be missed either. That is the point of the contrast between the sound teachers and teaching of Chapter 1 and the false teachers and teaching of Chapter 2. Noah and Lot had responsible decisions to make in the light of divine revelation. Twice Scripture reminds us that Noah did everything which God commanded him; and tardy and hesitant as Lot was, his tortured soul and his endangered body found safety as they dragged him away from Sodom in obedience to angelic advice.

The divine revelation of Scripture soundly taught and savingly obeyed brings about glorious results. Any false misrepresentation of the word brings confusion and death. This applies both to those within and without the people of God. We ignore these lessons at our peril. But Noah and Lot are sparks in the dark. The differing contexts of their righteousness make the application of instruction and comfort to Peter's readers amazingly versatile. As already noted, whether confident in trust like Noah or under-confident and beset by difficulties and doubts like Lot, Peter's advice makes God's grace vitally real and encouragingly reassuring, whatever the circumstances. Indeed, the experience of these two Old Testament characters becomes the sterling focus of Peter's advice in these verses on this dark and judgemental background. The false knowledge of God which leads to disobedience and disaster is set over against the true knowledge of God which brings grace and glory – encouragement indeed. The lurid judgement over the false teachers that dominates these verses is rightfully fearful and warns us against the dangers of false teaching. Noah and Lot, from their differing perspectives, are sparks in the dark. They offer rich comfort and hope, as well as warning, to both Peter's readers and to ourselves. Let us derive great benefit from them.

Chapter 13

FALSE KNOWLEDGE

ARROGANCE; SENSUALITY

2 PETER 2:10ᴮ–16

INTRODUCTION

Peter continues his description of the false teachers and their teaching. Chapter 2 with its false teaching is a constant foil to Chapter 1 with its true knowledge of God. Peter, in his letter, has briefly introduced his readers to these false teachers (2:1-3). He then gives three Old Testament examples of God's judgement of the wicked and his preservation of the righteous – the Angels, the Flood, the cities of Sodom and Gomorrah together with Noah and Lot (2:4-10ᵃ). Now, he returns to the subject of the false teachers and their teaching, detailing in the strongest of terms their sinful character and lifestyle (2:10ᵇ-16) and their destructive teaching and its effects (2:17-22).

In all of this, verse 10a is a hinge or bridge verse, where Peter teaches his readers that the Lord knows how to rescue the godly from trials and to keep the unrighteous under punishment until the day of judgement: "especially those who indulge in the lust of defiling passion and despise authority" (2:10). These words recall the lessons of Peter's three Old Testament examples and reintroduce the theme of the false teachers whose sins are itemized as *sensuality*: "the lust of defiling passion" and *arrogance*: "and despise authority". As Douglas Moo rightly suggests, Peter now reverses the order and details these aspects of the false teachers' character and lifestyle as he continues his letter:

ARROGANCE OF THE FALSE TEACHERS   (10^b-13^a)

SENSUALITY OF THE FALSE TEACHERS   (13^b-16)[117]

Peter condemns the arrogance of the false teachers. His language is aggressive and striking. His style is staccato and sharp. He angrily condemns these false teachers and their teaching, leaving his readers in no doubt as to how dangerous they are. In verses 10^b-13^a, he uses words from common biblical coinage and others quite unique in the New Testament to describe the teachers. He possibly employs word-plays on *blasphēmia* "blasphemy", "slander", *phthora* "destruction", "corruption", and *adikia* "wrongdoing", "unrighteousness" to drive these warnings home. The arrogance and pride of the false teachers is plainly to be seen.

Peter's Greek is sometimes difficult to follow in detail but the broad strokes are crystal clear. These fools of false teachers rush in where the very angels fear to tread. They rebuke and despise authority. They berate celestial beings while those very beings are silent and willing to leave the matter in God's hands. Their arrogance and rebellion are an affront to God and to those who are in a much better and stronger position to critique and calumniate but do not. Their pride is both appalling and sinful. Their arrogance is to be condemned, for it is a grave danger to God's people. In this vein, Peter declaims their character and, in all of this, parallel sections of Jude's letter, while not necessarily identical, are helpful and instructive for our understanding of this arrogance.

---

[117]   D. J. Moo, *2 Peter, Jude.* p120.

Peter's condemnation of the false teachers' sensuality in verses 13b-16 is equally indicting. His language is similarly strong. It has the directly opposite meaning, often literally speaking, from the descriptive terms of the godly teachers and believers. It is comprehensive, showing the total nature of their depraved condition, their outer demeanour and their inner thoughts, their actual sin as well as their state before God. It indicates the virus they inflict on others, especially on the Christian church. There are possibly word-plays similar to those in verses 10b-13a: *Beōr/Bosor* cf. *basar* "flesh"; *paranomias* "transgression" cf. *paraphronian* "madness" and, perhaps, *apatais* "deceptions", "pleasures" cf. *agapais* "love feasts" (cf. Jude 12) [see later]. Peter's entire presentation shows the depths and dangers of the false teachers' sensuality in the most lurid way, underlines the connection between false teaching and immoral living and, by implication, stresses the link between sound teaching and godliness. Peter's words call for detailed examination:

ARROGANCE	(2:10b-13a)
SENSUALITY	(2:13b-16)

EXPOSITION

ARROGANCE (vv10b-13a)

"Bold and wilful, they do not tremble as they blaspheme the glorious ones, whereas angels, though greater in might and power, do not pronounce a blasphemous judgement against them before the Lord. But these, like irrational animals, creatures of instinct, born to be caught and destroyed, blaspheming about matters of which they are ignorant, will also be destroyed

2 Peter - Growing in Christ amid False Teaching

> **in their destruction, suffering wrong as the wage for their wrongdoing" (10ᵇ-13ᵃ).**

Peter condemns the arrogance of the false teachers in the most vigorous terms comparing them to irrational wild beasts and showing how their behaviour brings God's judgement on them.

"Bold and wilful" "Bold" *tolmētai* describes a reckless audacity which defies both God and man. It is less found in the biblical literature than "wilful" but relates to a word-root in Jude 9 meaning "presumptuous" "wilful". **Wilful,** *authadeis* occurs much more in biblical works than the former. It connotes a strong determined attitude of self-pleasing and obstinacy to do one's own will at all costs. The two are twinned together in other literature. R. Bauckham suggests the meaning as "arrogant audacity",[118] which well gives the sense.

> **"they do not tremble as they blaspheme the glorious ones, whereas angels, though greater in might and power, do not pronounce a blasphemous judgement against them before the Lord"**

Peter uses Greek *blasphēmia* three times in various forms in these verses and, with its variety of meaning ranging from the strictly religious context of blasphemy to the more human and even legal connotation of "slander", "defamation", it creates an effective word-play on that general theme.

"Glorious ones" translates *doxas*, which has been variously rendered: "dignities" ᴬⱽ, "dignitaries" ᴺᴷᴶⱽ, "celestial beings" ᴺᴵⱽ, and "the glorious ones" ᴱˢⱽ. Some, as previously noted in verse 10ᵃ regarding *kuriotētos* "authority" ᴺᴷᴶⱽ, specify leaders in either state or church. *doxas* here may have a similar meaning.

---

[118] R.J. Bauckham, *Jude, 2 Peter*, p262.

"Angels" may, perhaps, be a preferable translation, though *doxa* is not normally used in this regard. The general context, however, with the immediate mention of **"angels"** *aggeloi* in verse 11, and the parallel reference at Jude 8-10 certainly points in this direction. If *doxas*, **"the glorious ones"** are angels, then it is conjectured that they are "evil" angels while the, *aggeloi*, the **"angels"** of verse 11, described as **"greater in might and power"** are seen as "good" angels. The point, then, Peter is making is that the false teachers, bold and self-willed like the "evil" angels, who reject and rail against God's authority, are to be deprecated, for even the "good" angels, greater in might and power, do not presume to do so.

This interpretation does not solve all the detailed problems of this difficult text, for the false teachers actually blaspheme **"glorious ones"** and, who are the "them", against whom the **"angels"** do not bring **"blasphemous judgement"**? In the light of these difficulties, the interpretation of **"glorious ones"** as either state or church leaders might seem preferable. However, on balance, we have opted for understanding **"glorious ones"** as implying evil angels. Whatever the resolution of these difficulties, the general meaning is clear: the false teachers are bold and self-willed. They rebel against authority, whereas the good angels do not presume to do so. False teachers rush in where angels fear to tread. The parallel passage at Jude, 8-10 is much more detailed regarding angelology, alluding to apocryphal writings, and though not necessarily identical, is similar in meaning. We quote it here in full as helpful elucidation, without necessarily committing to priority of 2 Peter or Jude:

> "Yet in like manner these people also, relying on their dreams, defile the flesh, reject authority, and blaspheme the glorious ones. But when the archangel Michael, contending with the devil, was disputing about the body of Moses, he did not presume to pronounce a blasphemous judgement,

but said, 'The Lord rebuke you'. But these people blaspheme all that they do not understand, and they are destroyed by all that they, like unreasoning animals, understand instinctively" (Jude 8-10).

The argument again is from the greater to the lesser. Just as Michael, a prince among the angels, did not presume to pronounce a blasphemous judgement but left the matter with the Lord, so the false teachers a lesser breed even below fallen angels, ought not to pronounce a blasphemous judgement but to leave it with the Lord: "The Lord rebuke you".[119]

---

[119] Michael the Archangel's name means 'who is like God?' In the book of Daniel, he is described as "one of the chief princes" (10:13) and "the great prince" who protects God's people (12:1). Michael opposes and overcomes demons sent by Satan to influence the rulers of Persia and Greece (10:13, 20). The term prince is equivalent to the word Archangel (cf. 1 Th. 4:16). In Revelation, Michael leads the battle against the Dragon and the evil angels (Re. 12:7).

At Jude 9 "Michael, contending with the devil, was disputing about the body of Moses, (he) did not pronounce a blasphemous judgement but said, 'The Lord rebuke you'".

The Old Testament says that God buried Moses and that no one knew where the grave was to that day (De. 34:6). A Jewish tradition arose connected with the apocryphal *Testament of Moses* and the related work *Assumption of Moses,* that Michael and Satan disputed about the body of Moses and Michael's prominence is also noted in *1 Enoch* (1 Enoch 9:1; 10:11; 20:5; 24:6).

Michael's pronouncement, 'The Lord rebuke you' alludes to Zechariah 3:2, where Satan accused Joshua, the high priest, but the Lord said to Satan, "The Lord rebuke you, O Satan!". While none of this detail is present at 2 Peter 2:11 as at Jude 9, it is obviously informative background to help us understand the gist of Peter's argument at this point.

Collating this data regarding Jude 9 confirms Peter's contention at 2 Peter 2:11. The arrogance of the false teachers is evident in this, that while they pronounce a blasphemous judgement against angels before God, angels fear to do so and leave the matter with the Lord. False teachers barge in where angels fear to tread.

Thomas R. Schreiner's summary is helpful and judicious:

> In conclusion, the false teachers did not fear demonic powers. Peter called them 'glories', not because they were good but simply because they were created by God himself, even though subsequently they fell into sin. Perhaps the teachers did not tremble before them because they disbelieved in their existence. This would fit nicely with the skeptical worldview they adopted about the coming of the Lord (3:3-7). Or they may have ridiculed any idea that human beings should be frightened about the power of spiritual beings. Bauckham and Moo suggest that the teachers ridiculed the notion that their sins would make them the prey of evil angels. By way of contrast, good angels do not even declare God's judgment against evil angels. They leave it with the Lord.[120]

"But these, like irrational animals, creatures of instinct, born to be caught and destroyed, blaspheming about matters of which they are ignorant, will also be destroyed in their destruction, suffering wrong as the wage for their wrongdoing"

Peter amplifies the rebellious mind-set of the false teachers by likening them to irrational beasts. Here, it is the negative lack of reason and the positive motivation of brute instinct that is stressed. This is effectively accomplished through Peter's strong expressions and inventive word-plays. **"Irrational"** is *aloga*, literally, "without logic". **"Creatures of instinct"** translates *phusika*, meaning "natural",

---

[120]   T.R. Schreiner, *1, 2 Peter, Jude*, pp348, 349.

"in accordance with nature", that is, programmed by animal stimuli, by urge and passion rather than by reason. **"Matters of which they are ignorant,"** is *hois agnoousin*, displaying an ignorance which contrasts strongly with the knowledge, *gnōsis* and *epignōsis*, repeatedly referred to in Chapter one (1:2, 3, 5, 6, 8). **"Born to be caught and destroyed"** underlines both the similar nature and ultimate fate of wild animals and false teachers. This fate or judgement is spelled out in three vivid word-plays: one from the religious and legal world, **"blaspheming about matters of which they are ignorant"**, one from the natural world, **"destroyed in their destruction"** and one from the commercial world, **"suffering wrong as the wage for their wrongdoing"**. These false teachers, like the brute beasts, suffer the rightful deserts of their outrageous, irrational behaviour. Their arrogance eventually entraps them. They become victims of their own rebel nature. M. Green puts it superbly:

> This, then, is the character of the false teachers as set out so far. They are dominated by lust; their passions are given free sway, with the result that they behave like animals, while the mental and spiritual sides of their humanity suffer atrophy. They are headstrong, rebellious against the will of God, and reckless of the consequences. They are contemptuous of other people, be these human or celestial. They are self-willed; the sensual man always is, for in the last analysis self is all that matters to him. His hell is this, that his world contracts until the only thing he has left is the self he has corrupted. Who can say that 2 Peter is irrelevant to our generation?[121]

Peter, thus, itemizes the arrogance of the false teachers. Their self-will and presumption know no bounds. It exceeds all reason.

---

[121] M. Green, *2 Peter and Jude*, p117.

They berate and blaspheme others before God in a way that the very angels, bad or good, fear to do. They are like vicious wild animals – in their vehemence, they destroy others, one another and ultimately, they self-destruct. Their arrogance eventually comes to rest upon their own heads as God judges them.

SENSUALITY (ᵛᵛ 13ᵇ-16)

"They count it pleasure to revel in the daytime. They are blots and blemishes, revelling in their deceptions, while they feast with you. They have eyes full of adultery, insatiable for sin. They entice unsteady souls. They have hearts trained in greed. Accursed children! Forsaking the right way, they have gone astray. They have followed the way of Balaam, the son of Beor, who loved gain from wrongdoing, but was rebuked for his own transgression; a speechless donkey spoke with human voice and restrained the prophet's madness" (13ᵇ-16).

Peter aggressively berates the sensuality of the false teachers at every level, their self-indulgent lifestyle with its revelling and carousing, their filthy minds, their evil hearts, and their condemnation in God's sight. They are like the false prophet Balaam, whose very dumb beast condemned him, and justifiably so.

"They count it pleasure to revel in the daytime. They are blots and blemishes, revelling in their deceptions, while they feast with you".

The progression begins with the false teachers' lifestyle. **"Revel"** is first mentioned as a noun *truphēn* though translated verbally in the context, literally: "deeming revelling in the day to be pleasure" and then as a present participle in verbal form, "revelling" *entruphōntes*. It means to "lead a life of luxury, self-indulgence, to revel, to carouse". Its double mention and intense form here probably indicates its excessive nature. "**In the daytime**" which translates *en hēmera*, "in the day", is also emphatic. Drinking or feasting during the day was regarded as a mark of degeneracy not only by Judeo-Christian society but also in the pagan world. (Ec. 10:16; Is. 5:11; Testament of Moses 7:4; Juvenal 1.103).[122] Pleasure and daylight properly used shows appreciation for God's providential goodness. This kind of behaviour, on the other hand, abuses God's gifts and is inappropriate for God's people (cf. Ro. 13:11-14).

"**Blots and blemishes**" translates *spiloi kai mōmoi* which, interestingly, Peter uses in a negative form, adding the Greek prefix 'A', namely A – privative, later in this letter to describe how Christians ought to live in the light of Christ's return: "without spot or blemish" *aspiloi kai amōmētoi* (2 Pe. 3:14) and also in his first letter, to describe Christ as the sinless and sacrificial lamb of God: "without blemish or spot" *amōmou kai aspilou* (1 Pe. 1:19). Such blots and blemishes in the Old Testament rendered an animal unfit for sacrifice (Le. 1:3) and a man unfit for priestly service (Le. 21:21). The false teachers were clearly culpable in this. Christians, on the other hand, must follow Christ in holiness and in purity of life and behaviour.

"**Revelling in their deceptions, while they feast with you**" The problem is further exasperated by the harmful influence the false teachers exert on the church. "**Deceptions**" *apatais* has as a primary meaning "deception", "deceitfulness" and tends to be related to the deceitfulness and trickery of sin. Peter is stressing the enticing effect the false teachers have upon other believers as they join together with them in meals. *Apatē* has also a secondary and derivative meaning of "pleasure", "pleasantness" and that relating to enjoyment in sin. The

---

122   cited R.J. Bauckham, *Jude, 2 Peter,* p265.

translation "pleasures" is also used by some here and the connection of the deceit with the pleasure can readily be appreciated. However, what is the precise context of **"while they feast with you"**? Does it refer to ordinary table fellowship, to a corporate fellowship meal within the church and/or to the so called AGAPE of which there is some evidence, to the Lord's Supper as instituted by Christ and observed by the church or to a combination of these last two? For there may have been a period when a unitary meal or AGAPE was eaten along with, before or after, the Lord's Supper rather than separately. The complexity grows as the comparative section in Jude indicates close similarities both in thought and language. It reads:

> "These are blemishes (*spilades* – with a primary
> meaning of 'rocks', 'hidden reefs' and a secondary
> of 'spots', 'stains') on your love feasts, *(agapais)* as
> they feast with you without fear" (Jude 12ᵃ).

There is also a variant reading here at 2 Peter 2:13 as at Jude 12 of *agapais* "love feasts" instead of *apatais* "deceptions/pleasures", though at 2 Peter 2:13, the latter would seem to be the original.

Taking all of this into consideration, Peter seems here to be referring to deceitful and sensual excesses brought in by the false teachers to meals eaten by the Christians in their assembly, something akin to the excesses mentioned by Paul as he writes to the Corinthian church regarding the Lord's Supper (1 Co. 11:17-34). The permissive, sensual behaviour of the false teachers was infesting the very heart of Christian fellowship and worship. The false teachers' lifestyle was having a harmful effect on the Christian church itself, including, perhaps, even its meetings.

> **"They have eyes full of adultery, insatiable for
> sin. They entice unsteady souls. They have hearts
> trained in greed. Accursed children!"**

Peter next describes the false teachers' mind-set, their inner life. Their eyes come in for comment, first of all. The language, again, is intense. Their eyes are not just "**full of adultery**" but, literally, "of an adulteress": *ophthalmous echontes mestous moichalidos* "having eyes mixed with an adulteress". That, too, is the constant habit of their gaze: "**insatiable for sin**". By way of contrast in his first letter, Peter uses a similar verbal root for "cease", when he claims that the Christian, like Christ, who has suffered in his body, "is done with sin" (1 Pe. 4:1[NIV]), in the sense that Christ died finally, once for all for sin. There is, and should be, a complete break with sin for the Christian. Not so with these false teachers. Every woman they look at is a potential prostitute, an object of lustful desire. Jesus warned about the sinfulness of this (Mt. 5:28). Job rightly made a covenant with his eyes not to look lustfully at a girl (Jb. 31:1). Again, even the pagan world recognizes the degeneracy of this in the popular ancient Greek proverb, based on the pun, that the shameless man did not have *koras* (the word can mean both 'pupils' and 'maidens') in his eyes but *pornas* 'prostitutes'.[123] How much less should the Christian be like this!

As with the carousing, the harmful effect on the church is noted: "**They entice unsteady souls**". "**Entice**" *deleazontes* is a word used in the world of fishing and snaring. "**Unsteady**" is *astēriktous*, literally, "rootless" and contrasts Peter's intention earlier in his letter of always reminding his readers of certain things, even though they knew them and are firmly established *estērigmenous* in the truth they have (1:12) and also recalls his closing warnings in the letter lest his readers fall from their "secure position" (*stērigmou*, 3:17 [NIV]), carried away by the error of lawless men. These, indeed, may well be among the "ignorant" (*amatheis* – literally "untaught") and "unstable" (*astēriktoi*), people who distort Scripture (cf.3:16). The link between false teaching and immoral behaviour again is evident.

---

123   Plutarch Moralia 528E cited D.J. Moo, *2 Peter, Jude*, p126 n14.

These dangers are as real and relevant in today's church as in Peter's day. The necessity for continual grounding in sound teaching and its application even among those established in the faith is as pressing as ever.

The hearts of the false teachers are next scrutinized. "**They have hearts trained in greed**" The "**heart**" in Scripture is the seat of the will rather than of the emotions. The "**heart**" is the very core of the false teachers' existence and their motivation. "**Trained**" *gegumnasmenēn*, from which our English "gymnasium", brings us into the world of sport. The false teachers have spent time, concentration, energy and discipline not training in godliness but in greed. They are, as the NIV meaningfully translates, 'experts' in it. "**Greed**" is *pleonexias*. Basically, it encapsulates that frame of mind of wanting more and more, regardless of whether the object of desire is beneficial or needful. "**Greed**" is covetousness. It includes sexual lust but the meaning extends beyond this to covetousness in general. Its downward spiralling base is well expressed at Colossians 3:5: and covetousness, which is "idolatry". It infringes not only the tenth, the first, the second but breaches all Ten Commandments. Peter's words here recall his introduction at verse 3: "in their greed they will exploit you with false words". It is hard to believe this of the Christian church but it happened then and it happens today. We must guard against it.

"**Accursed children!**" This climactic summary describes the false teachers' condition before both God and man. The phrase is, literally, "children of the curse" and means children characterized by a curse. They evince and deserve not God's blessing but his curse. It is a Hebraism, frequent in Scripture, and an understandable, if lurid, conclusion to Peter's description. Isaiah speaks of "children of perdition" (Is. 57:4 LXX), Hosea of "children of iniquity" (Ho. 10:9 LXX), Paul of "children of wrath" (Ep. 2:3) and "children of light" (Ep. 5:8). Peter in his first letter describes his readers as, literally, "children of obedience" (1 Pe. 1:14) and, lest we fall into magical or vindictive categories of thinking about curse and blessing apart from God, Scripture teaches that all who fail to trust in Christ, who bore man's curse, are under the curse of God (Ga. 3:10, 13). It is Christ who makes all the difference between curse and blessing and who alone qualifies us for the entitlement as "children" of God. This carries fearful implications for the spiritual state of the false teachers. **"Accursed children"** not only marks the depths of their depravity but also paves the way for Peter's Old Testament illustration of Balaam, where the idea of "curse" pervades the story.

> **"Forsaking the right way, they have gone astray.**
> **They have followed the way of Balaam, the son of**
> **Beor, who loved gain from wrongdoing, but was**
> **rebuked for his own transgression; a speechless**
> **donkey spoke with human voice and restrained**
> **the prophet's madness"**

Peter closes his remarks on the false teachers' sensuality with an illustration from the Old Testament story of the false prophet Balaam, which features the angel of the Lord and a 'dumb' donkey, just as he had rounded off his comments on the false teachers' arrogance with an allusion to angels and to brute beasts. The story of Balaam is told in detail at Numbers 22-24. Balak, king of Moab, hires the services of Balaam the prophet to bring a curse on Israel and curtail their advancing army. Balaam seeks God's direction but then swithers expecting reward for his services, though in the end he actually blesses rather than curses Israel. Within this story, a donkey miraculously speaks and rebukes Balaam for his evil intentions. Balaam also is responsible for leading the Israelites into idolatry and immorality. The story of Balaam's greed and sin was used as a pertinent warning in Scripture elsewhere (De. 23:4,5; Jos. 13:22; 24:9,10; Ne. 13:1, 2; Mi. 6:5; Jude 11; Re. 2:14). Peter adduces two main lessons from the story:

A. Just as Balaam, the false prophet, was led astray by putting personal greed and advance before his duty to God and the needs of Israel, so with the false teachers. The additional errors of idolatry and immorality were, perhaps, also in Peter's mind.

B. Just as the false prophet Balaam was rebuked by a 'dumb' donkey, so the false teachers are justifiably rebuked by Peter and God's people. The church should rebuke these false teachers and have nothing to do with them even if they feel themselves to be fools or are under–confident in doing so.

Some commentators baulk at the "speaking" donkey and divert the words to "the angel of the Lord" and to Balaam's "conscience". There is no need for such a modification. The writers of the New Testament were not at all embarrassed by the miraculous in the Old Testament, however incredible it might seem to be. The Old Testament was their 'datum point'.[124] So it should be with us. When we become sceptical about the miraculous in Scripture, it ultimately leads to denial of Christ's resurrection, without which, Scripture reminds us, we have no faith and are still in our sin (1 Co. 15:12-18 esp.14, 17). By faith, we accept and believe all that the word of God teaches, including miracles.

"Forsaking the right way, they have gone astray". In the Balaam story at Numbers 22:22,23, the term "way" is used literally and at Numbers 22:32 metaphorically (cf. LXX). Jude uses the expression "the way of Cain" along with "Balaam's error" and "Korah's rebellion" (Jude 11). The "right way" is an Old Testament metaphor indicating obedience to God's word (Ge. 18:19; 1 S. 12:23; Jb. 8:19; Pss. 18:30; 25:9; 119:14, 33; Pr. 8:20, 22 cf. Ac. 13:10). This entire biblical idiom makes clear Peter's description of the false teachers as abandoning

---

[124]   M. Green, *2 Peter and Jude*, p125.

the scriptural pathway and straying into another way. Peter has already remarked on this false teaching as to how many will follow their shameful ways and bring the way of truth into disrepute (2:2) and later remarks that it would have been better for them not have known that way of righteousness than to have known and turned their back on the holy command passed on to them (2:21). The connection between false unscriptural teaching and godlessness is as painfully evident here in Chapter 2 as that between sound scriptural teaching and godliness is pointedly evident in Chapter 1.

"They have followed the way of Balaam, the son of Beor". While most modern translations give Beor instead of Bosor (AV), the latter, according to some manuscript evidence, may well be original. It may be related to the Hebrew *basar*, "flesh". The suggestion that it was Peter's Galilean guttural pronunciation of the Hebrew is not without some credibility (cf. Mt. 26:73). If Bosor is correct and relates to *basar*, it emphasizes the "fleshly" nature of the greed and avarice.

"Who loved gain from wrongdoing" "Gain from wrongdoing" is *misthon adikias*. The exact same phrase is used to describe the arrogance of the false teachers at verse 13 and the same sentence harks back naturally to Peter's introductory remarks at verse 3: "in their greed they will exploit you with false words". This, above all, is the point of Peter's illustration. The covetousness, greed and avarice of the false teachers have so many parallels with the false prophet Balaam that the message is both a clear and forceful warning. Peter's readers need to take it to heart and so do we.

"But was rebuked for his own transgression; a speechless donkey spoke with human voice and restrained the prophet's madness" Peter's language, again, is aggressive, vivid and unique. **"Rebuked"** is *elegxin* which means to "rebuke sharply" or "confute". **"Transgression"** is *paranomias*. Both words are not found elsewhere in the New Testament. **"Spoke"** is *phthegxamenon*, a present

participle, "a word used of important, portentous utterance".[125]
There is probably an intentional word-play, yet again in this section,
between *paranomias* "**transgression**" and *paraphronian* "**madness**".
The "**madness**", of course, is metaphorical, though literal enough
to be understood as the lunacy of opposing God in any way or
"perverting the right ways of the Lord" (cf. Ac. 13:10 [NIV]). M. Green
catches the intended point well when he writes: "the oracular speech
of the (justifiably) disobedient donkey is contrasted with the madness
of the (culpably) disobedient prophet".[126]

The false teachers' sensuality in lifestyle, mind, eye and heart is
set on sin. They are experts trained in greed and greedy for more.
They do all this, inexcusably, in broad daylight and, hypocritically,
along with others in religious exercises. This sensuality is related to
their false teaching and means that they have forsaken the way of
truth. This mixture of arrogance and sensuality of the false teachers
and the relevance of the allusion to Balaam would not be lost on
Peter's readers. Nor should it be to us. False teaching and immorality
go hand in hand and are a constant danger to the church. Sound
teaching and godly living are the requisite antidote. They bring
strong assurance and healthful confidence to the people of God.

APPLICATION

The arrogance and sensuality of the false teachers fleshes out
the downward spiral of depravity mentioned at the beginning of the
Chapter 2. The lurid details of Peter's description fill the mind with
horror. Yet, listening to the news each day, world or local, reading
the tabloids or watching television reminds us that this weird world
of which Peter writes is so like ours today. The intriguing thing that
comes through is the interconnection between understanding and

---

[125]   M. Green, *2 Peter and Jude,* p125.
[126]   M. Green, *2 Peter and Jude,* p125.

behaviour, philosophy and lifestyle, doctrine, or the lack of it and living for good or for ill. A society that holds firm moral standards such as Scripture teaches and lives by them, even given the fallenness of human nature, has some chance of seeing a reasonably peaceful and happy state of affairs. As it is, of course, there are few or no principles or perimeters today. Anything goes, so most disastrous things come.

If that interconnection sadly intrigues and bewilders, what disgusts and frustrates is that this same arrogance and sensuality sometimes poisons the very church and its leadership and thus affects society as a whole. Yet this is indubitably so in our sophisticated, postmodern, well adjusted, twenty-first century church. When made up stories replace solid Scripture, when blurred idealistic principles take the place of clear spiritual teaching, when misrepresentation and compromise, twist, distort and even explain away biblical truths, miracles included, then a pretentious arrogance and a permissive sensuality take over. Even when we hear the truth and do not put it into practice, as Jesus reminds us, the same happens and the church sickens and comes near to death.

Peter here reminds Christians of the importance of laying a true foundation of Scripture: clearly taught, plainly understood and rigorously applied in daily life. This produces the additions to our basic faith, which make it effective and productive as so descriptively put earlier in his letter in Chapter 1 (1:3-11). Paul uses the metaphor of diet and healthy living to teach Timothy and Titus the same thing and avoid the errors of the false teacher both in Ephesus and Crete. Proper feeding makes for healthy living. Sound teaching produces godly behaviour. Of course, discipline and application within the process are ever necessary. But, that accepted, as Jesus taught: by their fruits you will know them. It applies to both teachers and taught alike. Otherwise arrogance and sensuality rule. Peter teaches similarly. We do well to heed him and to take his advice seriously in today's church.

Chapter 14

FALSE KNOWLEDGE.

EMPTINESS

2 PETER 2:17–22

INTRODUCTION

Peter continues his condemnation of the false teachers. He has described their arrogance and sensuality. Now he declaims their emptiness both as teachers and their teaching. But there is a change of emphasis here. Whereas previously in verses 10^b-16, he has related the damaging effect of their character and lifestyle on the church, now in verses 17-22, he outlines, in much greater detail, the harmful impact of their teaching both on the church and on the teachers themselves, while also continuing the fearful story of God's judgement on them because of their sin.

In showing the empty and insubstantial nature of this false teaching, Peter stresses the harm it does to the church. In verses 17-22, a clear pattern in his thinking emerges. In verse 17, he introduces his theme with three striking images from the world of nature, two focusing on the character of the false teachers and one on their condemnation: "waterless springs": "mists driven by a storm"; "gloom of utter darkness". In verse 18, he develops the first of these three images, "waterless springs": their empty words mean that they have nothing of value to say. In verse 19, he expands the second image, "mists driven by a storm", rounding it off with a proverbial saying: their insubstantial profession means that they promise what they cannot deliver. In verses 20 to 22, he amplifies the third image, "gloom of utter darkness", with one implied and two explicit proverbs: their apostasy or abandonment of their professed beliefs reduces them to a worse and yet more pitiful state than previously and brings them under an even greater judgement from God. Peter's language is, again, aggressive and his metaphors sharp. His words both recall and contrast earlier statements in his letter, while his message about the false teachers and their teaching was, obviously, not only fearful for his readers then, it is equally fearful and relevant for us today.

This outline is summarized under the following headings:

EMPTINESS   (2:17)
EMPTY WORDS   (2:18)
EMPTY PROMISES   (2:19)
EMPTY PROFESSION   (2:20-22)

The parallel section at Jude 12b-13 is, perhaps fuller, though the words and sentiments are similar to 2 Peter, especially the first and last line. It is worthy of comparison and consideration and we quote it in full:

> "waterless clouds, swept along by winds; fruitless trees in late autumn, twice dead, uprooted; wild waves of the sea, casting up the foam of their own shame; wandering stars, for whom the gloom of utter darkness has been reserved for ever" (12b-13).

EXPOSITION

EMPTINESS (2:17)

**"These are waterless springs and mists driven by
a storm. For them the gloom of utter darkness
has been reserved" (2:17).**

Peter uses three metaphors from the world of nature: dry springs,
mists blown away by the wind and blackest darkness. These images
describe the empty, insubstantial lives and teaching of the false
teachers, the disappointment and frustration which result and the
fearful judgement so anticipated.

"These are waterless springs" This shows the dashed hopes of
the thirsty desert traveller who, on coming to a spring, finds it has
dried up in the heat. Several similar sentiments are found in the
Old Testament. On the positive side, the mouth of the righteous,
the teaching of the wise and the fear of the Lord are all "a fountain
of life" (Pr. 10:11; 13:14; 14:27). But on the negative, Jeremiah, in
God's name, berates Israel on two scores: "They have forsaken me,
the spring of living water, and have dug their own cisterns, broken
cisterns that cannot hold water" (Je. 2:13 NIV). Jesus taught that he
alone could quench our spiritual thirst and, then, use us to help
quench the spiritual thirst of others (Jn. 4:13, 14; 7:37, 38). The false
teachers offered no real spiritual satisfaction, for they had found
none themselves.

"Mists driven by a storm" The sense of disappointment continues.
The transient clouds and early morning mists that hopefully
promised refreshing showers were soon blown away. The drought
persists. Alternatively, another way of taking this is that the **mists**
homichlai obscured the truth and produced confusion. Rather than
being 'driven away', they were 'driven along' by the fierce gusts of

ignorance and self-will, as by a demon. But the former seems to suit the context better. Frustration and dissatisfaction are the overall results of the false teaching.

"For them the gloom of utter darkness has been reserved"
"Gloom", *zophos*, has already been used to describe the state of the fallen angels at verse 4 and is here meaningfully translated by the NIV "blackest darkness". **"Reserved"** *tetērētai* comes from the root *tēreō* "keep, preserve, guard" and is emphatic. The verb is used both of the fallen angels being reserved for judgement (2 Pe. 2:4) and of the heavenly inheritance being reserved for believers (1 Pe. 1:4). It is a reservation with abiding consequences. Peter returns here to the theme of the false teachers' condemnation.

Some have thought the metaphor of gloom and darkness inappropriate alongside waterless springs and driven mists, but Peter, like others, may simply be using his metaphors for effect. Calvin, as ever, catches the fearful symbolism of the darkness reserved for the heretics when he writes: "that for the momentary darkness which they now spread, there is prepared for them a much thicker darkness which is to continue for ever".[127]

Clearly, their teaching is false, insubstantial, dissatisfying and deserves divine judgement.

EMPTY WORDS (2:18)

"For, speaking loud boasts of folly, they entice by sensual passions of the flesh those who are barely escaping from those who live in error" (2:18).

Peter expands the image of **"waterless springs"** (verse 17) by

---

[127]   J. Calvin, *Commentaries on II Peter*, p407.

likening it to the false teachers' empty words. They really have nothing of value to say. He also shows in some detail the harmful effects of these words. His language is vivid. It recalls and contrasts his earlier descriptions of true words in Chapter 1. Peter in verse 18 shows that the empty words, **"waterless springs"**, (v17) arise because of the *seduction* of the false teachers.

"For, speaking loud boasts of folly". **"Speaking"** is *phtheggomenoi*, a portentous, oracular utterance meant to be full of wit and wisdom. Here, the word is used facetiously. It was used meaningfully of the donkey's speech at verse 16. **"Loud boasts"** *huperogka* describes the manner of this speaking. The word means "swollen beyond natural size". Christopher Green writes: "Overblown, with exaggerated claims dressed in fancy words, these people were like spiritual puffer fish, inflating themselves to impress and intimidate".[128] **"Folly"** *mataiotētos* describes the substance of the speaking. It is an emptiness of futility and powerlessness. The word is used to depict paganism (Ac. 14:15; 1 Pe.1:18). It connotes the hollowness of the false teaching. Their loud words are meaningless.

"They entice by sensual passions of the flesh" **"Entice"**, again, is *deleazousin* from the world of fishing and snaring, already used at 2:14 of the false teachers seducing unstable souls. **"Sensual"** translates *aselgeiais* descriptive of the heretics' shameful ways at 2:2 and of the filthy lives of the Sodomites at 2:7. **"Passions"** is *epithumiais*, which is used in the New Testament minimally in a good sense, but in the majority of cases, as here, has an evil connotation. Peter has already used the term of a world corrupted by "evil desires", from which his readers have escaped (1:4). The Greek syntax is difficult at this point, but it seems better to take "sensual" as either adjectivally with or in apposition to "passions of the flesh". Bigg puts it summarily and

---

[128]   D. Lucas & C. Green, *The Message Of 2 Peter & Jude*, p116.

succinctly: "Grandiose sophistry is the hook, filthy lust the bait".[129] The contrast between boasted teaching and sensual lifestyle is again evident.

"**Who are barely escaping from those who live in error**" This translation is based on taking "**barely**" as *oligōs* and "**escaping**" as *apopheugontas*, a present participle. Alternatively, variant readings suggest *ontōs* "really and truly" and *apophugontas*, an aorist participle, "escaped". This the AV renders: "those that were clean escaped from them who live in error". The former however, both textually and contextually seems preferable. That the false teachers were attracting young Christians not yet established in their faith seems more likely than that they were subverting solid saints though that, of course, is possible. "**Error**" is *planē*, which is regularly used to describe paganism (Ro. 1:27; Tit. 3:3). The term carries overtones of deceit. Simon J. Kistemaker, changing the imagery, puts it well when he writes: "Like carnivorous animals that prey on the weakest members of a herd, so the false teachers focus their attention on recent converts".[130] The harm their emptiness does on other believers is most disconcerting.

EMPTY PROMISES (2:19)

"**They promise them freedom, but they themselves are slaves of corruption. For whatever overcomes a person, to that he is enslaved**" (2:19).

Peter develops the metaphor of "**mists driven by a storm**" (verse 17) by showing the hollow nature of the false teachers' promises. They promise what they cannot deliver. The reason for this is similar to that of their empty words. Peter in verse 19 shows, that the empty

---

129   C. Bigg, *The Epistles of St. Peter and St Jude*, p285 cited D.J. Moo, *2 Peter, Jude*, p143.

130   S. J. Kistemaker, *James, Epistles of John, Peter, and Jude*, p308.

promises, **"mists driven by a storm"**, (verse 17) arises because of the *slavery* of the false teachers.

"They promise them freedom, but they themselves are slaves of corruption". There has been much discussion as to the **"freedom"** *eleutherian*, which the false teachers promise. The following are the main views:

1. Freedom from moral constraint, which is the most popular, and probably the most likely view.

2. Freedom from fear of judgement, which draws strong support from the teaching of the false teachers as implied in Chapter 3.

3. Freedom from fear of evil spiritual beings related to Gnostic archons or demiurge. But while the danger of evil spiritual beings does present itself in the letter, the undeveloped ideas of Gnosticism at this point in time make the interpretation unlikely.

4. Freedom from **"corruption"** *phthora* in the sense of "perishability", while possible, is too Greek and too philosophical a concept to be a likely solution, though it might, perhaps, be a contributory theme.

5. Political freedom as suggested by Bo Reicke is again unlikely because of the context.[131]

The resolution of this also depends on the proper interpretation of **"corruption"** *phthora*, which Peter uses at 1:4 in the sense of moral corruption or depravity and at 2:12 in the sense of destruction

---

[131] For further study, see the helpful discussion in R.J. Bauckham, *Jude, 2 Peter*, p275-277.

through judgement. My own preference is for view (1.) though not excluding ideas expressed in view (2.) for the following reasons:

Jesus had promised true freedom and that exclusively through himself (Jn. 8:32, 36 cf.14:6). Paul confirmed this in his teaching (Ga. 4:1-7; Ro. 6:6, 7). The New Testament makes consistently clear that this freedom is not to be construed as freedom from God's law or freedom to do whatever one wishes, that is license, but rather a freedom from slavery to sin that is in essence a commitment of slavery to Christ and his teaching (e.g. Ro. 6:17, 18; Ga. 5:13, 14; 1 Pe. 2:16). The false teachers in advocating freedom from the law manifestly failed in this because they themselves were **"slaves of corruption"** and this is the main point Peter is making here. Calvin puts it well:

> He shews their inconsistency, that they falsely promised liberty, while they themselves served sin, and were in the worst bondage; for no one can give what he has not. This reason, however, does not seem to be sufficiently valid, because it sometimes happens that wicked men, and wholly unacquainted with Christ, preach usefully concerning the benefits and blessings of Christ. But we must observe, that what is condemned here is vicious doctrine, connected with impurity of life; for the Apostle's design was to obviate the deceptive allurements by which they ensnared the foolish. The name of liberty is sweet, and they abused it for this end, that the hearer, being loosed from the fear of the divine law, might abandon himself unto unbridled licentiousness. But the liberty which Christ has procured for us, and which he offers daily by the gospel, is altogether different, for he has exempted us from the yoke of the law as far as it subjects us to a curse, that he

might also deliver us from the dominion of sin, as
far as it subjects us to its own lusts.[132]

"For whatever overcomes a person, to that he is enslaved"
This proverbial saying has a military and slavery background. The
conquered enemies became slaves of the victorious conqueror who
overcame them and this practice became the ground of this proverbial
principle. It was known as a proverb outside Christian circles but
was later also evident in post-biblical Christian literature. That Jesus
knew, if not originated it, is evident from the close correspondence in
thought to Jesus' own statement at John 8:34: "Truly, truly, I say to
you, everyone who commits sin is a slave to sin". Paul too, used this
proverb as is clear in his words to the Roman Christians at Romans
6:16 in a context similar to Peter's word here: "Do you not know that
if you present yourselves to anyone as obedient slaves, you are slaves
of the one whom you obey, either of sin, which leads to death, or of
obedience, which leads to righteousness?" Clearly the false teachers
offered false promises of liberty, because they themselves were slaves
to sin. They misjudged the seriousness of sin, minimized the threat
of judgement and misconstrued the true nature of Christian liberty.
The same happens today when scripture truth is misinterpreted or
explained away.

EMPTY PROFESSION (2:20-22)

**"For if, after they have escaped the defilements of
the world through the knowledge of our Lord and
Saviour Jesus Christ, they are again entangled in
them and overcome, the last state has become
worse for them than the first. For it would have
been better for them never to have known the way
of righteousness than after knowing it to turn**

---

[132] J. Calvin, *Commentaries on II Peter*, pp408-409.

back from the holy commandment delivered to them. What the true proverb says has happened to them: 'The dog returns to its own vomit, and the sow, after washing herself, returns to wallow in the mire'" (2:20-22).

Peter emphasizes the third metaphor: "**the gloom of utter darkness**" (verse 17). He does this by showing how the teaching of the false teachers comes back upon them. The apostasy and abandonment of their professed beliefs makes their latter state worse than their former. This leaves them in a condition, where God's ultimate judgement will fall on them. Peter illustrates this with one implied and two explicit proverbs. Peter in verses 20-22 shows that the empty profession, which brings "**the gloom of utter darkness**" (v17) arises because of the *sin* of the false teachers.

"**For if, after they**" To whom does the "**they**" refer? Some have argued that the "**they**" are those who have been taught by the false teachers, that is, "**those who are barely escaping from those who live in error**" (v18), for the same word "escape" is used in verses 18 and 20. However, the participle "escape" is in different tenses in these two verses – "**escaping**" *apopheugontas* a present with ingressive force at verse 18 and "escaped" *apophugontes* implying past action at verse 20, the verb translated "**overcomes**" and "**overcome**" at verses 19[b] and 20 respectively, having the same Greek root, refers to the false teachers, the conjunction "**for**" *gar* clearly binds the two verses together and the immediate antecedent and the main subject throughout the verses is the false teachers. It is much more likely that the "**they**" are the false teachers than those whom they taught.

"**Have escaped the defilements of the world through the knowledge of our Lord and Saviour Jesus Christ**" is markedly similar in language and thought to that of 1:3,4: "through the knowledge of him who called us . . . having escaped from the corruption that is in the world because of sinful desire". The words for "**escaped**" *apophugontes*, "**knowledge**" *epignōsei* and "**world**" *kosmou* are the same in this context. The only exception at 2:20 is "**defilements**" *miasmata* with a nuance of cultic impurity, a transliterated word in English that conveys the same meaning in Greek: "a vaporous exhalation formerly believed to cause disease . . . an influence or atmosphere that tends to deplete or corrupt",[133] whereas at 1:4 "corruption" is *phthoras* with a focus on "corruption, not just in the moral sense but in the sense that sin and evil bring about death and its consequential corruption".[134]

"**They are again entangled in them and overcome**" "**Entangled**" is *emplakentes*. Though a different Greek word, it recalls the fishing imagery used at verses 14 and 18 to describe the false teachers' strategy: "seduce", "entice", "lure". "**Overcome**" is *hēttōntai* and is also used at verse 19, language suggestive of a warrior being overcome by his combatant. P.H. Davids comments creatively: "The picture that springs to mind is a graphic one, that of a person venturing back to the area of a giant spider's web that he or she has escaped (perhaps believing that they can handle the situation now) only to get entangled and be mastered by the huge spider".[135] It would appear that the false teachers only thought that they had escaped but had never really done so in the first instance.

"**The last state has become worse for them than the first**" This implicitly recalls the proverbial teaching of Jesus about the man cleansed of his evil spirit but then possessed by seven other more wicked spirits. The correspondence of language is almost identical and quite remarkable (cf. Mt. 12:45 = Lu. 11:26). Peter's turn of phrase almost implied that Jesus' prophecy according to Matthew about this "proverb" is now fulfilled in the false teachers: "and the

---

[133]   J. MacArthur, *2 Peter & Jude*, p106.
[134]   P. H. Davids, *The Letters Of 2 Peter And Jude*, pp248-249.
[135]   P. H. Davids, *The Letters Of 2 Peter And Jude*, p249.

last state of that person is worse than the first. So also will it be with this evil generation" (Mt. 12:45). Perhaps also related to this is Jesus' teaching which recalls Old Testament law and anticipates watchfulness on the part of the servant: "And that servant who knew his master's will but did not get ready or act according to his will, will receive a severe beating. But the one who did not know, and did what deserved a beating, will receive a light beating" (Lu. 12:47, 48 cf. De. 25:2). M. Green interestingly comments mentioning both these possible background sources:

> This would be a most natural adaptation of Jesus' words if Peter is indeed the author of this Epistle; in a forger it would be a most sophisticated touch.[136]

"For it would have been better". Peter drives his point home with the so-called *Tobspruch*, "one of those many proverbial statements in Hebrew and Jewish literature (including the literature of the early Jesus movement) in a 'better . . . than' form".[137] Biblical examples of *Tobspruch* include: Proverbs 15:16, 17; 16:19, 32; Ecclesiastes 7:1,2, 5; Mark 9:42, 43, 45, 47; Romans 14:21; 1 Corinthians 7:9; 1 Peter 3:17.

"Never to have known the way of righteousness". Peter continues in emphatic language. The **"way of righteousness"** is here a synonym explaining and emphasizing **"the knowledge (*epignōsei*) of our Lord and Saviour Jesus Christ"** (verse 20). The idea of "**the way of righteousness**" may well recall Jesus' words about John the Baptist: "Jesus said to them, 'I tell you the truth, the tax collectors and the prostitutes are entering the kingdom of God ahead of you. For John came to you to show you the way of righteousness, and you did not believe him, but the tax collectors and the prostitutes did.

---

136   M. Green, *2 Peter and Jude*, p130.
137   P. H. Davids, *The Letters Of 2 Peter And Jude*, p250 and n69.

And even after you saw this, you did not repent and believe him'"
(Mt. 21:31, 32 ᴺᴵⱽ).

"The Way" also becomes a popular title for the early Christian
movement (Ac. 9:2; 18:25; 19:9, 23; 22:4; 24:14, 22). Peter seems
to delight in this expression and has already listed it in this letter:
"**way of truth**" (2:2) and "**right way**" (2:15). The Old Testament
mentions "ways of righteousness" (Pr. 8:20; 12:28; 16:31; LXX) but
Peter here may well have in mind, by way of contrast, "**the way of
Balaam**" (2:15). The language of "the way", as already noted, has a
prominence in the Balaam story (Nu. 22-23). The story becomes a
frequent, proverbially notorious, negative example in Scripture for
this kind of wayward sinning. (De. 23:4, 5; Jos. 13:22; 24:9, 10; Ne.
13:1, 2; Mi. 6:5; Jude 11; Re. 2:14). The false teachers had never truly
entered the way of righteousness at all.

The implication of the use of this phrase here, as a synonym for
this knowledge of our Lord and Saviour Jesus Christ is clear. This
"knowledge" of Christ must be consistent with righteous living. The
false teachers were disproving this daily. Their behaviour pattern,
like their teaching, was not consistent with this "knowledge". They
were mastered by depravity, had never really escaped this corruption
and were obviously overcome by it and by its polluting influence.
Their way was not, nor ever had been, it would seem, the way of
righteousness but rather the way of Balaam. They were still in their
sin, whatever their profession might be.

"**Than after knowing it to turn back from the holy commandment
delivered to them**" Peter continues in a confirming note, now with
a negative thrust showing the lawless and antinomian tendencies
of the false teachers. All the forms here, both noun and verb, of
"knowing" are the emphatic: *epignōsis* and *epiginōskō*. The "**holy
commandment delivered to them**" is a further synonym for "**the
knowledge of our Lord and Saviour Jesus Christ**" (v 20) and, "**the

way of righteousness" (v 21). The forcefulness of these expressions, as they build up, is climactic. They emphasize the hideous nature of the false teachers' sin. Now, knowingly, these teachers even turn their back on the holy commandment. "**The holy commandment**", *hagias entolēs*, summarizes the entire Christian message. It is "**holy**" because it is from God. It is "**commandment**" in the singular *entolēs* because it "was standard Christian shorthand for the entire message, Old Testament, New, or both (3:2)".[138] *Entolē* consistently bears this significance throughout the New Testament (Mt. 15:3; Jn. 12:50; Ro. 7:12; cf. 16:26; 1 Ti. 6:14; He. 7:18; 1 Jn. 2:7; 3:23). Indeed, Peter uses it precisely with this meaning immediately after this section: "to remember the words spoken in the past by the holy prophets and the commandment (*entolēs*) of the Lord and Saviour through your apostles" (3:2, my translation).

The shocking nature of the false teachers' apostasy is exacerbated by the fact that this "**holy commandment**" was "**delivered** (*paradotheisēs*) **to them**". *Paradidōmi* is a technical term for handing on tradition. In Rabbinic circles it was done so orally, though the Jewish *halakah*, a Hebrew word meaning "walk" in the sense of 'walking a way of life', was originally an oral commentary on the Old Testament law and was eventually written down. *Paradidōmi* "to hand on", "to hand over" was used regularly in this sense in the New Testament for an authoritative handing over of dominical or apostolic teaching (Lu. 1:2; 1 Co. 11:2, 23; 15:1-3; 2 Th. 3:6; Jude 3). Some sense of the authority and importance of this process can be gauged by the expressions at Romans 6:17: "the form of teaching to which you were entrusted" NIV and at 2 Timothy 1:14 "the good deposit that was entrusted to you" NIV. Perhaps the closest parallel to this idea at 2 Peter 2:21 is Jude 3 where the phrase is "the faith that was once for all delivered (*hapax paradotheisē*) to the saints". M. Green's comment is appropriate: "though Peter here sees Christianity

---

138 D. Lucas & C. Green, *The Message Of 2 Peter & Jude*, p122.

more in terms of *the sacred commandment*, whereas Jude sees it in terms of 'the faith'. Ethics and doctrine are both crucial for new Christians".[139] That the false teachers should turn their back on the **'holy commandment'** was sin enough, that they should abort their responsibility by negating the authoritative handing over to them of teaching was aggravated sin in the extreme.

"'What the true proverb says has happened to them: 'The dog returns to its own vomit, and the sow, after washing herself, returns to wallow in the mire'". Peter rounds off his condemnation of the false teachers' teaching with two quite explicit proverbial sayings from the animal world. He has already described their behaviour as that of **"irrational animals"** (2:12). Here, he describes their teaching and its effects upon themselves in striking imagery once again drawn from the animal kingdom.

'The dog returns to its own vomit' seems to come directly from Proverbs 26:11:

> "Like a dog that returns to his vomit is a fool who repeats his folly".

The message is clear. The dog in Jewish society was not as with many of us 'a man's best friend'. These dogs were not household pets but often, wild creatures, vicious in their attacks, disease-ridden scavengers who literally returned to their own vomit, sniffed around it and even ate it! The false teachers having 'apparently' got rid of sin's pollution returned to it, to savour and feed on it.

The proverb **'and the sow, after washing herself, returns to wallow in the mire'** is more difficult to source certainly in Jewish literature, since, for the Jews, pigs were "unclean" animals (Le. 11:7) and they neither ate them nor, of course, kept them. Indeed, the Jews

---

[139]   M. Green, *2 Peter and Jude*, p132.

despised them and they were, in their country, necessarily "wild" animals. But their habits were universally known and proverbial. This precise proverb may well come from Heraclitus, though more probably from the ancient *Story of Ahikar,* where the Syriac version runs: "My son, thou hast been to me like the swine that had been to the baths, and when it saw a muddy ditch, went down and washed in it, and cried to its companions: come and wash".[140] **"Mire"** *borborou* is a rare poetic word found only in the Bible here and at Jeremiah 45:6 (LXX), describing the filth of Jeremiah's prison. **"Vomit"**, in reference to the dog, *exerama,* is only found here in the New Testament. *Emeton* is the corresponding term used in Proverbs 26:11 (LXX).

The illustration of the sow is equally clear. It is not necessary to presume that the main point is an unusual "washing in the mire", since "returns" is absent from the original of 2 Peter 2:22 as regards the sow but probably rightly supplied in translation. The sense is rather that, after a washing in water, the animal returns to its natural habitat, the mud and mire – so with the false teachers. There is no need to see any reference to baptism here. Such is purely conjectural.

"What the true proverb says has happened to them" "Proverb" *paroimias* is singular. This is probably because the saying is a joint proverb. Jesus himself, in proverbial expression and in a context of condemning both hypocritical and hypercritical behaviour, combines dogs and pigs in his famous statement: "Do not give dogs what is sacred; do not throw your pearls to pigs" [NIV] (Mt. 7:6; cf. Ph. 3:2; Re. 22:15). Simon J. Kistemaker helpfully comments: "Here is a conclusive observation: By vomiting, the dog relieves itself of *internal* impurities; the sow, when it is washed, is cleansed from clinging

---

140   see R.J. Bauckham, *Jude, 2 Peter,* pp279, 280, who also quotes the Arabic version which he claims is perhaps rather closer to 2 Peter's.

external mud. Nevertheless, both animals return to the selfsame filth".[141] What a blistering comment on the false teachers!

The "big issue" in verses 20-22 is theological. Had the false teachers ever been Christians in the first instance? Can a believer apostatize and abandon salvation? Is it possible to fall from grace? Michael Green argues that: "Apostasy would seem to be a real and awful possibility".[142] The forcefulness of the language here – knowledge of our Lord and Saviour Jesus Christ, the way of righteousness, the holy commandment delivered to them – all presuppose a genuine faith in Christ on the part of the false teachers and parallels with Hebrews 3:12-19, 6:6; 10:26, 38f.; 1 Corinthians 10:1-12; Jude 4-6 are so clear and unmistakable as to seemingly confirm this possibility.

However, this is not, we believe, necessarily so. The biblical teaching of the believers' eternal security, the perseverance of the saints in general and the fact that here in particular at verses 20-22, the yawing gap between the true assertions of salvation and the false teachers' belief and behaviour pattern of life seem so extreme as to make it clear that theirs was only an empty profession. They never had, in fact, been saved in the first instance. The Scripture passages quoted above are consistent with and fearful proof that they had "never" known Christ, not proof of their apostasy as believers (Mt. 7:21-23).

Edwin A. Blum puts it well, commenting on this passage when he writes:

> Is it possible, then, for Christians to lose their
> salvation? Many would answer affirmatively on

---

[141] S. J. Kistemaker, *James, Epistles of John, Peter, and Jude*, p315 (Emphasis his).

[142] M. Green, *2 Peter and Jude*, p131.

the basis of this and similar texts (e.g. Heb. 6:4-
6; 10:26). But this verse asserts only that false
teachers who have for a time escaped from world
corruption through knowing Christ and then turn
away from the light of the Christian faith are worse
off than they were before knowing Christ. It uses
no terminology affirming that they were Christians
in reality . . . The NT makes a distinction between
those who are in the churches and those who are
regenerate . . . So when Peter says, 'They are worse
off at the end than they were at the beginning', the
reference is to a lost apostate.[143]

Peter teaches that the empty words arise from the seduction
of the false teachers, the empty promises from the slavery of the
false teachers and the empty profession from the sin of the false
teachers. The combination of seduction, slavery and sin all point in
the one direction. The false teachers were not 'backsliders', who had
fallen away from faith. They never had faith in the first instance.
They were never saved or regenerated at all. Their fallen nature had
never been changed. They were dogs returning to their vomit, pigs
wallowing in their filth, leopards with unchanged spots, wolves in
sheep's clothing, bad not good trees, thorn bushes not vines, thistles
not fig trees. They related neither to the seed on the wayside nor
that of the good ground, but to the superficial on the rock and the
specious among thorns. The link between false teaching and false
lifestyle is as inexorable as the link between false teaching and false
teachers. E.A. Blum is correct. The reference is not to a believing
apostate but to "a lost apostate". True faith does not apostatize. It
may stumble but it does not fall. It may even 'fall' *within* grace but

---

[143] E.A. Blum, *"2 Peter"* In the *Expositor's Bible Commentary*, vol.12, ed. by
Frank E. Gaebelein, Grand Rapids Zondervan 1981, p282, cited by D.
J. Moo, *2 Peter, Jude*, p151, who also provides an excellent discussion on
apostasy from a biblical and theological perspectives, pp151-155.

never *from* grace. God's grace sees to that. The false teachers appear
to be unregenerate.

APPLICATION

The false teachers' behaviour is morally obtuse; their teaching is
doubly destructive. It harms not only the church, especially young
believers. It destroys themselves. Their latter state is worse than the
former. They worsen as they approach final judgement and appear
to go to their "own place" which they deserve and which, in large
measure, they have prepared for themselves.

This message, however, falls largely on deaf ears in today's church
and is regarded as both extreme and irrelevant, regarded rather
simply as a pique of Peter's ill-disposition toward his opponents, a
fit of bad temper lacking in grace. The same, of course, could be
said for Paul's invective against his opponents, especially in the
Pastoral Letters. Above all, it is regarded as irrelevant. By no stretch
of the imagination, it is claimed, could this kind of thing be so
rampant in today's church as to prove a problem – the principles of
Jesus' critique of the churches in Revelation, yes, but this kind of
immoral, erroneous heresy within the twenty-first century church,
today, certainly not.

Is it so exceptional, however? The plethora of pseudo-biblical
presentations of evangelism, the scripturally questionable forms of
church growth incentives, the pandering compromises that make good
business practice the rule of thumb for the church, the "health and
wealth" gospel and various "bindings" in need of liberation to effect
saving grace, not to mention the more blatantly heretical and aberrant
misrepresentations, which are plainly just twenty-first century heresies
within the church, all point up the necessity of refuting false doctrine
and being soundly instructed in solid biblical truth.

The sad thing is not simply the existence of these but the so-called "Christian umbrella" under which they shelter and are accepted in an ignorance parading as Christian charity by the church. "To the teaching and to the testimony! If they will not speak according to this word, it is because they have no dawn" (Is. 8:20). "Beware of false prophets, who come to you in sheep's clothing but inwardly are ravenous wolves. You will recognize them by their fruits. Are grapes gathered from thorn bushes, or figs from thistles?" (Mt. 7:15, 16). "Keep a close watch on yourself and on the teaching. Persist in this, for by so doing you will save both yourself and your hearers" (1 Ti. 4:16). "He must hold firm to the trustworthy word as taught, so that he may be able to give instruction in sound doctrine and also to rebuke those who contradict it" (Tit. 1:9). "Beloved, do not believe every spirit, but test the spirits to see whether they are from God, for many false prophets have gone out into the world" (1 Jn. 4:1). It is not without significance that prophets, apostles and the Lord of the church give us these warnings. We do well to heed, obey and implement them.

Chapter 15

PRACTICAL KNOWLEDGE

SCRIPTURE REMEMBERED

2 PETER 3:1, 2

INTRODUCTION

Second Peter Chapter 1 is about true knowledge of God. Chapter 2, by way of contrast, is about false knowledge of God. Chapter 3 is about practical knowledge of God. Chapter 3 shows what the outworking or application of this knowledge of God should be in the thinking and living of Peter's readers. If knowledge of God is really true, it will have practical results in the lives of those who profess it. It can never be purely academic. Jesus commands his followers not only to be hearers but doers of his words as well. They are to put them into practice, and that, necessarily so. Otherwise, the whole affair is a shambles. The building falls down (Mt. 7:24-29).

Knowledge of God and of his Son, the Lord Jesus Christ, is conferred through the Scriptures. That is the implication of the whole of Peter's second letter and certainly of 2 Peter 1:16-21, where the author reflects on the basic importance of apostolic and prophetic revelation. In this sense, Chapter 3, picking up from 1:16-21, returns to the main storyline of the letter, with Chapter 2 as a sort of vital and important interlude. Thus, Chapter 3, as a whole, focuses on Scripture. The main overt theme, of course, is Christ's return, his Second Coming. But the underlying structure by which the erroneous views of the false teachers are confronted, countered and corrected is Scripture. Hence, 2 Peter 3, as a "closing" letter of the New Testament canon, encapsulates views on Scripture both arresting and exciting. Here, the Holy Spirit not only corrects heresy but leads further in the glorious journey of biblical revelation. 2 Peter 3:1, 2 introduces this whole theme under the subject of "Scripture – remembered". It might be viewed in the following format:

SUBJECT OF SCRIPTURE REMEMBERED   (v1^a)

PURPOSE OF SCRIPTURE REMEMBERED   (v1^b)

SUBSTANCE OF SCRIPTURE REMEMBERED   (v2)

EXPOSITION

"This is now the second letter that I am writing to you, beloved. In both of them I am stirring up your sincere mind by way of reminder, that you should remember the predictions of the holy prophets and the commandment of the Lord and Saviour through your apostles" (3:1, 2).

SUBJECT

"This is now the second letter that I am writing to you, beloved"
Peter introduces the theme of Scripture remembered by earthing the subject in what he is writing in this letter. The implication seems to be that what he is writing in his letters is Scripture. **"Beloved"** translates *agapētoi* and is preferable to the weaker expression of

some translations, "dear friends". The idea is essentially of those who are recipients of God's unique love, *agapē*, in Christ, who are now accepted or, literally, "engraced" in Christ, God's "beloved", and sustain a bonding relationship to Christ their Saviour and to each other (cf. Ep. 1:6, where Christ is described as "the Beloved" (*tō ēgapēmenō*). Practically, the term **"beloved"** *agapētoi* marks a new beginning of theme and recurs throughout the chapter subdividing that theme (vv8, 14, 17). Peter has already used **"beloved"** in his first letter (2:11; 4:12), as does Jude (vv3, 17, 20) and John extensively (1 Jn. 3:2,21; 4:1,7,11; 3 Jn. 2,5,11). Paul also uses it but, in the light of his extensive writings, relatively rarely (Ro. 12:19; 1 Co. 10:14; 2 Co. 7:1; 12:19; Ph. 2:12; 4:1). Positively, the term **"beloved"** *agapētoi* not only introduces a new section but also expresses a note of warmth from writer to reader. A sense of contrast between the end of Chapter 2 and the beginning of Chapter 3 illustrates this warmth. Peter turns from warning and correction to admonition and instruction, "from harrying the heretics to encourage the faithful".[144] The **"beloved"** obviously contrast with the false teachers. The **"commandment of the Lord and Saviour"**, which Peter urges his readers to remember (3:2), is the same **"holy commandment delivered to them"** and is connected with the same **"Lord and Saviour Jesus Christ"**, on which and on whom, the renegade teachers have turned their backs (2:20, 21). Peter's **"beloved"** are far removed from the **"dog"** and **"sow"** just mentioned a few lines earlier in his letter. "Each time he uses the phrase *dear friends* in this chapter, he is increasingly wooing his readers away from friendship with the false teachers into a deeper love for God and his gospel".[145]

"The second letter that I am writing to you" Which is this **"second letter"**? A number of suggestions have been made:

---

[144] M. Green, *2 Peter and Jude,* p134.
[145] D. Lucas & C. Green, *The Message Of 2 Peter & Jude,* p125.

1. The first letter is 2 Peter 1 (and possibly 2), with 2 Peter 1:15 promising a further letter. This second letter is 2 Peter 3.

    Against this is the fact that there is really no definitive reason to question the unity of 2 Peter. As a whole, the letter is well interrelated and welded together and Chapter 3 flows easily from both Chapters 1 and 2. Furthermore in 2 Peter, the verbal links with Jude continue into Chapter 3.

2. The first letter is Jude written to Jewish Christians. The second letter is 2 Peter written to Gentile Christians. Both letters are authored by Jude.

    Against this, both letters bear different names and the natural implication for both the readers and ourselves is that the letters come from different authors. Further, if the author of 2 Peter is Jude, he certainly uses his "own" material in a very different way and from a very different point of view than he used it in Jude.

3. The first letter is lost. The second letter is 2 Peter.

    It would seem that there were 'lost' letters written by apostolic authors and, hence, not included in the New Testament canon, for example in Paul's correspondence the possible "severe letter" of 1 Corinthians 5:9, the possible "sorrowful letter" of 2 Corinthians 7:8 and, possibly also, the letter to the Laodiceans mentioned at Colossians 4:16.

    This is certainly a possibility but remains hypothetical and should probably only be adopted if no other option presents itself.

4. A more reasonable option appears to be the traditional understanding, namely, that the first letter is 1 Peter and the second letter is 2 Peter.

    Against this, it has been objected that the author of 2 Peter has a close knowledge of his readers whereas, the knowledge of the author of 1 Peter is much more distant and general. However, in both letters the author's knowledge is quite general and the differential between the two is insignificant.

A further objection to this view is that 1 Peter does not fit into the category of the description of 3:1, 2. As M. Green puts it: "However, it can hardly be said that 1 Peter is primarily a letter of reminder, still less a dissuasive against heresy, which seems to be implied in these two verses".[146]

While this is a more substantial objection than the former, the differences between 1 and 2 Peter have been somewhat exaggerated and the similarities understated.

The same word for "**mind**" *dianoia* is used at 1 Peter 1:13 as at 2 Peter 3:1 and there are a substantial number of references in 1 Peter to the Second Coming and the subsequent need for holy living in anticipation of this event, references which could easily be deemed as "reminders" by the author to his readers (1:13-17; 2:11, 12; 4:13, 17-19; 5:4). The **"prophets"** are centre stage in 1 Peter also (1:3-12). From this section many if not all, the exhortations in 1 Peter flow. Further, though from a slightly different view-point, 2 Peter 3:2 describes *primarily* the author's purpose in writing his second letter, though also embracing in a general way his first letter as well. Hence, there is no *prima facie* case for rejecting the traditional view that 1 Peter is the "first" letter and that 2 Peter is the "second" letter as is referred to at 2 Peter 3:1, 2 and indeed much more reason for accepting this less than has been averred by some. The traditional view is, in our opinion, the best option.

The subject of Scripture remembered is then introduced at 2 Peter 3:1, 2. It is written warmly to 'beloved' believers and embraces the whole tenor of 2 Peter. 2 Peter is Peter's second letter, 1 Peter his

---

[146] M. Green, *2 Peter and Jude,* p134.

first. Indeed, 2 Peter 3 encapsulates generally the complete ambit of
Scripture, as Peter goes on later to note, mentioning Paul's letters
in Chapter 3 (2 Pe. 3:15, 16). The specific subject of verse 1ᵃ is, of
course, Peter's "second letter". But the general context of both letters
is the complete revelation of Scripture. Peter is not writing his own
random thoughts, jottings, or opinions. "Both" his letters relate to
Scripture as a whole. The plain inference of this is that what Peter
writes, just as what Paul writes, is Scripture.

PURPOSE

**"In both of them I am stirring up your sincere mind by way of
reminder"** Peter here states the purpose of Scripture remembered.
The expression he uses is both strong and significant. **"I am stirring"**
diegeirō is, literally, to "arouse" or "awake" someone from sleep and
it is so cited elsewhere in the New Testament in that sense. While
"refresh" would be the natural translation in the context, as here,
of reminder, the force is even stronger and connotes "stirring" in an
arresting fashion. Peter has used these terms of reminder even more
expansively earlier in his second letter at 2 Peter 1:12-15. He will
always remind them of these things (1:12). It is right that he should
refresh their memory (*diegeirein en hupomnēsei* at 1:13 cf. *diegeirō en
hupomnēsei* at 3:1) while he is alive (1:13). After his departure, he
will make every effort to see that they recall these things (1:14, 15).
He returns to the same note here. The verbal resemblances are quite
remarkable. So, too, is the nuance of meaning. Earlier, refreshing
their memory is set in the fleshly context of living "in the tent of this
body" (1:13 ᴺᴵⱽ). Here, it is with a view to stirring up their **"sincere
mind"** in the proximate context of recalling prophetic, apostolic and
dominical teaching – Scripture – in the ultimate. Obviously, Peter
puts a high premium on this kind of recall. "Moffatt aptly cites Dr

Johnson, 'It is not sufficiently considered that men more frequently require to be reminded than informed'".[147] Calvin puts it well too:

> It now appears what is the use of admonitions, and how necessary they are; for the sloth of the flesh smothers the truth once received, and renders it inefficient, except the goads of warnings come to its aid. It is not then enough, that men should be taught to know what they ought to be, but there is need of godly teachers, to do this second part, deeply to impress the truth on the memory of their hearers.[148]

"Your sincere mind". The focus of this purposive remembrance is "**your sincere mind**". "**Mind**" is *dianoian*. It is used primarily but not exclusively of the cognitive faculty, a person's "thinking" or "understanding". Peter has already used it in his first letter for preparing the mind for action (1:13). Paul claims that the pagans are darkened in their minds (Ep. 4:18). The word in the New Testament implies not simply pure thought but the subsequent activities, which spring from this "understanding". "**Sincere**" is *eilikrinē*. It means literally "pure", "uncontaminated", "unmixed", "wholesome" and incorporates, particularly within Christian literature, the moral tones of "honest", "sincere": "that which will bear the full test of being examined by sunlight, and so it carries with it the sense of *transparent* sincerity".[149] The idea is germane to Greek philosophy and the actual term, in the doublet here, "**sincere mind**" is found

---

[147] J. Moffatt, *The General Epistles, James, Peter and Jude, (Moffatt New Testament Commentary)*, 1947, cited in M. Green, *2 Peter and Jude*, p134.

[148] J. Calvin, *Commentaries on II Peter*, p413.

[149] E.H. Plumptre, *St. Peter and St. Jude, Cambridge Bible for Schools and Colleges*, (Cambridge; Cambridge University Press, 1879, p189), cited D. Lucas & C. Green, *The Message Of 2 Peter & Jude*, p126 (cf. also Philippians 1:10).

in Plato for "pure reason" that is, thinking uncontaminated by the feelings or senses. Peter may, thus, be using the expression as a current philosophical "catch word" and filling it with distinctive Christian meaning, as noted elsewhere in this letter. It certainly contrasts the thinking and behaviour of the false teachers who are "**waterless springs**" and "**mists driven by a storm**", who challenged Peter's right to teach (2:17) and who "**deliberately overlook**" what they should remember (3:5). By way of contrast, here, Peter compliments and encourages his 'beloved' readers for their pure thinking and honest lifestyle.

T.R. Schreiner comments appositely:

> Believers need reminders about the truths they already know and accept precisely because such reminders, though including the mind, address the whole person. In biblical thinking reminders grip the whole person, so that we are possessed again by the gospel and its truth, so that we are energized to live for the glory of God.[150]

The specific subject of verse 1^b is, of course, Peter stirring or arousing his readers' minds. But the general context is with a view to affecting their behaviour. Peter is not penning a few pensive reflections or musing motley meditations to amuse or titillate their fancies. He is addressing their minds to focus their thinking and their living. Scripture does this both exclusively and to perfection. Hiding God's word in the heart is the practical antidote for sinful living (Ps. 119:11). The false teachers with their false teaching proved the obverse of this to be true. Their false teaching begat immoral living. Peter, secondly then, writes of the purpose of Scripture remembered and points up the biblical methodology of the same in the value for the Christian of true

---

150   T. R. Schreiner, *1, 2 Peter, Jude,* p370.

meditation of God's word. It is a life transforming exercise. It should affect their attitude, behaviour and lifestyle.

SUBSTANCE

"that you should remember the predictions of the holy prophets and the commandment of the Lord and Saviour through your apostles". Peter concludes this introductory section on Scripture remembered by indicating its substance, namely, Scripture and its biblical form. He has already, earlier in this letter, put the format of Scripture within the context of remembering: He will always encourage them to remember these things while he is alive. He will urgently refresh their memories. After his departure, he would want them also to remember these things (1:12-15). Peter goes on, too, in this earlier context, to show how apostolic witness combines with prophetic prediction to confirm all this, and that prophetic prediction is, quite obviously, not of human origin but has its source in the Spirit of God (1:16-21). It is as though Peter here, at 3:1, 2 picks up the story of Scripture where he had left off, with Chapter 2 as an instructful, if fearful, interlude. But the storyline is the same: Scripture remembered in its prophetic and apostolic format. Indeed, Peter, previously in his first letter, has already cited this prophetic prediction not only as the precursor of the message of salvation but as the motivation for the moral imperative he gives throughout his first letter. Prophetic prediction and apostolic injunction drive godly Christian living (cf. 1 Pe. 1:10-12 and 13ff).

Here, in his second letter, Peter emphasizes the same point. He mentions first the importance of prophetic prediction. The **"predictions"** are, literally, "the fore-spoken words". While the expression is used at Jude 17 of the apostles and could thus refer to New Testament prophets, it is much more likely to refer to the Old Testament prophets as previously at 2 Peter 1:19-21 and 1 Peter 1:10-12 (cf. Ac. 1:16; Ro. 9:29; He. 4:7 cf. He. 1:1). **"Of the holy**

prophets" The prophets are described as "**holy**" (*hagiōn*) which, for some, implies that Second Peter is both late and pseudonymous. But this is not necessarily the case. Peter uses "**holy**" of the prophets in his speech at Acts 3:21 and it is used of the prophets in Zechariah's song at Luke 1:70. It is the normal epithet used to describe prophets in the Old Testament and, if the whole people of God are called *hoi hagioi* – 'the holy ones' or 'the saints' in both Old and New Testaments, it can be clearly seen as applicable to both prophets and apostles. If anything, here, "**holy**" emphasizes the prophet's uniqueness as God's spokesman, for prophets were carried along by God's Spirit (1:21) and this contrasts the evident unholy words and behaviour of the false teachers, whom Peter berates in his letter. Both the authority and integrity of the prophet as recalled in Scripture are the effective counterblasts to the lies and lifestyle of the false teachers and scoffers who beguile Peter's readers.

"**And the commandment of the Lord and Saviour through your apostles**" Peter then turns to underline the other aspect of Scripture remembered: apostolic witness. Part of the problem, but also of the solution, is the piling up of genitival expressions. Literally, verse 2 reads: "to remember the fore-spoken words by the holy prophets and of your apostles the commandment of the Lord and Saviour". The purpose of this pile-up of genitives seems to be to accentuate the emphasis both of prophetic prediction and apostolic witness. This is effected by both prophetic prediction and apostolic witness and, extensively, in the case of the latter by linguistically linking them to "**the commandment of the Lord and Saviour**". Hence the translation: "that you should remember the predictions of the holy prophets and the commandment of the Lord and Saviour through your apostles". The purpose is to show that prophetic prediction is fulfilled in the person, work and words of Christ and that apostolic witness flows naturally from this same source, namely the person, work and words of Christ. This is completely consistent with all Peter has been saying in both letters and forms the basis of anything he or Scripture says. All the substrata of verse 2 point in the same direction.

"The commandment" *tēs entolēs* has been variously interpreted either specifically or generally. Peter has just mentioned the same term a few lines earlier in this letter (2:21). There the "**commandment**" is described as "**holy**" and as that which has been authoritatively "**delivered**" to the false teachers, upon which they have ignominiously turned their backs. In that context and here also, the "**commandment**" has been seen in a number of ways. It has been seen as the gospel in terms of repentance and faith which Jesus commands, the moral and ethical lifestyle required of those who follow Jesus, the fact and implications of Christ's Second Coming and even, though more doubtfully, as Peter's exhortations and warnings. It has been seen as one or other of these things, viewed in this letter specifically or as the entire corpus of scriptural teaching, prophetic and apostolic subsumed in Christ, viewed generally. It hardly seems necessary to make a definitive choice between the specific and general. One or some or all of the above in part may be in mind here.

However, if anything, the general interpretation is, perhaps, preferable but the emphasis seems to be on the responsibility and obligation to *obey* the "**commandment**". Peter's readers are to heed what he wrote as they reflected and remembered the entirety of Scripture, prophetic, apostolic but, above all, dominical. For the Lord Jesus was the source from which and the end to which all Scripture came and pointed. Christ and his teaching, predicted, fulfilled and expounded in Scripture is the ultimate authority. That is why it is to be remembered and obeyed. The rest of Chapter 3 underscores this point, especially vv15-16, where Paul's letters are viewed as Scripture.

"Of the Lord and Saviour". The phrase **"Lord and Saviour"** occurs four times in this letter, in three of which cases Peter adds the names "Jesus Christ" (1:11; 2:20; 3:18 and 3:2 without these names). This is emphatic in itself. Donald Guthrie noted that Peter teaches that this "sovereignty includes also salvation".[151]

"Your apostles" has elicited much discussion. This reading is much superior to that of "our apostles" which has very little manuscript support. As with **"holy prophets"**, **"your apostles"** has been regarded as proof of lateness and even of non-Petrine authorship. It is suggested that it would be unlikely that Peter would exclude himself if he were referring to the *original* apostles, the Twelve, as understood in the New Testament. But this is not necessarily the case. If Peter had written "our commandment" or "our apostles", he would just as likely have been open to criticism. Paul also has to affirm his apostleship even in as early a letter as Galatians. **"Your apostles"** does not necessarily exclude Peter from that company, if the emphasis is on "apostles". Nor, alternatively, can it be construed as being "apostles" in the sense of emissaries or church-planters rather than the original or founding apostles. When the New Testament uses "apostle", in this more general sense, it usually makes it clear. The mention of **"holy prophets"** or of **"your apostles"** is not proof of sub-apostolic lateness but rather of apostolic authority. The prophets predicted Christ. Christ came, taught, lived, died, rose again and will return. The apostles affirm all this from start to finish, just as the prophets predicted it before it all happened. This is the emphasis here in the context.

Paul's two descriptions, which include both apostles and prophets, come to mind here: "the household, of God, built on the foundation of the apostles and prophets, Christ Jesus himself being the cornerstone" (Ep. 2:20) and "the mystery of Christ, which was

---

[151]   D. Guthrie, *New Testament Theology*, pp300 n235.

not made known to the sons of men in other generations as it has now been revealed to his holy apostles and prophets by the Spirit" (Ep. 3:4.5). Both Peter and Paul affirm the authority of this glorious biblical revelation: prophetic, dominical, and apostolic. This is the substance of Scripture to be remembered. Michael Green, having mentioned the genitival expressions, summarizes the meaning of the passage excellently:

> At all events, the meaning is clear enough, and stresses the link between the prophets who foreshadowed Christian truth, Christ who exemplified it, and the apostles who gave an authoritative interpretation of it. God's self-disclosure was to be seen in the written word of God through the prophetic scriptures, and the spoken message through the apostolic proclamation (see Eph. 2:20; 3:5). The source of their authority was the Spirit who inspired both (Eph. 3:5; 1 Pet. 1:10-12; 2 Pet. 1:16-21).[152]

The specific subjects of verse 2 are, of course, "the predictions of the holy prophets and the commandment of the Lord and Saviour through your apostles". But the general context is Scripture itself. What a glorious summary of the substance of the Bible these words are: prophets foretelling, Christ fulfilling and apostles affirming God's self-revelation. Peter, thirdly, climaxes his introduction in the substance of Scripture remembered. The rest of Chapter 3 expands and expounds this theme.

---

[152]   M. Green, *2 Peter and Jude,* p135.

APPLICATION

The sentiments expressed in this section are pivotal, basic and fundamentally important. They are so, not only as far as Second Peter is concerned but also, as far as the entire biblical doctrine of scriptural revelation is involved. These verses are among those which spread through the whole Bible God's way of revealing himself to us. Their significance can hardly be overstated.

In Second Peter, they pick up the threads of this storyline from Chapter 1 about the importance of prophetic prediction and apostolic confirmation within biblical revelation. They forge, too, such a contrasting link with Chapter 2, that the dangers of erroneous teaching are fearfully seen. They introduce Chapter 3 and set the whole discussion of the Second Coming within a scriptural setting which leaves one in no doubt that not only is godly living but growth in grace a necessary concomitant of Christ's Parousia (2 Pe. 3:11-13, 18). If the integrity of Second Peter as an entire letter is at all questioned, it founders on this ground also – the consistent note of scriptural revelation which binds the letter, as a whole, together.

But these verses do far more than that. They are of 'cosmic' biblical importance, in that they teach us further of the whole way of God's self-revelation. We come to see here, again, the unfolding drama of the plan and purpose of Scripture itself. The nuance of prophetic prediction and apostolic confirmation evident here, as in other parts of the Bible, is invariably linked to Christ, the fullness of that revelation. Christ in his person, work and revelation is source, centre and purpose of biblical disclosure. The Bible inheres in Christ, God's Son and perfect Word. So, prophetic prediction, dominical instruction and apostolic confirmation bind the whole of Scripture together.

It is the rediscovery of this glorious doctrine of biblical revelation, of God's word as truth, which must shake the church again and keep its heart beating firm, its activities relevant and its growth majestic. Nothing less will do, for the God who has spoken fully and finally in his Son has bequeathed to us this glorious testimony of his written word as a gift and his Spirit to lead us into this truth. May the church in our day find again the wonder of such a discovery: "I have hidden your word in my heart that I might not sin against you" (Ps. 119:11 NIV). Remembering Scripture and being stirred to remember it in this way not only produces wholesome thinking, godly living and growth in grace, it also glorifies God throughout the whole process.

Chapter 16

PRACTICAL KNOWLEDGE

SCRIPTURE REJECTED

2 PETER 3:3, 4

INTRODUCTION

Peter turns from Scripture remembered (3:1, 2) to Scripture rejected (3:3, 4). He has just introduced Chapter 3, which we have designated practical knowledge of God, in what might be called one of the finest descriptions of scriptural revelation in the whole Bible. His readers are to recall Scripture within a scriptural context: "the predictions of the holy prophets and the commandment of the Lord and Saviour through your apostles" (3:2).

Peter continues with the on-going theme of his letter – the knowledge of God, true, false and, now, practical. The practical issue he deals with is scepticism regarding Christ's Second Coming on the part of his readers' opponents. They are described as "scoffers" (v 3). That they are a separate group from the "false teachers" of Chapter 2 is unlikely. The sad similarities in teaching and lifestyle of the two are plainly evident and their present threat is also patently obvious.

Peter seems here to be showing the danger of the false teaching of the false teachers in one specific area, that of Christ's return, and the havoc it produces not only for the knowledge of God but also for the growth in grace of those to whom he is writing.

Underlying this very practical instruction, however, indeed, underlying the whole of Peter's letter is Scripture and its importance. This is the basic theme behind the practical storyline. Scripture forms an unbroken link beneath the whole letter and rises to a climax in Chapter 3. Scripture is the key to true knowledge of God and to growth in grace in our Lord and Saviour Jesus Christ (3:18), and it is a necessary key.

Practically here, then, Peter deals with the rejection of Scripture by his readers' opponents. Three features characterize this rejection:

SCOFFING	(v3[a])
IMMORALITY	(v3[b])
DISBELIEF	(v4)

EXPOSITION

> **"knowing this first of all, that scoffers will come in the last days with scoffing, following their own sinful desires. They will say, 'Where is the promise of his coming? For ever since the fathers fell asleep, all things are continuing as they were from the beginning of creation'" (3:3, 4).**

SCOFFING

The scoffing is described emphatically.

"Knowing this first of all" **"Knowing"** *ginōskontes* is present participle and probably refers back to Peter's "beloved" readers (v1) and such knowledge possibly also to their opponents who may well recognize such knowledge but not accept it regarding themselves. The participle could well, as is often the case in the New Testament, have imperatival force: "but know this". **"First of all"** *prōton* has not so much the sense of priority as in a list with a second or third to follow but rather precedence in meaning, as at 1:20 namely, "above all". Peter's readers are to understand this above everything else as of primary importance, as they exercise memory recall.

"Scoffers will come in the last days with scoffing" **"Scoff"** *empaizō* means, literally, "to play with", "to dance around", "to take one's sport with someone" and, hence, "to mock" also "to deceive", "to defraud". The idea, of course, occurs throughout Scripture evident as far back as Satan's treatment of Eve in Genesis right up to maltreatment of Christ in his sufferings in the Gospels. The theme occurs in the Old Testament at Psalm 1:1; Proverbs 1:22; 9:7-8; 13:1 and also in the New Testament notably at 2 Peter 3:3 and Jude 18. Scoffing is not the same as jesting. The latter has the sense of poking fun but the former also includes ridiculing, mocking, deceiving, and despising with malevolent, knowledgeable intent and thus is much more culpable.

Here, the form **"scoffers with scoffing"** *empaigmonē empaiktai* compares in sense with Jude 18: "'In the last time there will be scoffers, following their own ungodly passions'", and is a Semitism using an infinitive absolute in the Hebrew for emphasis or continuity. A similar form is found at Luke 22:15: "I have eagerly desired (*epithumia epethumēsa*) to eat this Passover with you before I suffer"[NIV]. Thus, the expression is intense.

"Will come" *eleusontai* is future and has sometimes been used as proof of pseudonymity or even that the pseudonymous writer is referring to a prophecy of Peter. But there is no need to presume that. The future is also used in 2:1 in a similar fashion. Here, it reflects more the fulfilment of Scripture and that such fulfilment has already begun to take place with scoffers already present at the time of writing, as is implied in the use of the present tense later in the chapter (cf. 2 Timothy 3:1 for similar usage).

"In the last days" The **"last days"**, *eschatōn tōn hēmerōn* as a term is used throughout Scripture (LXX Ge. 49:2; Is. 2:2; Je. 23:20; 37:24; Eze. 38:16; Da. 2:28; Ho. 3:5; Mi. 4:1; Ac. 2:17; 2 Ti. 3:1; He. 1:2; Ja. 5:3 cf. Jude 18). Particularly in the New Testament it is used, not as is sometimes supposed, for the period *immediately* preceding Christ's return and the end of the world but of the entire period from Christ's first coming to his return inaugurated more especially by his death and resurrection (see esp. Acts 2:17; He. 1:2). These **"last days"** are characterized by the coming of false christs, prophets and teachers (Mt. 24:3-5, 11, 23-26; Ac. 20:29-31; 2 Ti. 3:1f; 4:1f; Ja. 5:3; Jude 18 cf. 1 Ti. 4:1f). Peter's readers will understand from their instruction that this is the case. M. Green sums up well the essence of this scoffing:

> Anthropocentric hedonism (*man-centred pleasure-seeking*) always mocks at the idea of ultimate standards and a final division between saved and lost. For men who live in the world of the relative, the claim that the relative will be ended by the absolute is nothing short of ludicrous. For men who nourish a belief in human self-determination and perfectibility, the very idea that we are accountable

and dependent is a bitter pill to swallow. No wonder
they mocked![153]

Today's postmodernism is similarly characterized by this attitude.
It is not content simply to question biblical truth but ultimately to
scoff at it in a superior fashion. Does anyone, in this enlightened
day and age, believe that the 'other-worldly' part of the Bible, either
the miraculous or otherwise in general, or, as here, the return of
Christ in particular, actually has or will take place? Even so-called
'Christian' nations with a formal or claimed biblical background
pick and choose from Scripture what they want to believe to suit
today's world.

In all of this, postmodernism is something of a misnomer.
Today's Christian church with a self-pitying pride and a self-
righteous arrogance would claim that she was the first to deal with
this problem. But think of the first-century society that Peter and
the apostles addressed with the gospel. Was it all that different, with
its philosophical, classical background, from today? The church's
answer then to scoffing scepticism was Scripture and Scripture alone.
Our emphatic answer in pulpit, market-place and philosophical
academia should be the same: Scripture, *Scriptura Sola*, God's
word as truth at every level of society — philosophical, scientific or
whatever. There should be no scoffing at God's word, the Scriptures.

IMMORALITY

The immorality is presented strikingly.

---

[153]   M. Green, *2 Peter and Jude,* p138. The words italicized in brackets are an
explanation of 'Anthropocentric hedonism' given by J. MacArthur, who
also gives this quotation by M. Green, in his commentary: J. MacArthur,
2 Peter & Jude, p113.

"Following their own sinful desires" **"Desires"** *epithumias* is etymologically neutral and can be used of good as well as evil desires, as noted above at Luke 22:15. However, as generally within the New Testament and throughout this present letter (1:4; 2:10, 18), the sense here is plainly that of evil desires. The links between the "scoffers" of Chapter 3 and the "false teachers" of Chapter 2 should not be overlooked. It is because of these evil desires that the teachers can be described as "trained in greed", "mists driven by a storm" and "slaves of corruption" (2:14, 17, 19). The interrelationship between false teachers and immoral lifestyle of those berated in Chapter 2 has already been noted. This is universal biblical teaching. False doctrine begets bad behaviour. Wholesome instruction produces spiritual health. Here, **"sinful desires"** has obviously a much wider context than that of teaching and plainly includes lifestyle as well. C. Green comments graphically:

> Although these people may present themselves as sophisticated and knowledgeable, having delicate qualms and posing courageous questions about the more difficult elements of Christian teaching, they are in reality driven by their greed and disobedience. It is sin, not sophistication, which is in the driving-seat, and the false teachers are merely *following*. How do they get away with this extraordinary bluff?[154]

The link between false teaching and immorality runs through Chapter 2 of this letter and here also. But too often we forget that. False teaching comes from false teachers, and all of this happens not outside but inside the church. These people were false teachers! So, the specialist nature of their teaching needs strikingly to be noted and strikingly to be condemned. As mentioned in respect of remembering Scripture (2 Peter 1:12-15; 2 Peter 3:1, 2), so also

---

[154] D. Lucas & C. Green, *The Message Of 2 Peter & Jude*, pp129, 130 (Emphasis his).

here regarding rejecting Scripture (2 Peter 3:3f), it is equally clear. We need to be wise, judicious, and firm so that the teaching of the church is "founded on and agreeable to the word of God".[155]

Otherwise, not only does erroneous teaching arise but immoral behaviour ruins the church and her witness. The knowledge of God, which should be practically wholesome becomes perniciously perverse.

DISBELIEF

The disbelief is marked by scepticism.

"They will say, 'Where is the promise of his coming?'" "Coming" here is *parousias*. Etymologically, it recalls the presence of a dignitary, the king. Theologically in the New Testament, it virtually becomes a technical term for Christ's return. Peter has already used the word at 1:16 referring to the Transfiguration in the phrase "the power and coming of our Lord Jesus Christ", where the emphasis, though primarily on the first coming, also includes the idea of the Second Coming as an ultimate fulfilment of the Transfiguration. Here, and also at 3:12, it obviously has a primary reference to Christ's return.

"'Where is the promise of his coming?'" is a question obviously expecting a negative answer. In this way, the scoffers express their disbelief in a scathing and sceptical manner. Scripture offers prominent examples of this same sceptical questioning, for example, in Satan's approach to Eve in the garden of Eden and to Jesus in his temptations in the desert. Clear parallels are found also in Jeremiah's critics who mocked him saying: "Where is the word of the LORD?

---

[155]   Formula of subscription to Westminster Confession of Faith, cited in The Book of the Constitution and Government of the Presbyterian Church in Ireland published by the Authority of the General Assembly, Belfast, 1980, reprinted with amendment, 2019, p73.

Let it now be fulfilled!" (Je. 17:15 ᴺᴵⱽ), and of the Israelites who 'wearied' God in Malachi's day "Where is the God of justice?" (Mal. 2:17 ᴺᴵⱽ cf. Ps. 79:10; 115:2; Jl. 2:17; Mi. 7:10). A similar reaction was evident in Ezekiel's time when many doubted coming judgement: "The days go by and every vision comes to nothing" (Eze. 12:22 ᴺᴵⱽ). The scoffers were not enquiring genuinely but disbelievingly. Rejection of God's word lay behind their questioning. It still does.

"'For ever since the fathers fell asleep'" The sceptical questioning gives way to categorical assertion of disbelief. "**The fathers**" is *hoi pateres*. Some claim that this refers to the first-generation of Christians and, as such, projects a later date for the letter, as "the fathers" used in this sense would be a second rather than a first century description. However, this seems unlikely. The plural "fathers" never refers to first-generation Christians in the New Testament but rather to the patriarchs in the Old Testament (Mt. 23:32; Lu. 1:55, 72; 6:23, 26; 11:47; Jn. 4:20; 6:31, 49, 58; 7:22; Ac. 3:13, 25; 5:30; 7:2, 11-12, 15, 19, 32, 38-39, 44-45, 51-52; 13:17, 32, 36; 15:10; 22:1, 14; 26:6; 28:25; Ro. 11:28; 15:8; 1 Co. 10:1; He. 1:1; 3:9; 8:9). Furthermore, the additional phrase "**from the beginning of creation**" would also point in the direction of the Old Testament patriarchs.

"'Fell asleep'" *ekoimēthēsan* is regularly used metaphorically as a euphemism for death. It was so used in Greek literature from the time of Homer onwards and has a similar meaning in the Old Testament. In the New Testament, this same terminology is used for believers who die, with an implicit emphasis on what the Christian understanding of death should be (Mt. 27:52; Jn. 11:11-12; Ac. 7:60; 13:36; 1 Co. 7:39; 11:30; 15:6, 18, 20, 51; 1 Th. 4:13-15). It is certainly not a theology of 'soul-sleep' or of unconscious existence between the point of death and resurrection but rather an affirmation for the believer that death anticipates that glorious resurrection awakening at the last day. The statement of the Westminster Catechism[156] is an excellent compendium of this truth: "The souls of believers are at their death made perfect in holiness,[157] and do immediately pass into glory[158]; and their bodies, being still united to Christ,[159] do rest in their graves till the resurrection[160]".

"All things are continuing as they were from the beginning of creation" The disbelieving scepticism is, thus, definitively expressed. There seem at least two points of reference behind this thinking, which are not necessarily mutually exclusive.

1. A general statement about a "closed" universe, into which, given past observation, it is unlikely that there will be divine intervention. Uniformitarianism, meaning that the universe is a divinely created but closed naturalistic system of cause and effect, has somewhat illogically allied itself with a belief in evolutionism and, of course, categorically denies divine intervention throughout world history, opposing both six-day creation and a global Flood. This may be part of the essence of the scoffers' attitude even though it pre-dates the actual term 'uniformitarianism' and denies what was earlier called the idea of *deus ex machina*. Interestingly, in recent years among secular geologists the concept of catastrophism, discarded because of uniformitarianism, seems to be gaining ground as a more acceptable thesis, though, of course, the majority of this school still denies a six-day creation and global Flood. If this were part of the scoffers' thinking,

---

[156] See Shorter Catechism 37 with Scripture proofs, *Westminster Confession of Faith*, Free Presbyterian Publications, Glasgow, 1995, pp297-298.
[157] He. 12:23.
[158] Lu. 23:43; 2 Co. 5:1, 6, 8; Ph. 1:23.
[159] 1 Th. 4:14.
[160] Is. 57:2; Jb.19:26,27. (Cf. Da. 12:2; Jn. 5:28-29; Ac. 24:15).

Christopher Green's pithy comment, helpfully set in the context of Peter's letter, is well worth noting:

> Our world, they would say, is a closed system which has no room for the intervention of God, and any such idea is 'no more than a vulgar myth'. Peter's three biblical examples will show that God stepped in once to create the world, and a second time to flood it; nothing stops him stepping in a third time to judge.[161]

2. A particular statement about the state of the dead in Christ and the promise of Christ's Second Coming. Here, the gist of the argument would be that both believer and unbeliever suffer the same fate in death with no observable difference and, therefore, any idea of the promise of God's final intervention through Christ's return must be discounted as flawed and mistaken. Interestingly, here, similar issues arose about the death and resurrection of believers and Christ's return in Corinth and in Thessalonica (cf. 1 Co. 15:1-58; 1 Th. 2:19; 3:13; 4:13-5:28; 2 Th. 1:1-3:18). Since, these would project a situation mid-50s/60s A.D., it would tend towards an earlier rather than a later dating of Second Peter, as, by a later date, this issue was not so rife.

Whether the 'scoffers' argue generally or particularly or both, the essence of their sceptical disbelief was a rejection of Scripture, as the rest of Chapter 3 shows. The issue was and is Scripture and it remains the root cause of disbelief. Calvin stresses the radical nature of such destructive thinking:

---

[161] D. Lucas & C. Green, *The Message Of 2 Peter & Jude*, p131 n17, citing J.H, Elliott, *1-2 Peter and Jude, with James, Augsburg Commentary on the New Testament* (Minneapolis: Augsburg, 1982) p153.

> It was a dangerous scoff when they insinuated a
> doubt as to the last resurrection; for when that is
> taken away, there is no gospel any longer, the power
> of Christ is brought to nothing, the whole of religion
> is gone. Then Satan aims directly at the throat of
> the Church, when he destroys faith in the coming
> of Christ. For why did Christ die and rise again,
> except that he may some time gather to himself the
> redeemed from death, and give them eternal life?
> All religion is wholly subverted, except faith in the
> resurrection remains firm and immovable. Hence,
> on this point Satan assails us most fiercely.[162]

Disbelief marks the end of the process in which scepticism plays a prominent part. Firstly, there is question and doubt as to what God says. Then, a reaction of indifference mixed with scepticism arises. Finally, scorn and derision form the inevitable conclusion. Disbelief is the upshot of all this. The pattern repeats itself in varying ways and to different degrees in Scripture – from Eve in Genesis, through Festus in Acts, to the false teachers in 2 Peter. The focus of this disbelief is against what God says, God's word, Scripture. This is the shocking thing here: those who were supposed to teach the church were actually uttering a travesty of instruction. They were authors not of belief but of disbelief. They aborted true and practical knowledge of God by rejecting Scripture. What a sad state of affairs within the church and its instruction!

APPLICATION

The thrust of the first psalm is, perhaps, the best comment on the theme of Peter's letter here about rejecting Scripture. The same sad progression of sceptical questioning is evident: walking in the

---

[162]   J. Calvin, *Commentaries on II Peter*, p415.

counsel of the wicked; standing in the way of sinners; sitting in the seat of mockers. The link between false teaching and immorality is implicit here also: a tree planted by streams of water; chaff that the wind blows away. The disbelief behind it all relates to Scripture itself, positively put: delight in the law of the Lord; meditation on it day and night; as well as negatively inferred: Satan's negative questioning, negating, maligning words to Eve persist from Genesis to Revelation, as the seed of the Serpent bruises the heel of the Seed of the woman. But the Seed of the woman deals that 'capital' blow to the head of the Serpent. The victory is ours in Christ! The point at issue in all this, clearly, is what God says in Scripture. God's word *is* truth.

The church of Jesus Christ needs to remember, recall, and remind herself constantly of this. Her apologetic before a disinterested and scathing secularism must not be timid but bold and biblical. The church's instruction must encourage by sound doctrine and refute those who oppose it (Tit.1:9), so that believers might grow in grace and in the knowledge of our Lord and Saviour Jesus Christ (2 Pe. 3:18). Scripture is not only the issue; it is also the answer to the problem. The sooner the church remembers, recalls, and reminds herself of this the better. Peter's words in his second letter drive us to Scripture, as do other New Testament directives (cf. 1 Cor. 15:1-11). Only then will we be like a tree planted by streams of water, not like chaff that the wind blows away. Scoffing, immorality and disbelief are best countered in this way.

> PSALM 1
> 1   Blessed is the one who turns away
>   from where the wicked walk,
>   Who does not stand in sinners' paths
>   or sit with those who mock.

2   Instead he finds God's holy law
        his joy and great delight;
    He makes the precepts of the LORD
        his study day and night.

3   He prospers ever like a tree
        that's planted by a stream,
    And in due season yields its fruit;
        its leaves are always green.

4   Not so the wicked! They are like
        the chaff that's blown away.
5   They will not stand when judgment comes,
        or with the righteous stay.

6   It is the LORD who sees and knows
        the way the righteous go,
    But those who live an evil life
        the LORD will overthrow.[163]

---

[163]   *Sing Psalms, New Metrical Versions of the Book of Psalms*, Free Church of
Scotland, Edinburgh, 2003.

Chapter 17

PRACTICAL KNOWLEDGE

BIBLICAL HISTORY

2 PETER 3:5-7

INTRODUCTION

Peter has just given a graphic description of the scoffers' views (3:3, 4). He has set these within the context of Scripture, which he has solemnly urged his readers to recall (3:1, 2). He now challenges these false views. They ignore biblical history (3:5-7), belie God's character (3:8, 9) and deny Christ's promise (3:10). They do all this because, fundamentally, they reject Scripture. Scripture is the on-going storyline of Chapter 3. Its rejection leads to amoral behaviour. Its acceptance produces a healthy Christian lifestyle: growth in the grace and knowledge of our Lord and Saviour Jesus Christ (3:18).

The basic premise of the scoffers' philosophy is that, since the beginning of creation and the death of the patriarchs, everything goes on in the same way. The earth, in other words, is a closed circuit with no divine intervention or probability of the same. The corollary of this, according to their view, is that, we ought not to

247

expect Christ's return. For the scoffers, the promise of Christ's return is flawed, unrealistic and illogical given the perimeters of the past. Peter counters this, by claiming that such an understanding fails to grasp the facts of biblical history: the creation and the Flood in particular. Hence, if the premise of the scoffers' argument is wrong the corollary is also wrong. If God initially brings about creation, intervenes with the Flood, there is no *prima facie* reason why he would not again intervene in the return of Christ, especially in view of the fact that he has already intervened in Christ's first coming.

So much of Peter's reasoning is tolerably plain. The form of the Greek here, however, has suggested to some that the details of what Peter is saying are somewhat opaque. Certainly, there are difficulties in the nuance of Peter's expressions. However, given the clear gist of his overall argument, even those details fall into place.

Peter in this section, stresses the sovereignty of God's word in Scripture in both the events of creation and Flood. He also indicates the different means God uses to fulfil his sovereign word both within a changing time-frame and a developing purpose. Things do not inevitably remain the same. God does intervene. All these factors serve to show the overall sovereignty of God's word and to illustrate how God intervenes to bring about his divine purpose. All things do not go on in the same way from the beginning of creation but continue to serve the purpose of a sovereign God, who carries out his sovereign will through the sovereign word of Scripture. The following analysis leads into the details of Peter's argument:

CREATION	(3:5)
FLOOD	(3:6)
JUDGEMENT	(3:7)

EXPOSITION

> "For they deliberately overlook this fact, that the heavens existed long ago, and the earth was formed out of water and through water by the word of God, and that by means of these the world that then existed was deluged with water and perished. But by the same word the heavens and earth that now exist are stored up for fire, being kept until the day of judgement and destruction of the ungodly" (3:5-7).

CREATION

The sovereign intervention of God in creation is all at points evident.

"**For they deliberately overlook this fact**". God's sovereignty is clear even as Peter introduces the subject. "**Overlook**" translates *lanthanei*, which basically means "something is hidden from someone" or "escapes someone's notice"; "**deliberately**" renders *thelontas* literally "willingly". If the participle *thelontas* modifies the verb *lanthanei*, the sense is "forget in a wilful way" or "**deliberately overlook**" (as in ESV and NIV). If the participle *thelontas* stands by itself, it has the nuance: "For when they maintain this, it escapes their notice" [NASB]. The difference is slight, but our preference is for the former. Bearing in mind what Peter has just said about remembering or recalling Scripture, the scoffers' attitude of incredulous questioning gives the impression that what Peter is saying is that their attitude of non-remembrance, even wilful hiding, is tantamount to deliberately forgetting God's word. It is an intentional act, a slighting rejection of God's sovereignty and, hence, culpable in the extreme, given the clear import of God's sovereignty in the context.

"**That the heavens existed long ago, and the earth was formed out of water and through water**" Peter's recall is that of Genesis. The combination of "**heavens**" and "**earth**" here implies this. Peter is not saying that God long ago, simply out of existing matter, made the "**heavens**" and formed "**the earth**". But rather that "long ago" by a divine fiat, God created the universe: "**the heavens existed**", *ouranoi ēsan*, and that "**the earth was formed**" or literally "stood" in the sense of "cohered", *gē sunestōsa*, at his divine command also. The sovereignty of divine creation is emphatic in the coupling of both "**the heavens**" and "**the earth**". Both these expressions regarding "**heavens**" and "**earth**" imply that divine creation was creation "*ex nihilo*", creation from nothing, not from existing matter. The Hebrew verb *bara*, used in Genesis, which gives the sense "to create from nothing" further emphasizes this.

That "**the earth was formed 'out of' water**", *ex hudatos*, aligns well with the initial picture of the Spirit of God hovering over the waters (Ge. 1:2), then, particularly on the second day, in the separation of the water (Ge. 1:6) and on the third day in the appearance of the dry ground from the middle of the waters (Ge. 1:9). This view is preferable to the idea of Thales that the 'substance' or 'matter' of the earth came from the waters. That the earth was also formed "**through water**" *di'hudatos* is more difficult to understand. It is possible to take it as a reference to the appearance of the earth in the midst of the waters (cf. Ge.1:9), less likely as a reference to God's providential care for his creation (cf. Ge.2:4-6f), and most likely as a general term referring to God's use of water as a means of creating the earth just as later he used water to destroy the earth, a sort of reversal of process (cf. Ge. 7:11, 12). In all, it is not the water which is sovereign but rather God. The water is simply instrumental, an agent under God's sovereign control in the whole affair, through a sovereign Scripture.

"By the word of God" *tō tou theou logō.* This marks the high point of the sovereignty of God's word in creation. The Genesis story stresses this by the constant repetition of the formula; "and God said, let there be . . . and there was" (Ge.1:3 cf. 1:6, 9, 11, 14, 20, 24, 26). The theme of God's creative activity by his word is further emphasized in Scripture: "By the word of the LORD were the heavens made, their starry host by the breath of his mouth" (Ps. 33:6 NIV); "By faith we understand that the universe was created by the word of God, so that what is seen was not made out of things that are visible" (He. 11:3). The Hebrew term for "word of the LORD", *debar jaweh*, as much expresses the deliberative action as the spoken word of God, for both are implied in *debar*, and finds its ultimate fulfilment in the Eternal Word through whom creation was accomplished (Jn. 1:3; He. 1:2 cf. Pr. 8:23-31; He. 11:3). Whether this is implied here or not, it certainly is a biblical theme.

The priority of God's word in creation is mentioned by other New Testament witnesses. John, alluding to the Genesis story, notes God's word as the source of all creation, light and life, indeed, the new birth and growth associated with it, which came through Jesus Christ, the enfleshed Word of God (Jn. 1:1-14). The writer to the Hebrews describes God's Son as the one through whom the world was not only created but is also sustained, God's final word to mankind, the word of his power, the creation of the visible out of the invisible (He. 1:1-3; 11:1-3). Paul relates God's commanding word at creation as a light shining out of darkness with his giving the light of the knowledge of the glory of God in the face of Jesus Christ (2 Co. 4:6 cf. 1 Pe. 2:9). James depicts believers as those whom God, by his own will, brought forth by the word of truth to be a kind of firstfruits of his creation (Ja. 1:18). Peter, among apostolic witnesses, was by no means alone in focusing on the priority of the word in creation.

God's word, then, is sovereign in creation. That is the point, above all, Peter is making here. The time-frame of "long ago" *ekpalai*, the agency of "water" *hudōr*, even the "the heavens" *ouranoi* and "the earth" *gē* are all, in a sense, incidental. The main point is God's sovereign word. Creation is a divine fiat. God's will is accomplished by his word, which when spoken, acts and activates through whatever instrument he chooses. The earth is not a closed circuit devoid of divine intervention. It is a divine fiat brought about through God's word as he uses whatever agency he chooses. The scoffers have got it all wrong. Calvin puts it well:

> The world no doubt had its origin from waters, for Moses calls the chaos from which the earth emerged, waters; and further, it was sustained by waters; it yet pleased the Lord to use waters for the purpose of destroying it. It hence appears that the power of nature is not sufficient to sustain and preserve the world, but that on the contrary it contains the very element of its own ruin, whenever it may please God to destroy it.[164]

In the biblical history of creation, "the heavens and the earth", then, Peter emphasizes *water* as the instrument through which God accomplishes this work. This recalls the Genesis account, where the Spirit hovers over the watery expanse and brings order out of chaos (Ge. 1:2, 3). Creation, according to Peter here is both "out of water" and "through water" (3:5). It, thus, echoes a divine creation "*ex nihilo*", out of nothing not from existing matter, as the Hebrew *bara* implies, as already noted. It also recalls the watery expanse, created by God "from nothing", "out of" and "through" whose instrumentality God created "the earth". Above all, it is creation "by the word of the God" (3:5), the repeated Scripture, as "God said" (Ge. 1:3, 6, 9, 11, 14, 20, 24, 26), a fact substantiated by other

---

[164] J. Calvin, *Commentaries on II Peter*, p416.

New Testament witnesses-John, the writer of the Hebrews, Paul, James as well as Peter, all in a context of creation by Jesus Christ, the eternal Word of God, a divine fiat, with water as instrumental but God's word as causative, controlling in both creation, providence and salvation.

<h2 style="text-align:center">FLOOD</h2>

The dynamic nature of the Flood stressed here amplifies God's power.

"And that by means of these" "By means of these" is literally *di'hōn. Dia* is a preposition of instrumentality "through" or "**by means of**". *Hōn* is a plural relative pronoun. To what antecedents does the plural refer? Some, as NIV, have suggested "**waters**", since verse 5 referred to two kinds of water (cf. Ge. 2:6, 9; 7:11). But the basic sense in verse 5 is water in the singular and this interpretation of water or waters provides a common thread running through verses 5-7. Some opt for "heavens" or "heavens and earth", but this is awkward, since it is difficult to see how either "heavens" or "heavens and earth" are the means by which the world was destroyed by the flood. The best interpretation, as implied by ESV, is to take the plural *hōn* as referring to both "the water" and "the word". "The word" is the immediate antecedent, is the key theme of the passage and this maintains a continuity of "the word" throughout verses 5-7. An expanded translation and sense would then be: "and that by means of the word and the water". This is our preference.

"The world that then existed" is literally "the then world". Time-frame language is used throughout verses 5-7: "the heavens existed long ago (*ekpalai*)" v5, also used at 2:3 of the false teachers' condemnation, "their condemnation from long ago (*ekpalai*)"; "the world that then (*tote*) existed" v6; "the heavens and earth that now (*nun*) exist" v7. Verse 5 depicts the distant past at creation, verse 6 the more recent past at the Flood and verse 7 the present, with, as we shall later suggest, a possible reference to the future (cf. 3:13). The overall significance of these temporal references seems to be that, whatever or whenever the context, God's dynamic intervention is not only possible but actual, for he holds the entire time-frame within his control. Far from things simply going on from the beginning without any divine interruption, the whole time-space module is formulated by God's ordering. The scoffers need to learn this truth.

"The world" is *ho kosmos*. There seems little doubt that the use of this term here as compared with "**the heavens and (the) earth**" of verses 5 to 7 is significant. The terms are not simply synonymous. The "**world**", *kosmos*, carries overtones of order, which was disrupted by the Flood almost in the sense of a return to primeval chaos (cf. Ge. 7:11; 17-23). It also means 'the world of men/mankind' and is used in Scripture in this way of man's fallenness as particularly evident in the Johannine writings in the New Testament. The occurrence of *kosmos* twice at 2:5 is an important guide here. At 2:5, again in the Flood context, it is used of "the ancient world", *archaiou kosmou*, and "the world of the ungodly", *kosmō asebōn*. Here at 3:6, the same feature of a sinful mankind under God's judgement is expressed. How far the destruction of the Flood affected "the heavens" is a moot point. But the primary emphasis here is on God's judgement on ungodly mankind and that plainly evidences God's dynamic intervention. Again, the scoffers have got it wrong.

"**Was deluged with water and perished**" "**Deluged**" is *kataklustheis*, from which our English word "cataclysm". The basic verb means "to deluge", "to submerge". Though used in this form only here in the New Testament, the related noun is *kataklusmos*, which the Greek Old Testament uses throughout the Flood narratives. "**Perished**" is *apōleto*. It does not imply "annihilation" but, as at verse 7, continuing judgement. This same dynamic interference of divine intervention continues. The Flood was God's judgment on a sinful world. T.R. Schreiner puts this dynamic intervention of divine judgement guardedly but incisively: "Bauckham is likely correct that 'world' here refers to a judgment that affects more than people, but it does not follow that it includes the heavens. A judgment of the earth is 'cosmic' enough".[165]

In the biblical history of the Flood, Peter replaces the expression "the heavens . . . and the earth" (3:5) with that of "the world" (3:6). The context is that of the sinful world of mankind, which God destroys in the Flood, since every intention of the thoughts of man's heart was only evil continually (Ge. 6:5). Noah was commanded by God's word to make, enter and remain within the ark until the dry land appeared. In that sense, the Flood was instrumental but God's word fundamental, paramount and authoritative. The Flood was time-limited but Scripture, God's word, is final and eternal.

JUDGEMENT

The future purpose of God in final judgement is completely consistent with his actions in both creation and Flood.

"But by the same word" "The same word" *tō autō logō* is emphatic. The sovereignty of God by means of his word dominates verses 5-7 and arises naturally from verses 1 and 2. It is "by the word of God" that the heavens existed and the earth was formed (v5). It is "by means of these" namely, in our understanding, by water and the word that the Flood convulsed the world (v6). Now, it is through this "**same**" word that the final judgement will come (v7). The word of God is not only a common but also a controlling factor in respect of creation, Flood and final judgement.

Donald Guthrie defines this well when he writes theologically of 'Man and his world':

---

[165]   T. R. Schreiner, *1, 2 Peter, Jude,* p 377.

In *2 Peter* reference is made to creation (2 Pet. 3:4ff.) and this is attributed to the Word of God. There is a clear allusion to the Genesis account in the fact that the earth is said to have been formed 'out of water and by means of water'. This comment on its beginnings is then immediately linked with the final destruction of the heavens and earth. The latter will occur only at the day of the Lord (2 Pet. 3:10, 12). In other words the beginning and end of the present material creation is wholly determined by God. The means for destruction is mentioned as fire (2 Pet. 3:7, 10, 12), a characteristic symbol of divine judgement. In two passages (2 Pet. 1:4; 2:20) the *kosmos* is specifically connected with corruption or defilement.[166]

"The heavens and earth that now exist" "That now exist" is, literally, "the now (*nun*) heavens and the earth". Peter continues to explore the purpose of God's sovereignty over all things. He returns to the heavens and earth mentioned in verse 5. The **"now"** *nun* of verse 7 obviously contrasts the, literally, **"then (*tote*) world"** of verse 6, but it is not only a qualitative distinction between **"world"** and **"heavens and earth"** but also temporal as evident in the Greek adverbs **"then"** and **"now"**. Indeed, even further, there is also a sense in which the contrast between the **"now"** heavens and earth of verse 7 and the "new heavens" and "new earth" of verse 13 is anticipated. The scoffers deny change but change there has been and will be, however long the time-scale, claims Peter.

"Are stored up for fire" **"Stored up"** *tethēsaurismenoi* is a surprising verb to use, for it means "store up", "treasure" and is more often used in connection with good things than bad. The tense, too, is

---

[166] D. Guthrie, *New Testament Theology*, pp147-148.

significant. It is perfect passive participle and denotes an action in the past that has lasting effects in the present. Coupled with the following "**being kept**" *tēroumenoi*, a present passive connoting continuing activity, it gives the overall literal sense: "having been stored up for fire, are being kept for the day of judgement".

"**For fire**". There *is* change and that very fact in this context is significant. It is change from water to fire. The world that was convulsed by water will never again suffer that fate, because God has so promised (Ge. 9:11-17). But it will be destroyed by fire. The instruments of water and fire are variable but the means, God's word, remains the same.

"**Fire**" *puri*. Peter is not reflecting Stoic or Iranian sources. There, the patterns are cyclic, a sequence of old worlds perishing by water and fire and new worlds arising as a result, but with Peter the sense is final. There, the theme is pantheistic, with Peter monotheistic. Rather, Peter is recalling biblical sources. "**Fire**" is regularly used in the Old Testament in connection with judgement, and sometimes at the end of history (De. 32:22; Ps. 97:3; Is. 30:30; 66:15, 16; Eze. 38:22; Am. 7:4; Zep. 1:18; Mal. 4:1). The New Testament is equally clear in this regard (Mt. 3:10-12; 1 Co. 3:13-15; 2 Th. 1:7-8; He. 6:7-8; 12:29; 1 Pe. 1:7; Re. 21:8). Jesus himself included fire frequently in his depiction of final judgement (Mt. 5:22; 13:40-42, 50; 18:8, 9; 25:41; Mk. 9:43-48; Lu. 12:49; 17:29). There is no *prime facia* reason to regard fire as purely symbolic or metaphorical but fearfully real in a literal sense (Le. 9:24, 10:2; Mt. 25:41; Mk. 9:[44, 46] 48; Lu. 17:29).

"**Being kept until the day of judgement and destruction of the ungodly**" The ultimate purpose of God's judgement is finally disclosed. It is not simply the destruction of the present heavens and earth and the creation of a new heavens and earth (cf. 3:10-12), but the judgement of God on the ungodly. There is a clear moral end within this cosmic scenario. Purpose marks every part of the climax of Peter's argument: **"being kept"** *tēroumenoi* recalls, in identical language, the fate of the ungodly angels mentioned earlier in the letter "kept until the judgement" (2:4); **"until the day of judgement"** *eis hēmeran kriseōs* expresses definitively that purpose in using the Greek preposition *eis*, "toward", "unto", and anticipates specifically "the day of the Lord", mentioned later by Peter (3:10); **"and destruction of the ungodly"** *kai apōleias tōn asebōn anthrōpōn* completes the sequence and reflects in like terms God's judgement in the Flood already noted: "upon the world of the ungodly" (2:5) namely, the purposes of God's final judgement on the godless. Christopher Green summarizes the entire section well:

> These three biblical examples have shown that the stability of the created order does not, as the false teachers suppose, argue against the reality of God's judgment. People do still die, just as they have always done, but neither the Old Testament nor the New promised that that would change until there is a completely new creation. The regular ordering of the seasons, the balance and interconnection of the universe from subatomic particle through to interstellar space, all argue for a creator God who is patient. But that does not mean that the world is closed to him. False teachers should realize that the same word that guarantees the stable world they delight in also guarantees the judgment they mock.[167]

In the biblical history of judgement, Peter contrasts the *fire* of judgement with the water of creation and Flood as an instrument of God's wrath. The world that was created through water and judged

---

[167] D. Lucas & C. Green, *The Message Of 2 Peter & Jude*, p135.

in the Flood will end in fire. But, again, God's word is supreme: "by the word of God" of verse 5, "by means of these" of verse 6, namely, the water and the word, and "by the same word" of verse 7 are the one and continuing theme – the word of God, the Scriptures. The very language and meaning of the words used to describe fallen angels, Sodom and Gomorrah and the false teachers in Chapter 2 continue in Chapter 3: "stored up for fire" (v7); "kept until the day of judgement" (v7); "destruction of the ungodly" (v7). The God who intervened in creation and Flood will intervene in judgement, in the Second Coming of our Lord and Saviour Jesus Christ, for Scripture says it. The world is not a closed circuit but under God's control and command. God has spoken and said that this is the way of it, according to Scripture.

APPLICATION

Peter's words about the biblical, historical events of creation and Flood substantiate his defence of the authority of Scripture against the scoffers. This is the first of a number of avenues down which he goes to affirm biblical truth against the scoffers' false position, and the bottom line in all this is God's word. God orders all things according to his word. Scripture is supreme. The agents and instruments God uses whether in terms of time or matter may vary, but they are subservient to his designs and those designs are rooted in his word.

The facticity and historicity of God's word in particular condemns the scoffers. The God who intervenes in such a sovereign and dramatic way is not shut out from the universe he brought into being. It is not impersonal nature but a personal God who is in charge of these things, and he works all together in a deliberately moral and righteous way. The end of this process is the judgement of the godless and the safety and preservation of his people. The God who, according to Scripture, intervened in creation and Flood will intervene, as he said, through his Son in final judgement.

This sovereignty stands foursquare on Scripture. The essential facticity and historicity of God's word must not be demythologized. Symbolic and metaphorical expressions there are, historical and cultural context there is, but God's word is truth. We are not at liberty to twist God's truth to suit our views. When we do that, we align ourselves with the false teachers and scoffers. When we thus handle the word of God inappropriately, where does fable end and history begin, fiction persist or fact rule, metaphor express or malignity distort truth?

Jesus unashamedly stood firm on biblical ground when he alluded to the Old Testament. He told it as it was. For Jesus, as for the apostles, what Scripture said, God said, and said it awesomely. Jesus is God and eternal truth resides in him. To do other than he did with Scripture is to follow the ways of Adam and Eve in their first transgression. The church must discover God's word as truth, factually and historically, whatever the cultural context or time setting. Scripture as God's word deserves that kind of respect.

Chapter 18

PRACTICAL KNOWLEDGE

GOD'S CHARACTER

2 PETER 3:8, 9

INTRODUCTION

Peter has repulsed the scoffers' attacks (3:5-7). They deny the promise of Christ's coming by claiming that the world is a closed circuit. Everything has gone on the same since creation. In view of this, they claim, there is no likelihood of a divine intervention such as in Christ's return. But Peter says their premise is wrong, as is their conclusion. In both creation and Flood, God has dramatically intervened in the course of events, why not further in Christ's return? These things the scoffers deliberately forget (v5).

The damage the scoffers and false teachers do, however, is not simply to themselves but to Peter's readers. Their insidious views affect them. The question "Where is the promise of his coming?" (3:4) plants the seeds of doubt in their minds. After all, Peter had already written to them: "The end of all things is at hand" (1 Pe.4:7) and that was apostolic teaching. Jesus had promised he would return,

261

had urged his people to be alert and watchful and the whole church throbbed with excitement at the prospect of the fulfilment of this promise when the Lord would come back and right all wrongs. Yet day after day passed and there seemed little prospect of this. Could the false teachers be right after all?

Peter now turns again to his readers who need direction. Reminder and recall has been his on-going theme; reminder of Scripture in particular in regard to Christ's return (3:1-3). The scoffers and false teachers deliberately forget (v5). Peter's readers must intentionally remember (v8f). Peter's method of reassuring them and of stifling their doubts is precisely the same, namely, recalling Scripture. Intriguingly, to do this, Peter reminds them of God's character from the Old Testament (vv8, 9) and then recalls Christ's promise from the New Testament (v10). The words spoken in the past by the holy prophets and the command given by our Lord and Saviour through the apostles continue to answer all the church's questions and deal with all her problems.

Peter focuses on Psalm 90 verse 4 particularly to delineate God's character:

> "For a thousand years in your sight
> are but as yesterday when it is past,
> or as a watch in the night."

Peter refers to this in verse 8 and then elaborates on it in verse 9. Of course, Dick Lucas and Christopher Green are right. It is not just that one verse but also the whole of Psalm 90 in context, which is in view. Psalm 90 as a whole confronts scoffers and false teachers and reassures questioning believers. It portrays God's character in a striking way. God is an eternal God (vv2, 4, 10), a creating God (v2), a judging God (vv3, 8,9), a saving God (vv1, 13-17) and a moral God (vv11, 12). "These five lessons are central to Psalm 90. Peter's

Christians were in danger of being distracted from recalling that God is the eternal Creator, who judges according to his moral law, and saves according to his covenant love".[168]

Peter fixes on the *eternity of God* in verse 8 and the *patience of God* in verse 9. Those are the attributes of God's character from the prophets in Scripture, which will reassure his doubting readers and deal a deathblow to the heresies of the scoffers and false teachers.

ETERNITY OF GOD   (3:8)
PATIENCE OF GOD   (3:9)

EXPOSITION

ETERNITY

"But do not overlook this one fact, beloved, that with the Lord one day is as a thousand years, and a thousand years as one day" (3:8).

God's eternal nature as compared with man's concept and experience of time is marked by a complete difference both in perspective and intensity and, recognizing this difference will help Peter's readers understand the perceived delay in Christ's return.

PERSPECTIVE

"But do not overlook this one fact, beloved," Peter turns from repulsing the scoffers and false teachers to reassuring his Christian readers. "You" *humas*, absent in translation, but present in the Greek text, is emphatic and points up the fact that Peter is now addressing his readers rather than the scoffers. It also has a controlling influence

---

[168]   D. Lucas & C. Green, *The Message Of 2 Peter & Jude*, p138.

on the context, which is specifically directed to Peter's readers. "**Overlook**" is *lanthanetō*. Peter has just used the same verb at verse 5 of the scoffers, who "deliberately overlook". This further stresses the contrast here. The scoffers deliberately forget; Peter's readers must "**not overlook this one fact**". They must intentionally remember. "**Beloved**", *agapētoi* completes the emphasis on the new addressees. Peter uses this expression intimately and warmly of his readers also at verses 1, 14 and 17.

"**That with the Lord one day is as a thousand years**" The point Peter is making, and it has obvious relevance to the perceived delay, is that time from God's perspective is totally different from our view-point. His perspective is utterly unique. Time, as far as God is concerned, cannot be reckoned by our finite conceptions. God, being eternal, is in a sense outside of time: "Before the mountains were brought forth, or ever you had formed the earth and the world, from everlasting to everlasting you are God" (Ps. 90:2 cf. Ps. 102:27; Da. 7:9; 1 Ti. 1:17; He. 13:8; Re. 1:4). And yet in a glorious sense he has entered into time of which he is in complete control: "Lord, you have been our dwelling place in all generations" (Ps. 90:1 cf. Mt. 1:23; Jn. 1:14; Ga. 4:4; He. 2:14; 1 Jn. 1:1-4). The impact of the comparison is well put by C. Bigg: "The desire of the Psalmist is to contrast the eternity of God with the short span of human life. What St Peter wishes is to contrast the eternity of God with the impatience of human expectations".[169] The implication of the comparison is equally incisively put by J.A. Bengel: "The *age-measurer* (so to speak) of God differs from the *hour-reckoner* of mortals".[170]

The remarkable, if somewhat sad thing, is that Jewish

[169]   C. Bigg, *The Epistles of St. Peter and St Jude*, p295, cited in T.R. Schreiner, *1, 2 Peter, Jude*, p379.

[170]   J.A. Bengel, *Bengel's New Testament Commentary*, vol.2 (1742, Grand Rapids: Kregel, 1981), p778, cited in D. Lucas & C. Green, *The Message Of 2 Peter & Jude*, p139.

commentators, intertestamental writers and early Christian Fathers missed this point and fixated on numerics and the concept of "day", Hebrew *yom*. They linked all this with the Genesis story, computing that the six days of creation were six thousand years and the seventh, the Sabbath, one thousand years, was to be linked with the millennium of Revelation 20:1-6. This way, known anciently as chiliasm more modernly as, pre-millennialism, which predicts a thousand years of rule by the saints in an earthly Jerusalem at the Parousia, obscures the deeper truth of God's eternal perspective from view.

Clearly, however, this numerical interpretation misses the point of Peter's quotation. Even exegetically it is flawed on a number of points. 1. Peter uses the expression "as" or "like" *hōs*: the analogy is a comparison not a statement. 2. If this is what Peter implies it does not fit the context and is certainly no real answer to the scoffers and false teachers. 3. It seems to misconstrue the continued statement of Peter **"and a thousand years as one day"** as simply reversing the order and confirming the validity of the numerical interpretation. The sense of the reversed repetition of these words seems to mean more than that.

INTENSITY

"And a thousand years as one day" It is true that this following phrase, a straight reversal of the former, could be viewed as simply confirming the thousand years/one day analogy. On the other hand, it could be viewed as negating the numerics and showing how a purely chronological interpretation falls short of the deeper meaning of Peter's use of the quotation or allusion to Psalm 90, which is to relate, as far as possible, the eternity of God to our human understanding. While the contention **"that with the Lord one day is as a thousand years"** illustrates the different perspective of God's view of time, the balancing statement **"and a thousand years as one day"** may well reflect the great intensity of God's use of time.

Dick Lucas and Christopher Green, picking up on Michael Green's excellent point that the quotation illustrates not just the perspective but also the intensity of God's eternity, make an astute observation: "In line with standard Jewish teaching on the passage, he adds the idea that *a day is like a thousand years*, which means that 'God sees time with a *perspective* we lack . . . [and] with an *intensity* we lack'. He can see the broad sweep of history in a moment, yet he can stretch out a day with patient care".[171] God, outside of time and controlling time, scans aeons pursuing his purposes and yet fills hours and days full of significances, which completely baffle our human understanding of chronology. "For waiting seems very long on this account, because we have our eyes fixed on the shortness of the present life, and we also increase weariness by computing days, hours, and minutes. But when the eternity of God's kingdom comes to our minds, many ages vanish away like so many moments".[172]

Richard Bauckham, who investigates the minutiae of Jewish and other writings behind this concept, sums it up so well when he writes:

> The point is rather that God's perspective on time is not limited by a human life span. He surveys the whole of history and sets the times of events in accordance with his agelong purpose. His perspective is so much more comprehensive than that of men and women who, accustomed to short-term expectations, are impatient to see the Parousia in their own lifetime.[173]

---

[171]   D. Lucas & C. Green, *The Message Of 2 Peter & Jude,* p137, alluding to both R. J. Bauckham, *Jude, 2 Peter,* pp308-310, and M. Green, *2 Peter and Jude,* p146 (for further implications), (Emphasis M. Green).

[172]   J. Calvin, *Commentaries on II Peter,* p418.

[173]   R. J. Bauckham, *Jude, 2 Peter,* p310.

Peter's readers must consider time from God's perspective not from a human point of view, if they are to make sense of the perceived delay in Christ's return, and to refute the scoffers' ridicules. To put it in a Greek form thought: God's sense of time is in terms of *kairos*, time as a season or significant period; man's sense of time is *chronos*, time in years, days, and minutes.

PATIENCE

"The Lord is not slow to fulfil his promise as some count slowness, but is patient towards you, not wishing that any should perish, but that all should reach repentance" (3:9).

The purpose of God's eternity from this perspective introduces another of his perfections: God's patience. God's patience evinces not slowness of reluctance but compassion of willingness and is the reason for the perceived delay in Christ's return. Peter here elaborates on the allusion to Psalm 90:4, almost hinting at an explanation along the lines of Psalm 90:3: "You return man to dust and say, 'Return, O children of man!'" and Psalm 90:12: "So teach us to number our days that we may get a heart of wisdom".

SLOWNESS

"The Lord is not slow to fulfil his promise" "**The Lord**" as in verse 8 is better understood as God rather than Christ. While the expression "The day of the Lord" (v10) in the New Testament usually connotes the return of Christ, the title "**Lord**" here is better attributed in context to God the Father. "**Promise**" *epaggelias* may well recall the wider context of 1:4 "promises", but also quite naturally alludes to the particular promise of Christ's *parousia* or coming as so referred to at 3:4: "Where is the promise of his coming?" "**Slow**", of which "**slowness**" later is definitive, is *bradutēta*. It means "delayed" or "late" usually in the context of "hesitation" or "loitering". The promise of the perceived delay of God's action was a problem in the Old Testament, which led to questioning or doubting God's promise. The classic description is at Habakkuk 2:3 where the prophet gives the Lord's answer to the problem, an answer where the subject can be taken as either the "vision" or the "Lord" himself:

> "For still the vision awaits its appointed time;
> it hastens to the end—
> it will not lie.
> If it seems slow, wait for it;
> it will surely come; it will not delay".

The writer to the Hebrews quotes Habakkuk 2:3-4 (LXX) to encourage his readers to persevere to the end and receive what God has promised (He. 10:36-38). The problem also interestingly arises in Greek literature where Epicurus' argument against providence appealed to the delay of divine judgement (Epicurus 548C 549B *bradutēs* "lateness" as in 2 Peter 3:9) while Plutarch explains that the delay demonstrates God's "gentleness and magnanimity" (Plutarch 551C: *praotēs kai megalopsuchia*) and gives opportunity for "repentance" (Plutarch 551D: *metanoian*).[174] Linguistic parallels notwithstanding, the abundant *Jewish* background on this subject, would account for Peter's thought here.

Peter follows the same line as the writer to the Hebrews. It is not God's lack of ability, indifference, forgetfulness or general apathy, which are the cause of the delay but rather the positive aspect of his patience and mercy.

"As some count slowness" **"Some"** *tines* could refer either to the scoffers and false teachers or to Peter's readers. A touch of irony about the expression would point to the false teachers but Peter seems

---

[174] R. J. Bauckham, *Jude, 2 Peter*, p314.

rather to be thinking of those influenced by their views, namely Peter's readers. Calvin pertinently comments: "For our minds are always prurient, and a doubt often creeps in, why he does not come sooner. But when we hear that the Lord, in delaying, shews a concern for our salvation, and that he defers the time because he has a care for us, there is no reason why we should any longer complain of tardiness".[175]

COMPASSION

"**But is patient**" Peter now develops the glorious positive side of God's patience as a purposeful answer to any perceived delay inimical to God's being. "**Patient**" *makrothumei* combines in a verbal form the two ideas of "large" with "great anger". "Peter used it here to show that God has a vast capacity for storing up anger and wrath before it spills over in judgment (cf. Ex. 34:6; Joel 2:13; Matt. 18:23-27 Rom. 2:4; 9:22)"[176] This particular idea of God's patience also recalls the Old Testament 'slow to anger' and is abundantly explicated throughout Scripture as a divine attribute (Ex. 34:6; Nu. 14:18; Je. 15:15; Jona. 4:2; Ro. 2:4; 9:22).

"**Towards you**" *eis humas* is emphatic specifying not the false teachers, though they may by inference be included, but particularly Peter's faithful readers. There is a variant "toward us" *eis hēmas,* which is followed by AV and NKJV but this reading is less substantiated and the other preferable. "**Towards you**" is not only emphatic but controlling in the context and grammatically governs the following "**any**" *tinas* and "**all**" *pantas.* Peter's Christian readers are particularly the subjects of address.

"**Not wishing that any should perish, but that all should reach repentance**". This amplifies the divine patience by giving the reason

---

175   J. Calvin, *Commentaries on II Peter*, p419.
176   J. MacArthur, *2 Peter & Jude*, p122.

for the perceived delay as God's desire for the salvation of his people. All the words of the phrase bristle with the wonder of divine long-suffering: "**not wishing**" is *mē boulomenos*, the present middle participle of *boulomai* (I wish) denoting cause; "**any**" *tinas* is the particular and individual person; "**perish**" *apolesthai* means "utterly destroyed" and refers to eternal judgement in hell, as is typical of the term; "**all**" *pantas* is the sum total of the earlier mentioned "**any**" who repent; "**reach**" *chōrēsai* is often taken passively in the Greek and so would describe God "gathering" or "collecting" the wandering to "**repentance**"; "**repentance** *metanoian*," "a complete change of mind", "a right about turn in will and life" involves that which, according to Scripture, is absolutely necessary for eternal life. These words describe not only the divine patience but also the purpose and manner of its object, the way and manner of salvation. This promise gives the reason for any perceived delay, draws Peter's readers from the doubts implanted in them by the scoffers and false teachers and reassures them not only of the return of their Lord but of the salvation he has bestowed upon them.

Of course, the problem here is to whom do these words refer – to all men without exception or to elect sinners?

1. Some maintain here universalism, which this, together with other Scriptures, means that all mankind will eventually be saved. But this cannot be the case, for even in the immediate context Peter speaks of the heavens and earth "stored up for fire, being kept until the day of judgement and destruction (*kriseōs kai apōleias*) of the ungodly" (3:7) and the Scriptures clearly teach elsewhere a hell of eternal destruction.

2. Some, threading together Scriptures speaking pointedly of God not wanting the death of the wicked but rather that they might repent and live (Eze. 18:23, 32; 33:11; Jn. 3:16; Ro. 11:32; 1 Ti. 2:4), have argued that the choice is sovereignly in

man's hand and that he is ultimately responsible for his own eternal destination. As M. Green has put it commenting on this verse: "the plain meaning is that, although God wants all men to be saved, and although he has made provision for all to be accepted, some will exercise their God-given free will to exclude God. And this he cannot prevent unless he is to take away the very freedom of choice that marks us out as men. Some will indeed perish (v7), but this is not because God wills it".[177] The problem with this view is that it makes man not God sovereign in salvation and ignores the biblical evidence for a sovereignly divine work of grace and for the bondage of the human will in sin.

3. Some see Scripture as teaching that God sovereignly ordains and wills the salvation of only some. They are convinced of this because of the teaching of certain Scriptures such as John 6:37; 44-45, 65; 10:16, 26; Acts 13:48; Romans 8:29-30; 9:1-23; Ephesians 1:4-5, 11. Whatever other view of salvation Scripture may appear to teach must be held consistently with these truths. This view is my personal preference.

In this particular instance regarding 2 Peter 3:9, two lines of reasoning persist.

a. Theologically, Scripture teaches two aspects of God's will. There are those places where Scripture speaks of God "wishing or "desiring" salvation and in these cases, it is the salvation of all men without exception. Alternatively, Scripture speaks of God "willing" or "decreeing" salvation and in these cases, it is the salvation of God's elect or chosen people that is in view. There is a distinction then,

---

[177]   M. Green, *2 Peter and Jude*, p148.

it is claimed, between God's *desired* and God's *decreed* will; sometimes, as it is put, between his "*revealed*" and his "*hidden*" will. God wants all men to be saved but only wills the salvation of some. This is not theological double-talk but capable of theological definition.[178] On this understanding, it would be God's *desired* will as offered to all men without exception, to which 2 Peter 3:9 refers.

b. Exegetically, it is possible to take the whole phrase "**not wishing that any should perish, but that all should reach repentance**" as controlled by the preceding "**towards you**" *eis humas*. If this, as seems reasonable, refers not to the scoffers and false teachers but to Peter's Christian readers who were questioning and wavering under the influence of these heretics and needed reassurance, then the "**any**" *tinas* and the "**all**" *pantas* would also refer to Peter's Christian readers. R. J. Bauckham comments: "The author remains close to his Jewish source, for in Jewish thought it was usually for the sake of the repentance of his own people that God delayed judgment. Here it is for the sake of the repentance of 2 Peter's Christian readers. No doubt repentance from those sins into which some of them have been enticed by the false teachers (2:14, 18; 3:17) is especially in mind. We need not suppose that the author put the false teachers themselves entirely beyond possibility of repentance and salvation, but here he addresses his readers, who are distinguished from the false teachers (3:5, 8, 17)".[179] Both a. and b. combined, offer a perfectly reasonable exposé of what Scripture, as a whole, teaches.

As a conclusion to this section, we quote in full Calvin who sums up admirably:

---

178 See, for example, J. Piper "Are There Two Wills in God?" in "*Still Sovereign*", pp 107-31 cited by T. R. Schreiner, *1, 2 Peter, Jude*, p382 n56.

179 R. J. Bauckham, *Jude, 2 Peter*, p313.

Not willing that any should perish. So wonderful is his love towards mankind, that he would have them all to be saved, and is of his own self prepared to bestow salvation on the lost. But the order is to be noticed, that God is ready to receive all to repentance, so that none may perish; for in these words the way and manner of obtaining salvation is pointed out. Every one of us, therefore, who is desirous of salvation, must learn to enter in by this way.

But it may be asked, if God wishes none to perish, why is it that so many do perish? To this my answer is, that no mention is here made of the hidden purpose of God, according to which the reprobate are doomed to their own ruin, but only of his will as made known to us in the gospel. For God there stretches forth his hand without a difference to all, but lays hold only of those, to lead them to himself, whom he has chosen before the foundation of the world.[180]

Both perfections of God, his eternity and his patience, provide Peter's readers with the key to understanding the perceived delay in Christ's return and the answer to the scoffers' ridiculing attacks; and both God's eternity and God's patience rest foursquare on Scripture. The answer to the false teachers' teaching rests on God's character, his eternity and his patience, in general. But the premise of this answer rests on Scripture itself, Old Testament Scripture: Psalm 90, verse 4, in particular, with the implications of Psalm 90, verses 3 and 12, also in view.

---

[180]   J. Calvin, *Commentaries on II Peter*, pp419-420.

APPLICATION

Peter's readers are to approach the subject of Christ's return not from a human but from a divine perspective. They are to contemplate it not so much in terms of the Greek, *chronos*, time computed in minutes, hours, months and years as in terms of the Greek *kairos*, a divinely appointed and appropriate season.

Of course, Christ will return within a human time-frame. Christ will come again in like manner as he was seen leaving (Ac.1:11). Every eye will see him, even those who pierced him and all the earth will wail on account of him (Re.1:7). The manner of his coming is clearly delineated. But the time of his coming is of a different nature. It is not for us to know the times and the seasons fixed by the Father's authority (Ac. 1:7). But concerning that day and hour no one knows, not even the angels of heaven, nor the Son, but the Father only (Mt. 24:36). God's eternity is sovereign. The issue is not the Father's flawed delay but rather his reasoned deliberation, not his pernicious covenant-breaking but his purposeful covenant-keeping. The delay is graciously part of the revelation of God. Its slowness is justly measured not vindictively dispensed. It is tender rather than tardy, caring rather than callous, sovereignly directive rather than maliciously destructive. God's patience is just.

As Peter's readers contemplate the perfections of God's eternity and patience, promised in the prophets, fulfilled in the Lord and confirmed in the apostles, this alone will answer the false ridicule of the scoffers concerning Christ's return. The Christian church does well to follow God's character and words, his eternity and patience, with similar intensity and to similar effect.

Chapter 19

CHRIST'S PROMISE

2 PETER 3:10

INTRODUCTION

Peter has urged his readers to remember Scripture (3:1, 2). He has itemized the views of the scoffers and false teachers who reject Scripture and deny the Lord's return (3:3, 4). Peter has done this by going back to Scripture and using it to refute his opponents. He has reassured his readers that things do not inevitably go on in the same cyclic fashion without change by citing the intrusive biblical events of creation and Flood (3:5-7). He has reaffirmed the reality of Christ's return in spite of its perceived delay by emphasizing God's character (3:8, 9) and will now do so by means of Christ's promise (3:10). And he has done all this precisely in accordance with his opening gamut about Scripture: "that you should remember the predictions of the holy prophets and the commandment of the Lord and Saviour through your apostles" (3:2). Intriguingly, everything in this third chapter of Peter's second letter follows that pattern and exhibits that *modus operandi*. What an illustration of this scriptural principle the whole of Chapter 3 is.

Specifically, Peter has turned to the Old Testament to refute the perceived delay by recalling Psalm 90 and expounding God's character: his eternal nature and purposeful patience. The method Peter adopts is that he quotes Psalm 90:4 to substantiate, first, God's eternity (3:8) and, then, he expounds Psalm 90:4, secondly, to explain God's patience (3:9). This was to redress doubts, which produced Christian apathy about or even denial of Christ's return. Peter now, at 3:10, underscores Christ's promise to correct misunderstandings about that return.

The striking thing is that Peter uses precisely the same scriptural method to make his point in verse 10 as he did in verses 8 and 9. In verses 8 and 9, Peter uses the words of the holy prophets from the Old Testament to drive his point home. Now, in verse 10, it is the command given by Christ through the apostles in the New Testament, which animates Peter's claim. God's character and Christ's promise, biblically orientated, effectively remove doubts and misunderstandings fostered by the scoffers and false teachers about Christ's return and about the delay that, according to them, belies that event. Here, too, in verse 10, particular aspects of Christ's return are taught by this methodology:

SUDDENNESS OF CHRIST'S RETURN (3:10ᵃ)
SOLEMNITY OF CHRIST'S RETURN (3:10ᵇ)

EXPOSITION

SUDDENNESS

"But the day of the Lord will come like a thief"
(3:10ᵃ).

The apostolic quotation original to Peter, but mentioned also by other apostles and sourced in Christ's own teaching, evinces the sudden and unexpected nature of Christ's return.

"But the day of the Lord" "The day of the Lord" *hēmera kuriou*: describes throughout Scripture God's judgemental interventions in history which point to that final day when God will definitively judge his enemies and vindicate the righteous. Of such, there is abundant biblical evidence, Old Testament and New, prophetic and apostolic.[181]

"Will come" *Hēxei* is first in the Greek sentence and emphatic. The following adversative "but" *de* separates verse 10 from verse 9 and stresses the emphasis. This makes abundantly clear that any inference from verse 9[b] that God's forbearance cancels the day of judgement is completely mistaken. "**The day of the Lord**" will undoubtedly take place regardless of any delay or prescribed patience on God's part connected with it. Of this, Peter's readers should be in no doubt whatsoever.

"Like a thief" is *hōs kleptēs*. The source of this "thief" imagery obviously comes from Jesus' own sayings (Mt. 24:43-44; Lu. 12:39-40; cf. Mk. 13:34-37). In this, the vigilance that a householder should have towards the sudden and unexpected intrusion of a thief is compared with the vigilance Jesus' disciples should have toward the coming of the of Son of Man. In the apostles, the image is naturally transferred to the vigilance necessary in the light of the sudden and unexpected nature of Christ's return. Here, again, the obvious scriptural principle is evident: the predictions of the holy

---

[181] Is. 13:6, 9; Eze. 13:5; 30:3; Jl. 1:15; 2:1, 11, 31; 3:14 – cf. Peter on Jl. 2:28-32 in Ac. 2:17-21; – Am. 5:18, 20; Obad. 15; Zep. 1:7, 14; Mal. 4:5 cf. Ac. 2:20; 1 Co. 5:5; 1 Th. 5:2; 2 Th. 2:2 – cf. in the New Testament also as the day of Christ or Lord Jesus Christ et var. [et = and; var = variations]; 1 Co. 1:8; 2 Co. 1:14; Ph. 1:6,10; 2:16.

prophets and the commandment of the Lord and Saviour through your apostles (3:2). "Peter does not simply quote the apostles, for he is an apostle, and he would have heard from Jesus' own lips the warning, 'Keep watch, because you do not know on what day your Lord will come. But understand this: If the owner of the house had known at what time of night the thief was coming, he would have kept watch and would not have let his house be broken into. So you also must be ready, because the Son of Man will come at an hour when you do not expect him'".[182]

Peter's knowledge of Paul's letters, to which he alludes here at 3:15-16, makes it possible that he knew 1 Thessalonians 5:2: "For you yourselves are fully aware that the day of the Lord will come like a thief in the night". The closeness of the format of 2 Peter 3:10 to 1 Thessalonians 5:2 makes this even more probable, though it does not necessarily imply dependence. The fact, too, that Paul mentions the sudden unexpectedness of a nocturnal break-in (1 Th. 5:3, 4) adds to the general closeness of the allusion.

The apostle John seems equally aware of this saying of Jesus. He refers pointedly to Jesus' words at Revelation 3:3, where Sardis had twice in its history been overcome through failure to watch and the enemy had scaled the precipitous sides of the Acropolis and broken in like a thief[183] and at Revelation 16:15, where neglect of watchfulness might lead to shameful judgement: ("Behold, I am coming like a thief! Blessed is the one who stays awake, keeping his garments on, that he may not go about naked and be seen exposed!"). The fact, too, that the angel with the little scroll "swore by him who lives for ever and ever, who created heaven and what is in it, the earth and what is in it, and the sea and what is in it, that there would be no more delay" (Re. 10:6) adds a poignant eschatological note which

---

[182]   D. Lucas & C. Green, *The Message Of 2 Peter & Jude*, p141 (Quotation is from Mt. 24:42-44).

[183]   M. Green, *2 Peter and Jude*, p149.

makes it clear that John shared the whole context of perceived delay and animated it with this sudden, unexpected but sure affirmation of last day events.

All of this "thief" imagery shows not only the sudden expectedness of the coming and the necessity for watchfulness in view of it but also Peter's methodology of adducing it all from the command given by our Lord and Saviour through the apostles (2 Pe. 3:2).

T.R. Schreiner sums it up helpfully:

> The image of the day coming like a thief is notable in Peter, for the readers are reminded to be ready. Circumstances may suggest that the day will not arrive. The false teachers may have scorned the notion of a sudden change in history. The day of the Lord, however, will arrive suddenly, and so no definite signs of its coming can be trumpeted. The signs that precede it, apparently, are ambiguous enough to lead to other conclusions. The teachers will be humiliated and judged when it comes, and Peter implored his readers to be ready.[184]

The point that consistently comes through in all this "thief" imagery, then, is not only the sense of loss that the break-in emphasizes but the need for watchfulness it requires. This begins with the clear and incisive instruction of Jesus himself in the Gospel records with their pointed allusions to the coming of the Son of Man and specifically to that of the "thief". The insistent note of watchfulness is struck not only by Peter in both the letters (1 Pe.5:4, 8, 9; 2 Pe.3:9-15) but also by Paul, John, James and the writer to the Hebrews on the same theme. This confirms not only the fact of

---

[184]   T. R. Schreiner, *1, 2 Peter, Jude*, p383.

Christ's return but also the methodology behind it: "the predictions of the holy prophets and the commandment of the Lord and Saviour through your apostles" (3:2).

SOLEMNITY

"and then the heavens will pass away with a roar, and the heavenly bodies will be burned up and dissolved, and the earth and the works that are done on it will be exposed" (3:10[b]).

Peter's explanation, now given, is couched in vivid apocalyptic from Old Testament and New Testament, and stresses the solemnity and fearfulness of the last day. The main gist of what he says is frighteningly plain, for he paints the lurid picture in broad-brush strokes, which reflect the three items he records:

1. The heavens will pass away with a roar.
2. The heavenly bodies will be burned up and dissolved.
3. The earth and the works that are done on it will be exposed.

It is as we look in further detail at each of these events that there is a degree of complexity.

To approach this, we scan some of the possible Old Testament and the New Testament background, namely, "the predictions of the holy prophets and the commandment of the Lord and Saviour through your apostles" (3:2), for these obviously filled Peter's mind. We look, then, at each of the three events in more detail.

Old Testament apocalyptic passages which may well have animated Peter here include Isaiah 13:10-13, 24:19; 34:4; 64:1-4; 66:16, Joel. 2:28-32 (cf. Ac. 2:17-21) and Micah 4:1, all of which

280

describe cataclysmic upheaval in heaven and on earth. Of these Isaiah 34:4 is typical and, perhaps, the most relevant to our discussion:

> "All the host of heaven shall rot away,
>   and the skies roll up like a scroll.
> All their host shall fall,
>   as leaves fall from the vine,
>   like leaves falling from the fig tree."

New Testament apocalyptic, of course, includes Jesus' sayings at Matthew 24:1-51 with parallels at Luke 21:5-36 and Mark 13:1-37. Specifically of interest are those passages in the Gospels in which Jesus specifically speaks of heaven and earth as "passing away" or "disappearing". Also, among the sayings of Jesus, the same verbal root from *parerchomai* ("go by, pass by"; "pass"; "pass away, come to an end, disappear") is used as occurs here at 2 Peter 3:10 (cf Mt. 5:18; 24:35; Mk. 13:31; Lu. 16:17; 21:33). Of these Gospel sayings, perhaps the most typical and relevant would be Mark 13:24-26, Jesus' quotation of Isaiah 13:10 and his subsequent comment:

> "But in those days, after that tribulation, the sun
> will be darkened, and the moon will not give its
> light, and the stars will be falling from heaven, and
> the powers in the heavens will be shaken. And then
> they will see the Son of Man coming in clouds with
> great power and glory".

It is also worth noting the reflection of Isaiah 34:4 through Matthew 24:29 to Revelation 6:12f especially verse 14: "The sky vanished like a scroll that is being rolled up, and every mountain and island was removed from its place" and that of Psalm 102:25-27 and Hebrews 1:10-12, is like a sort of "uncreation at the end". As well as elucidating Peter's methodology (3:2), this background also enhances the solemnity and fearfulness of the last day.

"And then the heavens will pass away with a roar"

"**Heavens**" is the usual plural term *ouranoi* and can be taken pictorially as the sky like an envelope above the world.[185] Some see it markedly "the spiritual sphere rather than just the sky (1:18; 3:5, 7, 13)"[186] or "that part of the creation that is unseen – the spiritual realm"[187]. It seems better, however, to take it in the more traditional biblical sense as the upper air, the entire universe, where "heavens" reverts back to verses 5 and 7 and where, in tandem with the earth, it refers to all that God has created in the universe.[188] So the picture is of the atmospheric heavens vanishing as John described events on the last day: "'The sky receded like a scroll, rolling up' (Rev. 6:14 see Isa. 34:4)".[189] J. MacArthur puts it in modern language that helpfully updates the nuance and certainly reflects the imagery well: "**Heavens** refers to the visible, physical universe of interstellar and intergalactic space. Like Christ, Peter foresaw the disintegration of the entire universe in an instant 'uncreation', not by any naturalistic scenario, but solely by God's omnipotent intervention".[190]

"**Will pass away with a roar**" "**Pass away**" or "disappear" is *pareleusontai* which, as earlier noted, is the same verbal root used of Christ's teaching about the heavens and earth passing away. "**Roar**" translates *roizēdon* a colourful onomatopoeic word found only here in the New Testament but with a vivid variety of usage elsewhere. It connotes the swish of an arrow through the air, the rumbling of thunder, the screaming of a descending lash, the rushing of mighty water, the hissing of a serpent and the crackling of flames. While allowing for the noise of the conflagration itself, R. Bauckham

185 M. Green, *2 Peter and Jude*, p150.
186 D. Lucas & C. Green, *The Message Of 2 Peter & Jude*, p142.
187 D. J. Moo, *2 Peter, Jude*, p189.
188 T. R. Schreiner, *1, 2 Peter, Jude*, p383.
189 S. J. Kistemaker, *James, Epistles of John, Peter, and Jude*, p336.
190 J. MacArthur, *2 Peter & Jude*, p124.

suggests "the thunder of the divine voice".[191] Most commentators associating the great noise with fire, a notable theme in both Peter's letters, hear at this point the noise of the "crackle of flames". The imagery is certainly arresting.

The first event describes disintegration of the universe in terms that strikingly affect both eye and ear and stress the solemnity and fearfulness of the day of the Lord.

"And the heavenly bodies will be burned up and dissolved"

"Heavenly bodies" is *stoicheia*. It means the "basics" and is used in this way of a list or table of first principles, as in the letters of the alphabet, notes on a scale of music or figures representing numbers. Paul uses the term, and interpretation is somewhat difficult, of "the elementary principles of the world" in a pejorative sense at Galatians 4:3, 9 (cf. Col. 2:8, 20) in a context where spiritual forces adverse to Christianity may well be at work. The word is used at Hebrews 5:12 of the "elementary truths of God's word" NIV, the basics of the Christian faith, in a non-pejorative sense. The word has some associations with Stoic philosophy. By the second century within Christian circles it was used, as by some here at 2 Peter 3:10 and 12, for the heavenly bodies in the sense of sun, moon, stars of the universe. Literally, the term describes the basic substance of the entire universe, the building blocks of the world, as it were, and is used in this sense in the Sibylline Oracles. Arising from this, there have been three main interpretations of *stoicheia* here as listed by D. Moo:[192] 1. The basic elements of the physical universe, according to most ancients: fire, water, air and earth. 2. The heavenly bodies: sun, moon, stars, and planets. 3. Spiritual beings.

---

[191]   R. J. Bauckham, *Jude, 2 Peter*, p315.

[192]   D. J. Moo, *2 Peter, Jude*, pp189-190.

1. The basic elements of the physical universe. The common understanding of *stoicheia* in terms of "first principles" as the building blocks or basic stuff of which things are made: fire, water, air, and earth is certainly a strong linguistic contender as an interpretation. It is found in this sense, as noted above, in the Sibylline Oracles, notably at 3:80-81 "all the elements (*stoicheia*) of the world will be widowed (*chēreusei*)" and in later Sibylline writers who interpreted these elements as air, earth, sea, light, heaven, days, nights (Sib.Or.2:206-7; 8:337-339), "a list which suggests not so much the four elements as the various constituent parts of the universe".[193] This view fits reasonably well into the context, for at verse 7, Peter announced that the totality of God's creation – "**heavens and earth**" are "**stored up for fire**". Now, he moves on one step further, claiming that the elements of the earth will actually be destroyed by fire. Furthermore in verse 12, Peter mentions only the "**heavens**" and the "elements" (*stoicheia*), which suggests that "elements" (*stoicheia*), and the earth are closely related.[194]

Against this view it is claimed that to identify the "elements" with heaven and earth is redundant in the context of this verse.[195] Further, it is suggested that a reference to the four elements or to this Sibylline list of elements is not very appropriate at 2 Peter 3:10 between a reference to the heavens and a reference to the earth, and also against this in verse 12 and in verse 10 also, *stoicheia* corresponds to the LXX of Isaiah 34:4, which refers to "all the powers of the heavens".[196]

---

[193] Sibylline Oracles 3:80-81 and 2:206-7, 8:337-39, cited in R. J. Bauckham, *Jude, 2 Peter*, pp315-6.

[194] D. J. Moo, *2 Peter, Jude*, p190.

[195] S. J. Kistemaker, *James, Epistles of John, Peter, and Jude*, p336.

[196] R. J. Bauckham, *Jude, 2 Peter*, p316.

2. The heavenly bodies. This is the position held by most commentators. The strength of this interpretation is based on the links with Old Testament texts especially Isaiah 34:4 and on the continuation of this theme through the New Testament especially at Revelation 6:12f and particularly v14, as noted earlier, where not only the stars will be dissolved but the sky rolled up like a scroll. S.J. Kistemaker writes: "The expression *elements* signifies the celestial bodies – the sun, moon, and stars. This prophecy reflects the Jewish belief that in the last day even the stars will be destroyed. Other parts of Scripture also indicate the heavenly bodies will be affected when the day of the Lord appears (e.g. Joel. 2:10; Matt. 24:29; Mark. 13:24; Rev. 6:12-13). As sun, moon, and stars are mentioned in the creation account (Gen. 1:16), so in the day of consummation these celestial light-bearers will disappear".[197]

This position is strengthened by the fact that stars and sky are differentiated and, in one version of the LXX of Isaiah 34:4 (B, Lucian), corrected by an emendation, it reads "all the powers of the heavens will melt".[198] *Stoicheia* as "heavenly bodies" is well attested by the second century.

Against this, would be the preference for *stoicheia* linguistically as in sense 1 and, possibly, the general lateness of second century evidence as weak support for such an interpretation.

3. Spiritual beings. This interpretation of *stoicheia* derives from usage at Galatians 4:3, 9 and Colossians 2:8, 20 as that of "spiritual powers", the "spiritual" nature of the "**heavens**"

---

[197]   S. J. Kistemaker, *James, Epistles of John, Peter, and Jude*, p336.
[198]   R.J. Bauckham, *Jude, 2 Peter*, p316 cf. P. H. Davids, *The Letters Of 2 Peter And Jude*, p286.

and the possibility that the "host of heaven" in the Hebrew of Isaiah 34:4 is not simply the stars but astral and angelic powers.

However, the view is not widely accepted. The difficulties of interpretation at Galatians 4:3, 9 and Colossians 2:8, 20, the alleged "physical" nature of "**heavens**" and Peter's general interest in the physical universe, with little predilection as to whether spiritual powers inhabit stars or planets, makes it the least likely interpretation of the three.

Regarding *stoicheia* argument 3 seems redundant. The strength of argument 1 is primarily linguistic usage, that of argument 2 Old Testament and related New Testament background. There seems, in the final analysis, no reason why arguments 1 and 2 could not be combined. What Peter seems to be saying is that, while the physical "**heavens**", the universe, meets dissolution, the "**heavenly bodies**" – the substance of the earth and, indeed, of the universe – melts, literally, melts down through burning. Interpretations 1 and 2 are not incompatible. It is the "elements" of heaven and earth which Peter avers will be substantially destroyed by burning. This second event of the last day simply supplements the first in terms of solemnity and fearfulness.

"And the earth and the works that are done on it will be exposed"

Difficulties of understanding the third event arise because of a mixture of variants and interpretation, which are largely focused on the final verb translated "**exposed**", of which there are at least two other variants:

1. "Disappear" *aphanisthēsontai* is notably weak in manuscript evidence, plausible in meaning though probably a scribal interpretation.

2. "Burned up" *katakaēsetai* has more manuscript support, fits into the context but is manifestly the easiest reading and, hence, suspect.

3. "Expose" or literally "found" *heurethēsetai* with reasonable manuscript support seems better solo than either negatively "will not be found" or combined with *luometha* "will be founded dissolved". Being obviously the most difficult reading of the three and, therefore, possibly producing the two and other variant explanatory readings, it is best accepted as original.

As to meaning, *heurethēsetai* literally "found" on the background of the Hebrew *masa* which has judicial overtones may be taken as "found before God" or "manifest before God" and, thus, **"exposed"** to God's judgment.[199]

"And the works that are done on it" could refer to the contents of the earth or to the persons within it. Again, while strict judgement would incline to the former, it need not exclude the latter. R. Bauckham's opinion as to **"earth"** *gē* is helpful: "it can easily mean the physical earth *as the scene of human history*, the earth as the dwelling-place of humanity (cf. Matt. 5:13; 10:34; Luke 12:49, 51; 18:8; John 17:4; and especially Rom. 9:28)".[200]

The third event drawing heaven, earth their elements and their contents to judgement completes the solemnity and fearfulness of that great and final assize; **"the heavens will pass away with a roar, and the heavenly bodies will be burned up and dissolved, and the earth and the works that are done on it will be exposed"** – what an awesome and fearful day that will be.

---

[199]   See especially both: R.J. Bauckham, *Jude, 2 Peter*, pp 316-321 and T.R. Schreiner, *1, 2 Peter, Jude*, pp 385-387.

[200]   R.J. Bauckham, *Jude, 2 Peter*, p320, (Emphasis his).

The combined effect of so many features of this climactic conclusion confirms the solemnity of Christ's return. The vivid imagery to both eye and ear of these truths, the source of Jesus' teaching in the prophets and the intriguing way this teaching is continued in both apostles and Apocalypse but, above all, the sense of loss and destruction at the final judgement is more than compensated for in a "new heavens and a new earth in which righteousness dwells" (3:13), for God's people and according to God's promise. This shows the purpose of God in all this and finally clarifies "the predictions of the holy prophets and the commandment of the Lord and Saviour through your apostles" (3:2), with which Peter prefaces this instruction. As a practical knowledge of God, the same is well worth both waiting for and living for.

APPLICATION

John Calvin's comments form an insightful guide here to application:

> What afterwards follows, respecting the burning
> of heaven and earth, requires no long explanation,
> if indeed we duly consider what is intended. For it
> was not his purpose to speak refinedely of fire and
> storm, and other things, but only that he might
> introduce an exhortation, which he immediately
> adds, even that we ought to strive after newness of
> life. For he thus reasons, that as heaven and earth
> are to be purged by fire, that they may correspond
> with the kingdom of Christ, hence the renovation
> of men is much more necessary. Mischievous, then,
> are those interpreters who consume much labour on

refined speculations, since the Apostle applies his
doctrine to godly exhortations.[201]

There is a real sense in which Calvin is right. If all our labours,
preaching and hearing, in the field particularly of apocalyptic,
are aimed at "refined speculations", we are wrongly motivated.
Knowledge and understanding we must seek, but always toward
applying what we hear to "godly exhortations".

Sadly, so much apocalyptic within and, indeed, without
Christian circles has been refined (and not so refined) speculation.
Scary horror images like Apocalypse Now, which equivocate more
to intergalactic wars with aliens than to facing biblical truth, can
reduce the word to entertainment rather than challenge. Crystal ball
gazing on the part of believers can leave them enquiring into details
which Jesus claimed neither to know nor to expect his people to want
to know either (Mk. 13:32; Ac. 1:7). The suddenness and solemnity
of the day of the Lord should produce faith and godliness on earth.
We must go, preach, and so hear truths like 2 Peter 3:10 that sinners
will be fearfully brought to repentance and faith and saints will be
encouragingly matured in sanctification, so that the glory will be all
of God who has ordained such awesome events.

"But the day of the Lord will come like a thief, and then the
heavens will pass away with a roar, and the heavenly bodies will be
burned up and dissolved, and the earth and the works that are done
on it will be exposed".

Peter recalls both aspects of Christ's return, its suddenness, and
its solemnity from Jesus' own teaching: the suddenness from the
vivid imagery of the thief in the night (Mt. 24:43-44; Lu. 12:39-40
cf. Mk.13:34-36); the solemnity from the graphic details of the Son
of Man's coming (Mk. 13:24-27; Mt. 24:29-31; Lu. 21:25-28). Both

---

[201] J. Calvin, *Commentaries on II Peter*, p420.

counter effectively the attacks of the scoffers and of false teachers, conform excitingly to the predictions of the holy prophets and the commandment of the Lord and Saviour through the apostles and induce practically not idle speculation but godly living. The message of Chapter 3, thus, gloriously continues.

> That day of wrath, that dreadful day,
> When heaven and earth shall pass away,
> What power shall be the sinner's stay?
> How shall he meet that dreadful day?
>
> When, shrivelling like a parchèd scroll,
> The flaming heavens together roll;
> When, louder yet, and yet more dread,
> Swells the high trump that wakes the dead;
>
> O, on that day, that wrathful day,
> When man to judgment wakes from clay,
> Be Thou the trembling sinner's stay,
> Though heaven and earth shall pass away!
> *Walter Scott, 1771-1832*[202]

---

[202] The Church Hymnary revised edition, Presbyterian Church in Ireland, Oxford 1997, Hymn 161.

Chapter 20

GODLY LIVING – OLD TESTAMENT

2 PETER 3:11-13

INTRODUCTION

Peter continues two major themes which he has already introduced in Chapter 3:

Scripture, Old Testament and New. Peter's declared purpose for his readers is to recall the words spoken in the past by the prophets and the commandment of the Lord and Saviour through the apostles (v.2). Hence, the creation, preservation and ultimate destruction of heavens and earth all come about "by the word" (vv5, 7). It is through the Old Testament word that the perfection of God's eternity and patience are seen and it is through the New Testament word that the suddenness and solemnity of Christ's return and the subsequent judgement of mankind are revealed (vv8-10). Now, in this next section, Peter goes on to explain how the destruction of the existing heavens and earth and the appearance of a new heavens and earth are confirmed both by the Old Testament prophets (vv11–13) and by the Lord through the New Testament apostles (vv14-16). God, through Scripture, is not only in sovereign control of everything but graciously reveals this sovereignty to reassure and encourage his doubting people. That is why Peter's readers are to recall these things from start to finish.

The Return of Christ and the Day of Judgement. Peter also majors on this theme in Chapter 3. The scoffers and false teachers deny both these events and add immoral behaviour to their disbelief. They also try to dissuade Peter's readers from the truth (vv3-7). But Peter assures them that these events will, indeed, take place and will lead to a fearful and yet glorious conclusion (vv8-13).

Peter now factors into the equation two other considerations, which, to some degree, have already been present, but are now made much more explicit:

APPLIED TEACHING

Applied teaching, practical knowledge of God, is the norm of all Scripture. Moral imperatives follow biblical indicatives. This is the general rule of all Scripture. Jesus had taught his followers not only to hear his words but also to put them into practice (Mt. 7:24-29). Indeed, that was the acid test in the context of the Sermon on the Mount by which false teachers were to be deemed genuine or otherwise: "Thus you will recognize them by their fruits" (Mt. 7:20), where "fruits" were the outcome of their own obedience to Christ's words evident in godly living (cf. Mt. 5-7 esp. 7:15 – 23).

Of course, apostolic instruction followed the same pattern, especially in the light of Christ's return and the day of judgement. All the apostles apply prophetic and dominical (Jesus') teaching in this particular way.[203] The false teachers and scoffers succumbed to immorality. Genuine believers, however, ought to be characterized by godliness. Chapter 3 of Second Peter is primarily about practical knowledge of God in this applied way. False teachers were marked by immorality. Genuine believers should be marked by godliness.

CONCLUDING REFLECTIONS

Concluding reflections, alongside applied teaching, also mark Second Peter, as Peter closes his letter. Peter refers to this as his "second" letter to his readers. In our understanding, his "first" letter was First Peter. Both letters are reminders to stimulate his readers to wholesome thinking (3:1,2). Peter had earlier in this second letter alluded to this "recall" theme in similar language (1:12-15). Perhaps these two points, one at the start the other at the conclusion of Peter's second letter, are another of those *inclusios* explaining the purpose of his writing. While references throughout this letter recall earlier themes, now, increasingly as he closes his writing, this recurs. Words, phrases, ideas pick up quite pointedly not only on earlier themes of Second Peter but on First Peter also – a further indication of authenticity – as though Peter gathers up his thoughts in a climactic conclusion. Chapter 3 brings practical knowledge of God to a very real, urgent, and climactic finale.

As both this section (3:11-13) and the next (3:14-16) fall into a natural concluding applicatory sequence, the former drawing inspiration from the Old Testament prophets, the latter from the New Testament apostles, we examine this section in the following terms:

---

[203] Applied teaching with moral imperatives arises from a wide spectrum of apostolic eschatological doctrine Ac. 3:19-21; – Peter speaking – 1 Co. 15:58; Ep. 5:10-16; Ph. 4:5; Col. 4:5; 1 Th. 4:13-5:11; 2 Th.1:11, 12; 2:15-17; 3:4-15; 1 Ti.6:14; 2 Ti.4:1-5; Tit.2:13-15; He. 10:19-25 esp. 25; 13:14-21; Ja. 4:13-17;1 Pe. 5:1-10; 1 Jn. 3:1-3; Jude 17-25; Re 22:7-21.

HOLINESS AND GODLINESS: MORAL IMPERATIVE   (vv11,12ᵃ)
ISAIAH AND THE PROPHETS: BIBLICAL MOTIVATION   (vv12ᵇ,13)

EXPOSITION

HOLINESS AND GODLINESS: MORAL IMPERATIVE

"Since all these things are thus to be dissolved, what sort of people ought you to be in lives of holiness and godliness, waiting for and hastening the coming of the day of God" (3:11, 12ᵃ).

The moral imperative arising from Peter's biblical and eschatological teaching about the last day should lead his Christian readers to holy and godly living.

"Since all these things are thus to be dissolved" "All these things" *toutōn pantōn* probably refers to the totality of events mentioned in verse 10: "the heavens will pass away with a roar, and the heavenly bodies will be burned up and dissolved, and the earth and the works that are done on it will be exposed", whatever the particular determination of "heavens" "heavenly bodies" "earth" or "works" may be, whether predominantly physical or personal. These may also include, of course, those events in the further antecedents mentioned in verse 7. **"Dissolved"** *luomenōn* is from the same verbal root *luō* as is used in verses 10 and 12. This tends to confirm the interpretation of **"all these things"** given above. Its form is present passive participle and, having a future definitive nuance in respect of "the day", it also gives the impression that the process is already taking place, if waiting final, cataclysmic completion. The present form of things is already passing away and will ultimately do so. Therefore, ultimate trust ought not to reside in ephemeral things.

Life for the Christian ought not to be moulded by passing earthly entities, but by abiding, eternal verities.

"What sort of people" is *potapous.* The term is used positively as a question by the disciples about Jesus' person and pejoratively by the Pharisee of the sinful woman approaching Jesus in his home (Mt. 8:27; Lu. 7:39). Here, however, it may be more as, indeed, also at Matthew 8:27, an exclamation of astonishment not requiring a response, with the nuance, "how wonderful, how marvellous"!! This seems to be the case more particularly at Mark 13:1 and 1 John 3:1. It certainly heightens anticipation in a positive way in the context: what wonderful, marvellous people ought you to be in lives of holiness and godliness, as you wait for and hasten the coming of the day of God!

"In lives of holiness and godliness" *en hagiais anastrophais kai eusebeiais* is literally "in holy forms of behaviour and godly acts". One remarkable feature here is the *plural* form of both nouns, which stresses not only the practical side of the holiness and godliness, but also suggests pursuing many different kinds of holy behaviour and godly activities. Another intriguing aspect is the fact that Peter in his first letter mentioned the importance of holiness "in all your conduct" in a context of hardship and persecution (1 Pe.1:15) and in his second letter in a context of false teaching and immoral living as a fundamental and an extension of basic faith (2 Pe.1:3; 5-7). Both references in both letters occur early on and may well have a controlling influence on the specific exhortations to both holiness and godliness, which Peter later gives throughout the remainder of both letters. Peter is here actively recalling teaching already given. As the scoffers and false teachers are marked by amoral and immoral acts, so Peter's Christian readers are to be characterized by holy behaviour and godly living. Such should be the abiding features of their lives.

"Waiting for" is *prosdokōntas* and is repeated three times here in verses 12, 13 and 14 and so becomes a prominent theme towards the end of the letter. It designates the eager expectation that believers should have in anticipating the coming of Christ and in the fulfilment of God's future promises.[204] Peter H. Davids comments helpfully:

> The connection of this verb to eschatological hope is common in the NT, for the question of whom one is waiting for comes up in Matt 11:3 (par. Luke 7:19; cf. Luke 3:15) and future expectation (or the danger of a lack of it) in Matt 24:50 (par. Luke 12:46). As seen in the teaching of Jesus, this expectation also has the sense of being prepared for the Day. There is a moral side to waiting; it is not merely an intellectual stance. It is, in fact, very similar to the idea of 'watching' (often in the teaching of Jesus, and of course also in the letters, and translated 'be alert' in 1 Pet 5:8 and a number of other places in the NT). This fits with the likely origin of this idea of waiting, that is, Hab. 2:3, 'Though [the revelation] linger, wait for it; it will certainly come and will not delay'.[205]

"And hastening the coming of" **"Hastening"** is *speudontas* and like **"waiting for"** is a present active participle. It derives from *speudō* "I hasten" and should not be taken as intransitive or reflexive "exert oneself" but rather with *parousian* "coming". *Speudō* can also mean "strive", "make an effort", "be eager" and Peter uses the substantive form at 1:5 where "make every effort" is the meaning. If this is the sense here, as some take it both reflexively and intransitively, it would mean: "as you wait eagerly for the day of God to come". They are

204 T. R. Schreiner, *1, 2 Peter, Jude,* p390.
205 P. H. Davids, *The Letters Of 2 Peter And Jude,* p290.

to both practically and personally anticipate and encourage the day of Christ's return.

Calvin understands it proverbially and translates "Hasten slowly (*festina lentè*)".[206] Indeed, "hasten" rather than "strive" is a more natural meaning (cf. Lu.2:16; 19:5, 6; Ac. 20:16; 22:18) and the sense, if difficult, is better rendered, transitively "hastening the coming of".

But how can believers "hasten" or "speed" the coming of the day of God? Does this not interfere with the idea of God's sovereignty? Various answers have been given to the first of these questions for example: by evangelism – "And this gospel of the kingdom will be proclaimed throughout the whole world as a testimony to all nations, and then the end will come (Mt. 24:14); by prayer – "Your kingdom come" (Mt. 6:10 cf. Re. 8:4); by Christian behaviour – "what sort of people ought you to be in lives of holiness and godliness, waiting for and hastening the coming of the day of God" (v11 cf. 1 Pe. 2:12); by repentance and obedience – "Repent therefore, and turn again, that your sins may be blotted out, that times of refreshing may come from the presence of the Lord, and that he may send the Christ appointed for you, Jesus, whom heaven must receive until the time for restoring all the things about which God spoke by the mouth of his holy prophets long ago" (Ac. 3:19-21 – Peter's words). The Rabbis went as far as suggesting that if Jews would repent or perfectly keep the Torah for one day the Messiah would come!

However, how does this "hastening" or "speeding" the day of God's coming relate to God's sovereignty? Douglas J. Moo answers that second question well:

> We may think that the idea of Christians hastening
> the coming of Christ takes away from the sovereignty

---

[206] J. Calvin, *Commentaries on II Peter*, p421.

of God, for doesn't the Bible make clear that God determines the time of the end? We have here another instance of the biblical interplay between human actions and God's sovereignty. Human acts are significant and meaningful, but God is nevertheless fully sovereign. As Bauckham argues, what Peter is suggesting is that God graciously factors his peoples' actions into his determination of the time of the end.[207]

"The coming of the day of God" The replacement of the "day of Christ" or the "day of the Lord" with the "**day of God**" is striking. M. Green comments adroitly: "The remarkable expression for the usual 'day of the Lord' (attested here in some MSS) smacks of the Old Testament 'Day of Yahweh', as does the only other New Testament occurrence, Revelation 16:14. The return of Jesus Christ is the *day of God*".[208]

Peter thus suggests many Christian activities to fill this waiting period, which will, in fact, paradoxically yet biblically, 'speed on' the 'sovereign' day of God's coming in Christ's return. Believers *can* do something to speed things on in regard to this sovereign day!

ISAIAH AND THE PROPHETS: BIBLICAL MOTIVATION

"because of which the heavens will be set on fire and dissolved, and the heavenly bodies will melt as they burn! But according to his promise we are waiting for new heavens and a new earth in which righteousness dwells" (3:12^b, 13).

---

[207]   D. J. Moo, *2 Peter, Jude*, p198, compare R. J. Bauckham, *Jude, 2 Peter*, p325.

[208]   M. Green, *2 Peter and Jude*, pp153-154, (Emphasis his).

A consideration of the words of Isaiah and of the prophets will drive Peter's readers through the destruction of the present heavens and earth to the discovery of a new heavens and earth. Here, the predictions of the holy prophets have a definitive and motivating part to play for believers.

"Because of which the heavens will be set on fire and dissolved, and the heavenly bodies will melt as they burn!" The major motivation behind this section comes from the Old Testament, mainly from Isaiah though from others as well, and is then picked up eventually in the New Testament. Peter firstly indicates the destruction of the existing heavens and earth. The language and theme is strongly reminiscent of verse 10. Indeed, it has been described as a refrain of verse 10. It also harks back to the details of verse 7. Indeed, these three verses 7, 10 and 12[b] form a progression regarding the destruction of the present heavens and earth: verse 7 speaks of the present heavens and earth being reserved for fire; verse 10 recalls the heavens disappearing with a roar, probably of crackling fire, and the heavenly bodies being destroyed by burning; verse 12[b] confirms the heavens being dissolved by fire and the heavenly bodies melting in the heat. There are, of course, differences and difficulties – the definition of "heavens" "heavenly bodies" "earth" and "works", the differential between verses 10 and 12[b], namely, the absence of "earth" in verse 12[b]. However, the general lines are clear: reserved (v7); actioned (v10) confirmed (v12[b]). Simon J. Kistemaker distinguishes this:

> Notice also a difference of purpose in relation to these two texts. In verse 10 Peter presents the manner, that is, how the day of the Lord will come; in verse 12[b] he indicates the result of this day, namely, 'the destruction of the heavens by fire'.[209]

---

[209]   S. J. Kistemaker, *James, Epistles of John, Peter, and Jude*, p339.

In all this, verses: 7, 10, 12[b], Peter here forcefully describes the destruction of the present heavens and earth in language reminiscent of Isaiah and other Old Testament writers. The new feature, implicit in verses 7 and 10, but quite explicit in verse 12 is the verb **"melt"**. **"Melt"** is *tēketai*, the present passive from *tēkō* (passive: melt, be melted, dissolve), which in the context conveys a future sense. It is this term **"melt"**, which in the general context of **"fire"**, recalls the Old Testament background:

"If thou wouldest open the heaven, trembling will take hold upon the mountains from thee, and they shall melt (*takēsontai*), as wax melts (*tēketai*) before the fire" (Is. 64:1.2) LXX; "And all the powers of the heavens shall melt", (*takēsontai pasai hai dunameis tōn ouranōn*) and the sky shall be rolled up like a scroll; and all the stars shall fall like leaves from a vine, and as leaves fall from a fig-tree" (Is. 34:4) LXX; [210] "And the mountains shall be shaken under him, and the valleys shall melt (*takēsontai*) like wax before the fire, and as water rushing down a declivity" (Mi. 1:4) LXX. [211]

Isaiah among the Old Testament prophets provides the specific background from which Peter describes this fearful dissolution of the present heavens and earth, with the creation of new heavens and a new earth (Is.65:17; 66:22) and then, Peter points to the fulfilment of these prophetic predictions in the New Testament, both destruction and renewal. What prophets predict; apostles confirm.

"But according to his promise we are waiting for new heavens and a new earth in which righteousness dwells"

Peter teaches how Christians not only look forward to the

---

[210]   Is. 64:1, 2 LXX cf. Is. 34:4 LXX [*Vaticanus*].
[211]   cf. Mi. 1:4 LXX.

destruction of the universe but to its renewal.[212] Again, this teaching is rooted firmly in the Old Testament, particularly in Isaiah among the prophets.

"But according to his promise" The adversative **"but"** *de* turns our attention from the destruction of the old to the creation of the new. **"Promise"** *epaggelma* is mentioned in verses 4 and 9 and at 1:4, the root of the noun being the same with a slightly different ending. Certainly in this final chapter, it focuses on Christ's return as the day of the Lord. The promise is questioned by the scoffers at verse 4 and affirmed by the apostle at verse 9. Here, at the verse 13, it is anticipated, as something Peter and his readers are looking forward to in terms of fulfilment. It will surely come, for the Lord has promised it. Again, as in verses 3:7; 3:10; 3:12^b, so in verses 1:4; 3:4 and 3:9, the same climax. What prophets predict; apostles confirm.

"Waiting for" *prosdokōmen,* mentioned again, is here a verb not a participle as at verses 12 and 14. But the effect is similarly cumulative and climactic. They are eagerly awaiting the destruction of the universe (v12), its renewal (v13) and keenly anticipating its results in Christian behaviour (v14). The entire effect is again climactic. What prophets predict; apostles confirm.

"New heavens and a new earth" **"New"** is *kainos,* new in nature or in quality not *neos,* new in time or origin.[213] **"New heavens and a new earth"** is emphatic being first in the Greek sentence and being without the definite article. This combines heavens and earth in a unity, a feature accentuating the emphasis.

The biblical background is predominantly from Isaiah. While

---

[212]   D. J. Moo, *2 Peter, Jude,* p199.

[213]   A.A. Hoekema, *The Bible and The Future* (Grand Rapids; Eerdmans. 1979), p280, cited in D. Lucas & C. Green, *The Message Of 2 Peter & Jude,* p148.

Isaiah 11:6-9 and Isaiah 32:1-20 hint in this direction, Peter would probably have two passages specifically in mind regarding "**new heavens and a new earth**":

> "For behold, I create new heavens
>> and a new earth,
> and the former things shall not be remembered
>> or come into mind" (Is. 65:17).

> "'For as the new heavens and the new earth
>> that I make
> shall remain before me, says the Lord,
>> so shall your offspring and your name remain'"
> (Is. 66:22).

This theme of restoration or recreation seems to be later developed in other New Testament references as here in 2 Peter 3:13. Jesus speaks of the renewal of all things, when the Son of Man sits on his glorious throne (Mt. 19:28). Peter proclaims the coming of Christ, even Jesus, who must remain in heaven until the time comes for God to restore everything, as he promised long ago through his holy prophets (Ac. 3:20, 21). Paul writes that the creation itself will be liberated from its bondage to decay and brought into the glorious freedom of the children of God (Ro. 8:21). John climaxes this theme in the two closing chapters of Scripture introducing it with a clear demarcation between the emergence of the new and the dissolution of the old world in language reminiscent of the opening chapters of Scripture: "Then I saw a new heaven and a new earth, for the first heaven and the first earth had passed away, and the sea was no more"(Re. 21:1). "Paradise Lost will become Paradise Regained, and God's will shall eventually be done alike in earth and heaven".[214] The pattern again recalls 3:2: "the predictions of the holy prophets and

---

[214]   M. Green, *2 Peter and Jude*, p154.

the commandment of the Lord and Saviour through your apostles". What an amazing world of newness and righteousness Christians have to look forward to!

How precisely this would come about neither Peter nor, indeed, the New Testament clarifies in definitive detail. "Did Peter teach that the old heavens and earth will be annihilated and that God will create something brand new? Or is the idea that God will purify the old world and create out of the same elements a new one? It is difficult to be sure, and we would do well to be cautious in postulating how God will fulfill his promises".[215]

Some have held from the earliest days a view of annihilation as, for example, Justin Martyr and Minucius Felix, whereas Irenaeus and Origen argued for purification and renovation. R. Bauckham, analysing biblical and Jewish apocalyptic writings on the subject, comments: "Such passages emphasize the radical discontinuity between the old and the new, but it is nevertheless clear that they intend to describe a renewal, not an abolition, of creation".[216] Anthony Hoekema seems to agree, for he claims that what is taught here, is "not the emergence of a cosmos totally other than the present one, but the creation of a universe which, though it has been gloriously renewed, stands in continuity with the present one".[217]

Whichever the case, Christians look forward to a future world that is real, the birth of a brave new world. They "look forward" to this world, the day of God, the fulfilment of God's promises. What a

---

[215] T.R. Schreiner, *1, 2 Peter, Jude,* p392, who cites, Overstreet, "2 Peter 3:10-13", pp362-65, for the former, and both Wolters, "2 Peter 3:10", pp405-13 and Thiede, "A Pagan Reader of 2 Peter", pp79-91 for the latter.

[216] R. J. Bauckham, *Jude, 2 Peter,* p326.

[217] A.A. Hoekema, *The Bible and the Future* (Grand Rapids; Eerdmans, 1979), p280 cited in D. Lucas & C. Green, *The Message Of 2 Peter & Jude,* p148.

prospect! How gloriously the promise and purpose of God is fulfilled in this new heavens and new earth (3:13)!

"In which righteousness dwells" From the beginning and throughout his letter Peter has been anticipating this glorious promise and future hope. So now at the close, he is gathering up the threads of this theme and reminding his readers of it. Believers will participate in the divine nature and escape the corruption in the world caused by evil desires, for they have, through the righteousness of our God and Saviour Jesus Christ received a faith of equal standing with the apostles (1:1, 4). They will, thus, receive a rich welcome into the eternal kingdom of our Lord and Saviour Jesus Christ, (1:11). For all the horrific scene around them, Noah, a herald of righteousness (2:5) and Lot, a righteous man (2:7), were preserved and rescued by the sovereign grace of God. So believers, by dint of that preserving and redeeming grace, will eventually live in the new heavens and new earth, **"in which righteousness dwells"** (3:13). And it is no transitory dwelling but a permanent one, for **"dwells"** is *katoikei* not *paroikei*. The new heavens and earth will provide a continuity of life analogous to here but on a transformed level and in an eternal, permanent setting. This further enhances the glorious prospect before them. 'Paradise Lost' in this striking way, as John Milton suggests, has become 'Paradise Regained'. What a glorious promise and a glorious fulfilment, all according to the purpose and plan of God in Scripture, the return of Christ will be.

APPLICATION

In Paris 1953, David Helm recalls how Samuel Beckett premiered his greatest play, *Waiting for Godot (En Attendant Godot)*.[218] The play was more about "waiting" than it was about "Godot", a mystical

---

[218]   D. R. Helm, *1 & 2 Peter and Jude*, p263.

figure who never arrives. "Godot" made up of the English word "God" and the French "ot" combines to give the idea of a diminutive and endearing god-like figure who will meet every need. The play, about waiting, pendulates between endless frenetic activity and dazed purposeless boredom.

How different is Peter's prescription for waiting for the day of God! Peter's "waiting" is marked by tiptoe like anticipation full of joy, excitement, interest and purpose. It focuses not on cyclic unreality but on a definitive arrival of the living and true God. It aims to produce lives of holiness and godliness, in plurality: holinesses and godlinesses. It heads up and gives purpose to sanctification in day-to-day living. That is what waiting for God is all about for the Christian. Spurgeon puts it this way: "As you walk the streets of London, remember you've got the reputation of God in your hands".[219]

This waiting is driven by Scripture, particularly in this instance, the promise of the day of God in the Old Testament. The blend of dissolution and transformation animates the whole scene. The present heavens and earth become the new heavens and earth, a virtual unity. As Anthony Hoekema puts it: "Since where God dwells, there heaven is, we conclude that in the life to come heaven and earth will no longer be separated, as they are now, but will be merged. Believers will therefore continue to be in heaven as they continue to live on the new earth".[220]

It is a transformed unity that purposefully links present existence in a fallen context with future life in a glorious scenario. A.A. Hodge comments "As to the location of the place in which Christ and His glorified spouse will hold their central home throughout eternity,

---

[219]   C. H. Spurgeon, cited by D. R. Helm, *1&2 Peter and Jude*, p266.
[220]   A.A. Hoekema, *The Bible and the Future*, p285.

a strong probability is raised that it will be our present Earth, first burned with fire and then gloriously replenished".[221]

Edward Donnelly helpfully directs avoiding both dangers of apathetic neglect and hyper-spiritualized surrealism and closes our discussion as he writes:

> An awareness of the future renovation of the earth casts a flood of light on many statements of the prophets and psalmists which we can tend to overlook. Some Christians believe that these prophecies refer to a golden age before Christ's return. But others spiritualize them completely, bleeding them of any material fulfilment and seeing them as no more than pictures of spiritual blessings. Yet there is a literalness here which we should not ignore, for they are telling us what will indeed happen to this present world.[222]

We wait for the day of God driven by the words of Scripture, like that: "that you should remember the predictions of the holy prophets and the commandment of the Lord and Saviour through your apostles" (3:2). "But according to his promise we are waiting for new heavens and a new earth in which righteousness dwells" (3:13). What prophets predict; apostles confirm. What a day, more, what a life that will be! Hallelujah.

---

221 A.A. Hodge, *The Confession of Faith*, 1869, repr. London: Banner of Truth, 1958, p383, cited E. Donnelly, *Heaven and Hell*, p115.

222 E. Donnelly, *Heaven and Hell*, p114.

Chapter 21

PRACTICAL KNOWLEDGE

GODLY LIVING – NEW TESTAMENT

2 PETER 3:14–16

INTRODUCTION

Peter encourages moral imperatives through biblical and eschatological indicatives. He applies teaching about the Second Coming in terms of the practical knowledge of God. The destruction of the old world and the re-creation of the new must find expression in the lives of his readers and, by implication, in all Christians, who hold that biblical hope not just in theory but in reality. Peter's teaching method goes back to his theme at 3:2: "the predictions of the holy prophets and the commandment of the Lord and Saviour through your apostles".

In 2 Peter 3:11-13, Peter enjoins holy and godly Christian living motivated by the Old Testament prophets, chiefly Isaiah. In 2 Peter 3:14-16, he requires spotless and blameless behaviour from believers on the background of the New Testament apostles, notably Paul. This lifestyle stands in stark contrast with the immoral and permissive ways of the scoffers and false teachers.

Peter continues to factor in his concluding reflections at the close of his letter. As noted in the last section, but now increasingly, words and phrases recur, backward references spring up not only to this second letter but to First Peter as well, and *inclusios*, bracketing earlier teaching with closing exhortations, pour out. It is obvious that Peter is rounding off his thoughts and bringing his letter to a climactic conclusion.

The format here is similar to that of the previous section. We categorize it accordingly:

SPOTLESSNESS AND BLAMELESSNESS: MORAL IMPERATIVE (14-15ᵃ)
PAUL AND THE APOSTLES: BIBLICAL MOTIVATION (15ᵇ-16)

EXPOSITION

SPOTLESSNESS AND BLAMELESSNESS:
MORAL IMPERATIVE

"Therefore, beloved, since you are waiting for these, be diligent to be found by him without spot or blemish, and at peace. And count the patience of our Lord as salvation" (3:14, 15ᵃ).

The moral imperative of Peter's teaching about the old and new worlds, couched in both poignant and reflective language calls his readers to a spotless and blameless life-style. Every phrase in this section adds its own contribution to this cumulative picture.

"Therefore, beloved" *Dio, agapētoi* both in the emphatic position of "therefore" at the beginning of the Greek sentence and in the warm sentiments of the title "beloved", picking up on the same address from 3:1 and 8, marks the beginning of a new section though closely related to the former. A similar expression of division at 3:17 is not as strong. This particular introduction at 3:14 signals the close of the letter and recalls the close bond of relationship between Peter and his readers.

"Since you are waiting for these" **"Waiting for"** is again *prosdokōntes*. It continues this same verbal form used by Peter at verse 12 for looking forward to the "day of God" and at verse 13 for awaiting "new heavens and a new earth". This forms a concluding theme to his letter, nuanced by a sense of anticipation and expectancy, which recalls the alertness of Jesus' command to his disciples to "watch" and the urgency of Peter's own words earlier to the crippled beggar in Jerusalem to "look at us". **"These"** translates *tauta*, a plural, and is better than "this", the singular. The expression includes all those things Peter has been mentioning: the patience of the Lord, the dissolution of the old world but is, perhaps, most referring to the immediate antecedent, a new heavens and a new earth. Michael Green catches the atmosphere well when he comments pithily: "The look of hope must produce the life of holiness".[223]

"Be diligent" is *spoudasate* "to be zealous", "to make an effort". It seems to be a favourite word of Peter's. He used it in the early stages of his letter and, now, it recurs *inclusio*-like at the end. His readers are to "make every effort", the same word, to add to their faith (1:5) and "be all the more diligent" to make their calling and election sure (1:10). Personally, Peter will "make every effort" to see that after his departure, presumably his death, they will always be able to remember these things (1:15) Paul, too, uses this same Greek verb

---

[223]   M. Green, *2 Peter and Jude*, p155.

quite a number of times, which is interesting in the light of Peter's remarks about Paul's letters in this context (Ga. 2:10; Ep. 4:3; 1 Th. 2:17; 2 Ti. 2:15; 4:9, 21; Tit. 3:12 cf. He. 4:11).

Peter Davids helpfully comments:

> The appropriate lifestyle of a follower of Jesus does not just happen; it requires effort, especially since the forces of the surrounding culture will attempt to make apprentices of Jesus adjust their behavior back to that of the majority culture.[224]

It is exactly the same with the majority culture today. The same warm conclusion, wrapt anticipation and earnest diligence is intentional. The world does not live that way.

"To be found by him" "Found" is *heurethēnai*. This is the object of the exercise of their effort. Again, Peter has just used the term at 3:10, though there are quite a number of variants of which this particular word is the most difficult and, probably, the most likely reading. There, in verse 10, it is used of the earth being "exposed" in a judicial sense or "found" before the judgement of God. Here, in verse 14, Peter enjoins his readers to exert themselves in this direction, so that ultimately their appearance before their Lord will be pleasing. The "reflective" aspect of Peter's penmanship is again evident. T.R. Schreiner notes a wide spectrum of references to "be found" in this judicial sense, many of which again, are Pauline (2 Pe. 3:10 cf. 1 Co. 4:2; 15:15; Ga. 2:17; Ph. 3:9; 1 Pe. 1:7; Re. 5:4).[225] **"By him"** is *auto* and is best taken in a judicial rather than a cultic sense, namely, "before him" and accords well with the judicial "found".

Douglas Moo adroitly notes:

---

[224] P. H. Davids, *The Letters Of 2 Peter And Jude*, p 294.
[225] T. R. Schreiner, *1, 2 Peter, Jude*, p393.

'To be found' has judicial overtones. It conjures up the scene of the court of law, where the judge 'finds' defendants guilty or innocent. Peter, we suggested, used this same verb in a similar manner in verse 10, speaking about the whole physical earth being 'found' before God – that is, 'laid bare' to his searching and infallibly correct judgment.[226]

"Without spot or blemish, and at peace" "Without spot or blemish"** is *aspiloi kai amōmētoi*. *Aspilos* "without spot", though not an Old Testament word, describes sacrificial animals in a New Testament context (1 Pe. 1:19). *Amōmos* "without blemish" is the usual LXX (Greek Old Testament) term for sacrificial victims without defect. Peter here uses the rare word *amōmētos* "without blemish", which means substantially the same and continues the sacrificial metaphor, though also including the idea of moral blamelessness. "The two words describe Christians as morally pure, metaphorically an unblemished sacrifice to God".[227]

"And at peace" The **"peace"** *eirēnē*, can be either the peace of reconciliation (Ro. 5:1), relating to justification or the peace of a satisfied conscience (Ph. 4:7), relating to sanctification. It is less likely here to mean "peace" with fellow Christians as well, though of course it should involve that. Peter writes, at the beginning of this letter, that peace in abundance might be his readers' experienced blessing (1:2) and now recalls this at the close (3:14), a further *inclusio* phenomenon.

Interesting from our point of view is the fact that, where this double idea of "spotless and blameless" occurs, it is necessary fruit of eternal life, though not necessarily implying moral perfection in

---

226   D. J. Moo, *2 Peter, Jude,* p207, (Emphasis his).
227   R. J. Bauckham, *Jude, 2 Peter,* p 327.

this life.[228] The majority of these double or single references are in an eschatological context and many of them refer to the state Christians or the church ought to be found in when Christ returns (Ep. 1:4; 5:27; Ph. 2:15; Col. 1:22; Jude 24; Re. 14:5). There is no idea of sinless or moral perfection of the believer in this life here.

Equally interesting as relating to reflection and recall, is the fact that precisely the opposite positive description, the Greek term minus the *negative a prefix*, is used by Peter to describe the false teachers previously in this letter. They are "blots" *spiloi* and "blemishes" *mōmoi* (2:13), another possible *inclusio* with 3:14. Additionally, these double terms are used in their negative and in virtually the same form to describe Christ's sacrificial death by Peter in his first letter: "without blemish" *amōmou* or "spot" *aspilou* (1 Pe. 1:19), a possibly even wider *inclusio* yet again, if Petrine authorship of both letters is accepted. John MacArthur makes the interesting observation that "**spotless**" can denote Christian character and "**blameless**" Christian reputation.[229] At any rate, the main message of these comparative references is clear: looking to Christ to become Christ-like marks the Christian who truly waits for the Lord's return, while the opposite features characterize those who do not, regardless of their profession.

Calvin, as ever, notes penetratingly:

> But we must notice what he says, that we ought to be *found blameless* by Christ; for by these words he intimates, that while the world engages and engrosses the minds of others, we must cast our eyes on the Lord, and he shews at the same time what is real integrity, even that which is approved by

---

228 J. Calvin, *Commentaries on II Peter*, p423; T. R. Schreiner, *1, 2 Peter, Jude*, p393.

229 J. MacArthur, *2 Peter & Jude*, p133.

his judgment, and not that which gains the praise of men.[230]

"And count the patience of our Lord as salvation" "Count" is *hēgeisthe* "think" "consider" "regard" and is emphatic in meaning. Peter has used it earlier of himself thinking it right to refresh his readers' memory (1:13) and of the false teachers who think it pleasure to carouse in broad daylight (2:13). Critically for our purpose here, he has just used the same verb at verse 9 to describe how the scoffers wrongly regard the delay in the Second Coming as "slowness" on God's part. Peter, of course, argues both at verse 9 and at verse 15 that the delay is an example of God's "patience" *makrothumia*. Christians are to "count" or "regard" the patience of our Lord not as slowness but as patience, indeed, as he puts it here, as **"salvation"**. "Salvation" *sōtēria* covers, of course, the entire gamut of covenant grace in Scripture. Here, however, at 3:15 as elsewhere also, Peter uses the term "salvation" in an eschatological sense of ultimate deliverance from sin at the end of life, as seen, for example, in his first letter (1 Pe.1:5, 9, 10). Again, concluding reflections here in Second Peter, as in respect of both letters, provide meaningful *inclusios*. These are clearly Peter's reminders to his readers of an obligation to godly living. They equally clearly contrast with the thinking of the false teachers and scoffers. Not only the way in which Peter's readers *live* should be markedly different from these divisive heretics. The way in which they *think* should be totally different as well.

Douglas Moo makes the point in this way:

> Peter would not be writing as he does to these believers if some of them, at least, were not in danger of succumbing to the false teachers' pernicious influence. As a result, he wants them to consider

---

[230]   J. Calvin, *Commentaries on II Peter*, p422, (Emphasis his).

the time they have before Christ's return as an
opportunity to secure their relationship before the
Lord.[231]

Peter thus puts the moral imperative to live "without spot or
blemish" (v14), motivated by Christ's return. He goes on now to
give Paul and the apostles in the New Testament as the biblical
motivation for such behaviour.

PAUL AND THE APOSTLES: BIBLICAL MOTIVATION

**"just as our beloved brother Paul also wrote to
you according to the wisdom given him, as he
does in all his letters when he speaks in them
of these matters. There are some things in them
that are hard to understand, which the ignorant
and unstable twist to their own destruction, as
they do the other Scriptures" (3:15[b], 16).**

Just as Isaiah and the prophets in the Old Testament drive
Peter's readers to holiness and godliness, so Paul and the apostles in
the New Testament should stir them to a spotless and the blameless
lifestyle. We have already noted how many of Peter's sentiments
are echoed in Paul and in the other apostles. So, Peter here warmly
describes Paul as a Christian colleague, endowed with the wisdom of
revelation, who has written to Peter's readers, and who, indeed, in all
his letters refers to the same subjects as did Peter. Admittedly, within
Paul's writings, there are issues difficult to interpret. But some, who
do not understand Paul, and perhaps do not want to understand him
are, as a result, insecure in matters of doctrine. Sadly, these people
distort what Paul writes, and do this to their own destruction. Peter
obviously has the false teachers, scoffers and their followers in mind
here, as he writes.

---

[231]   D. J. Moo, *2 Peter, Jude*, p209.

The implication of this, here at the close of Peter's letter, the "bottom line" as it were, is that Paul writes "Scripture". This has massive implications as Peter well knows. Scripture, whether Old or New Testament, the words of the holy prophets or the commandment given by the Lord and Saviour through the apostles, is the real motivation for godly living, whether the subject is Christ's return or anything else. The glaring moral difference in behaviour between true Christians, hopefully Peter's readers, and the false teachers and scoffers, is inextricably bound up with belief, understanding, lifestyle and character. Jesus was right when he taught: "Thus you will recognize them by their fruits" (Mt. 7:20). Jesus' followers must not only hear and heed his words but also put them into practice. Now, all of this underlies Peter's words about Paul here. It is not so much a personal matter, though inevitably it is that, as a scriptural matter, and every word and phrase of Peter's description here points in that direction.

"Just as our beloved brother Paul" This description has occasioned much discussion as to difficulties in Peter addressing Paul in such terms and, as a consequence, if there were difficulties, giving further proof of pseudepigrapha and denial of Petrine authorship. However, this is unlikely, since the overall picture of New Testament relations between Peter and Paul is not one of enmity but rather one of amity. The so-called differences between the two men has largely been occasioned by the sharp disagreement mentioned at Galatians 2:11-21, but this was the only case so mentioned and other evidence points in the opposite direction:

1. Theologically.   Both Peter and Paul are shown to be in agreement over the inclusion of Gentiles in the church and denial of the need for Gentile circumcision (Ac. 11:2-18; 15:1-21).
2. Personally.   Even in the context of Galatians 2, we note that the disagreement was quite openly

about Peter's inconsistency in behaviour not a difference of opinion in principle. Further, if Christian forgiveness and reconciliation mean anything, the issues were resolved and over. Paul on his part clearly avers Peter as an apostle to the Jews, as himself to the Gentiles (Ga. 2:7,8) and a pillar of the church (Ga. 2:9). Paul, furthermore, recalls a fifteen day visit with Peter earlier (Ga. 1:18), mentions Peter in no critical but, rather, in quite an open and respectful way in his Corinthian correspondence (1 Co. 1:12; 3:22; 9:5; 15:5) and shares work and service with Peter's fellow-worker, Silas/Silvanus (Ac. 15:22-18:5; 2 Co. 1:19; 1 Th. 1:1; 2 Th. 1:1 cf. 1 Pe. 5:12).

3. Naturally.

The phrase **"beloved brother"** or similar expressions were used quite widely for fellow-workers within the Christian church in the first century: (Ep. 6:21; Col. 4:7 of Tychicus; Ph. 2:25 of Epaphroditus; Col. 4:9; Philemon 16 of Onesimus; 1 Th. 3:2; 1 Co. 4:17 of Timothy; 1 Pe.5:12 of Silas/Silvanus) and contrasts with the much more venerated terminology used of Paul, for example, in the second century: "the blessed and glorious Paul" (Polycarp); "the blessed Paul" (Clement); "the sanctified Paul . . . right blessed" (Ignatius). There is nothing particularly unusual or anachronistic, then, in Peter's description. It is simply expressive of familial affection quite normal in the New Testament church. **"Our"** is possibly better taken in the sense of "my", since epistolary plurals are rare, if extant at all, within the New Testament. The term **"beloved brother"** may either imply being numbered within the apostolic and leadership circle or simply a reference to Christians in general, though probably the former rather than the latter, in this case.

In all, the idea that this one incident mentioned in Galatians 2:11-21 "turned into a life-long jealousy is a mere guess"[232] or that it proves pseudepigrapha is flawed: "If 2 Peter is a pseudepigraph, it is a very good one!".[233] Compare this with D. Guthrie who comments: "Would a pseudepigraphist have adopted the view that Peter did not understand Paul's writings?".[234] Rather, as a natural expression of respect, love and affection between the two readers of the apostolic Church, it is perfectly acceptable. Simon J. Kistemaker comments:

> We receive the distinct impression that a warm relationship existed between Peter and Paul.[235]

"Also wrote to you . . . as he does in all his letters when he speaks in them of these matters". **"Wrote"** is *egrapsen*. Peter here clearly states that Paul wrote to Peter's own readers. But to which of Paul's writings does this refer? A number of suggestions have been made:

1. Geographically If Peter's addressees are the same in his second letter as in First Peter, then the area known in the ancient world as Asia Minor would qualify. Those Pauline letters specifically sent to this destination include

---

[232] D. Lucas & C. Green, *The Message Of 2 Peter & Jude*, p151.
[233] M. Green, *2 Peter and Jude*, p159.
[234] D. Guthrie, *New Testament Introduction*, p834.
[235] S. J. Kistemaker, *James, Epistles of John, Peter, and Jude*, p344.

Galatians, Ephesians and Colossians and some have suggested the same.

2. Thematically

If subject matter in terms of these issues referred to be in mind, then a different line of enquiry arises. In terms of the "day of the Lord", 1 and 2 Corinthians and 1 and 2 Thessalonians would be likely possibilities. However, if the issue were more particularly the projected delay in Christ's return and God's patience, then Romans would be a likely candidate, since there are a number of allusions throughout this letter, which would be especially relevant to this scene (e.g. Ro. 2:4 but also 3:25; 9:22-23; 11:22,23). Romans may, indeed, be particularly suitable if, as Romans 16:4 may suggest, the letter was 'circular', that is, destined to circulate around a number of congregations. Ephesians also, by dint of the absence of stated destination in a number of manuscripts, may also qualify as 'circular' as well.

3. Generally

The above may be drawing the areas of enquiry too narrowly. Hence, for those who would conjecture alongside specific issues a more general provenance of eschatological admonitions and ethical interpretations, many portions within Paul's letters would be applicable (e.g. Ro. 13:11-14; 1 Co. 7:27-35; 15:58; 2 Co. 7:1; 9:6; Ga. 5:21; 6:7-8; Ph. 2:15-16 ; 3:20; 4:5; Col. 3:4-6; 23-25; 1 Th. 5:4-11 cf. Ep. 4:30; 5:5, 16, 27; 6:13). If the yet more general concept of practical application of scriptural teaching were taken as the yardstick, references within Paul would be even more numerous. There is the added probability that Paul's writings to these specific readers may be among letters which are now lost (cf. 1 Co. 5:9; Col. 4:16) and the possibility, too, that in the light not only of 'circular' letters but of further dissemination of Paul's letters actually taking place (Col. 4:16), yet more material may be worth considering. Details, in context, allow of such possibilities: **"You"** most likely refers to specific addressees, namely, Peter's readers, but could also imply Christians of all generations. **"All his letters"** does not necessarily imply a completed Pauline corpus but all of Paul's letters which Peter had seen or letters extant at the time. **"These matters"** seems to have been generally covered in our discussion but the term can have the widest of connotations. Simon J. Kistemaker's brief judgement below is judicious but further research into this issue may well be of some benefit: "Perhaps we should refrain from guesswork and simply admit that we do not know which letter Paul wrote to the readers of II Peter".[236]

"According to the wisdom given him" Paul's letters evidence divine wisdom. He often claimed that his ministry was from the "grace given to me" (Ro. 12:3; 15:15; Ga. 2:9; 1 Co. 3:10; Ep. 3:2, 7; Col. 1:25). Here, the formula changes somewhat to **"according to the wisdom given him"**. But the implication is clear. Just as his ministry

---

[236] S. J. Kistemaker, *James, Epistles of John, Peter, and Jude*, p344.

was divinely not humanly directed, so also his writings. **"Given"** is *dotheisan* a "divine passive" and emphasizes this point. The language implies "inspiration" (2 Ti. 3:16). Douglas J. Moo puts it well:

> What he wrote in his letters came not from his own study or imagination; it came from God himself, who gave Paul the wisdom to understand and apply the gospel in his generation.[237]

"There are some things in them that are hard to understand, which the ignorant and unstable twist to their own destruction, as they do the other Scriptures".

"Hard to understand" is *dusnoēta* literally "hard to understand" "obscure" "ambiguous". It is a rare word. It was used of oracles in antiquity such as the Delphi oracle or of pronouncements notoriously capable of more than one interpretation. The word, then, has the additional connotation of "difficult to interpret", where misunderstanding could take place. It does not mean impossible to interpret and is not a dissuasive against studying Paul or any other difficult Scriptures. It is, rather, great comfort to realize that others recognize such difficulties and that we should try to find a meaning consistent with the context and with other scriptural principles relevant to the theme. **"Which the ignorant and unstable"** Misunderstanding is one thing; misinterpretation is something very different. This is Peter's main concern here, namely, those who are **"ignorant and unstable"**. Again, we have another of Peter's couplets, which also recalls earlier themes in his letter as he draws his teaching to a conclusion. **"Ignorant"** is *amatheis*. It is not simply "ignorant" in the sense of "not knowing" but is, literally, "untaught" in the sense of being "uninstructed". Richard Bauckham makes the valid point:

---

[237]   D. J. Moo, *2 Peter, Jude*, p210.

"These people have not received sufficient instruction in the faith to be able to interpret difficult passages in the Scriptures correctly".[238] Perhaps the word harks back to Peter's description of those distracted by the false teachers at 2:18: "those who are barely escaping from those who live in error". **"Unstable"** is *astēriktoi* and has a similar nuance. It describes those insecure spiritually and easily misled perhaps because their understanding and experience of Christianity is relatively superficial. The word intriguingly again harks back to 2:14 where false teachers are said to "entice unsteady souls" and the same term is used, *astēriktous,* and contrasts the positive form of the word at 1:12, of those who are "established (*estērigmenous*) in the truth". A degree of blame may connote both words in the couplet as Bauckham suggests: "There may be an element of condemnation in the description: these people are ignorant because they are *unwilling* to learn, and unstable because they *allow themselves* to be misled".[239] In the light of this, it may be better to infer a reference not only to the false teachers but also to those duped by them.

"Twist to their own destruction" Misrepresentation certainly comes to the fore now. **"Twist"** is *streblousin,* a vivid metaphor. It means to "twist" or "distort". It literally means to *"tighten with a windlass"* and conjures up a picture of twisting a rope or torturing on a rack as of "pulling Paul out of shape in a deliberate desire to make him say something other than his clear intention . . . The hallmark is not simply an antipathy to Paul but an antipathy to this theme, consistently presented in Scripture, for their abuse of him is merely a symptom of their abuse of the whole Bible".[240] What a dangerously insidious activity!

---

[238]   R. J. Bauckham, *Jude, 2 Peter,* p331.

[239]   R. J. Bauckham, *Jude, 2 Peter,* p331, (Emphasis his).

[240]   D. Lucas & C. Green, *The Message Of 2 Peter & Jude,* p152.

"To their own destruction" **"Destruction"** is *apōleian*, a typical term for eschatological punishment. Thomas R. Schreiner fearfully and rightly comments:

> The verbal and noun form of the term are used quite often in 2 Peter to designate God's judgment on the wicked (2:1, 3; 3:6-7, 9). Their errant use of Paul's writings landed them in hell – hardly an innocent peccadillo . . . Those who were twisting and distorting Paul's writings lacked the humility to learn from others, but they were perverting what Paul wrote to justify their licentious lifestyles.[241]

"As they do the other Scriptures**"** The plain implication of these words seems to be that Peter is describing Paul's letters as Scripture. Some, however, question this on the grounds that while Peter is saying that the false teachers twist the other Scriptures, the **"other"** may imply a different category and they claim that **"Scriptures"** does not always imply canonical Scripture as in the Old Testament but could simply be a term meaning Writings. Some, however, would maintain that Peter is affirming Paul's writings as Scripture for:

1. The Greek word for **"other"** *loipos* specifically refers to "other" of the same kind. Thomas Schriner explains this well: "This is evident where 'other' (*loipos*) functions as an adjective. In each instance the 'other' refers to others of the same kind: 'other virgins' (Matt. 25:11 NASB, ESV), 'other apostles' (Acts 2:37), 'other churches' (2 Cor. 12:13), 'other Jews' (Gal. 2:13; cf. also Rom. 1:13; 1 Cor. 9:5; Phil. 4:3). Peter clearly identifies Paul's writing as Scripture".[242]

---

[241] T. R. Schreiner, *1, 2 Peter, Jude,* p397.
[242] T. R. Schreiner, *1, 2 Peter, Jude,* pp397-398.

2. The term **Scripture** *graphē* does imply the same level of authority as Old Testament canonical Scripture. "But the term 'scripture' (*graphē*) occurs fifty times in the New Testament and invariably refers to the Old Testament Scriptures, even in Jas 4:5."[243] "In the New Testament the term *Scripture* in both the singular and plural 'is used exclusively of Holy Scripture'".[244] "But the word 'Scriptures' (*graphai*) always refers in the New Testament to those writings considered not only authoritative but canonical – in a word, it refers to the Old Testament . . . Peter therefore implies that the letters of Paul have a status equivalent to that of the canon of the Old Testament itself".[245] In view of this, it is difficult to affirm that the term simply means "Writings".

3. In spite of the suggestion that this is too early to place Second Peter in the first century, other evidence at that time is contrary to this. For example, in 1 Timothy 5:18 Paul introduces as "Scripture" a verse from the Old Testament: "You shall not muzzle an ox when it treads out the grain" (cf. De. 25:4) and a reference to a saying of Jesus: "The labourer deserves his wages" (cf. Lu. 10:7; Mt. 10:10).

4. This is consistent with how Paul regards the authority of his own writings (1 Co. 14:37 cf. Ro. 1:2; Ga. 1:1) and how authoritatively Peter viewed his writings, by implication, also (cf. 1 Pe. 1:10-12; 2 Pe. 1:19-21; 3:1, 2).

Clearly, Peter's usage here implies that Paul's letters are regarded

---

[243] T. R. Schreiner, *1, 2 Peter, Jude,* p398.

[244] Colin Brown in *New Testament Dictionary of New Testament Theology,* Exeter, The Paternoster press; U.S.A., Zondervan, 1978, Vol.3 p490, cited in S. J. Kistemaker, *James, Epistles of John, Peter, and Jude,* p346 n58.

[245] D. J. Moo, *2 Peter, Jude,* p212.

as "**Scriptures**". The implications of Peter maintaining that Paul's letters were Scripture is massive. It marks a high point in Peter's reasoning regarding the importance of Scripture toward the close and climax of his letter.

APPLICATION

Biblical theology is intriguing in the light of progressive revelation. Of course, that progression can become counter-productive, where it posits diametric changes through the Bible, so that what is taught at one point is contradicted at the other. But, where it shows true progression, it both enlightens and excites the mind about Scripture. Augustine averred this in his famous dictum about the Testaments, when he claimed that the New is in the Old concealed and the Old is in the New revealed.

However, it is not only from Old to New Testament that we see this process, but even within Old and New Testaments themselves. We see it particularly as we come to study the later books of the New Testament canon as we have been doing in Second Peter. The same is true with Second Timothy also and, in both these letters, it is particularly true in regard to the doctrine of revelation or Scripture.

As we set side by side what Paul and Peter teach about Scripture in these closing writings of the New Testament canon, just as we have seen Peter do, we learn so much about the doctrine of revelation in general and of the Bible itself in particular:

Paul expresses his thoughts with those words to Timothy:

> "But as for you, continue in what you have learned
> and have firmly believed, knowing from whom
> you learned it and how from childhood you have

been acquainted with the sacred writings, which are able to make you wise for salvation through faith in Christ Jesus. All Scripture is breathed out by God and profitable for teaching, for reproof, for correction, and for training in righteousness, that the man of God may be competent, equipped for every good work" (2 Ti. 3:14-17).

Peter's two letters have much to say on that important subject too. His first letter recalls that glorious progression from prophet to apostle in the sovereign purpose of God's revelation of salvation (1 Pe. 1:10-12). His second letter picks up the theme and explores the 'mechanics' behind prophecy and its 'production' (2 Pe. 1:19-21). But those closing remarks of that second letter put it all into context and align it with Paul's remarks about Scripture too. It is an awesome and impressive finale:

"This is now the second letter that I am writing to you, beloved. In both of them I am stirring up your sincere mind by way of reminder, that you should remember the predictions of the holy prophets and the commandment of the Lord and Saviour through your apostles" (2 Pe. 3:1-2).

and

"And count the patience of our Lord as salvation, just as our beloved brother Paul also wrote to you according to the wisdom given him, as he does in all his letters when he speaks in them of these matters. There are some things in them that are hard to understand, which the ignorant and unstable twist to their own destruction, as they do the other Scriptures" (2 Pe. 3:15-16).

It is, however, an open-ended finale. Paul urges Timothy to use those Scriptures to advance his own ministry and Peter wants his readers to use them to avoid heresy and immorality and to live godly Christian lives, to grow in grace and in the knowledge of their Lord and Saviour. Paul and Peter, monumental leaders of the early church, the one, the apostle to the Gentiles, the other, the apostle to the Jews, combine to show the way forward as Scripture, from start to finish. This climaxes all that God says in Old and New Testaments in his majestic word. It gives a solid foundation for all our Christian teaching, is chart and compass to all our Christian pilgrimage and is the heartbeat of all our Christian living, as well as guarding us against all the heresy and immorality of false teachers and scoffers: the Holy Scriptures. What a final open-ended word from all the holy prophets through the commandment of our Lord and Saviour by the apostles to us. What a treasure from the covenant God to his covenant people – his firm word, the Scriptures. Our hearts continue to burn within us as he walks and talks with us in the way, as he opens our minds to understand these Scriptures. The Scriptures are the surest of guidelines to growing in Christ amid false teaching. Thus, in this closing cadence of his second letter, at the close of his life, as he reflects on earlier themes and recalls many *inclusios*, Peter stresses the massive importance of Scripture revelation both for himself and for Paul. *Scriptura Sola* is the firmest of foundations for the practical knowledge of God amid false teachers and scoffers.

> How firm a foundation, ye saints of the Lord,
> Is laid for your faith in His excellent word!
> What more can He say than to you He hath said,
> To you who for refuge to Jesus have fled?
>
> "Fear not, I am with thee, O be not dismayed,
> For I am thy God, and will still give thee aid;
> I'll strengthen thee, help thee, and cause thee to
> stand,

Upheld by My righteous, omnipotent hand."

"E'en down to old age all My people shall prove
My sovereign, eternal, unchangeable love;
And then, when grey hairs shall their temples adorn,
Like lambs they shall still in My bosom be borne."

"The soul that on Jesus hath leaned for repose,
I will not, I will not desert to his foes;
That soul, though all hell should endeavour to shake,
I'll never, no, never, no, never forsake!"[246]

---

[246] "K" in Rippon's Selection of Hymns (England), 1787, alt. https://www.
hymnal.net/en/hymn/h/339

In John Rippon's A Selection of Hymns (1787, plus numerous subsequent editions), "How Firm a Foundation" (no. 128) is attributed simply to "K–". Two other hymns in the collection bear the same mark, "In songs of sublime adoration and praise," and "The Bible is justly esteemed." The author of the hymn has never been definitively identified, but the most common candidates are listed below. I. Robert Keen(e) The most likely possibility is Robert Keene, who served as precentor at Rippon's church. The evidence for connecting K with Keene comes (1) from his close acquaintance with Rippon, (2) Rippon's tune book, and (3) the testimony (of sorts) of Thomas Walker. After Rippon started publishing a tune book, A Selection of Psalm and Hymn T… Go to person page > https://hymnary.org/person/K.

Chapter 22

CONCLUSION

2 PETER 3:17-18

INTRODUCTION

Personal letters of the day including those in the New Testament often tended to dwindle to a close. They petered out. Public letters of that period including those in the New Testament seemed to close in a much more ordered and planned fashion. Regularly these New Testament letters, aside from some, where personal greetings and details were mentioned, closed by summarizing in a succinct and pithy manner the contents of the letter, ending with a concluding benediction or doxology. Second Peter ends in this way as do other New Testament letters for example, Romans 16:25-27; 1 Corinthians 16:22; 2 Corinthians 13:7-11; Galatians 6:11-16; 1 Thessalonians 5:23-24; 1 Timothy 6:20-21; 2 Timothy 4:1-8; 1 Peter 5:8-10; 1 John 5:13-21; Jude 24-25.

We have already noted this concluding, summarizing tendency in Second Peter in the last two sections, with *inclusios* or bracketing recalls going back to the middle or opening of the letter and even back to First Peter. The same is true, now, as we come to the final words of Peter's second letter. It seems to follow quite an organized pattern too, as Peter recalls his main theme in writing.

These final words open with an exhortation in verses 17 and 18ª corresponding to the purpose statements concluding Greek secular letters of the day. The keyword in verse 17 is "watch" *phulassesthe*, connoting "being alert", "being on one's guard". The subject matter relates to external influences. The sentiments reflect warnings about the false teachers mentioned in Chapter 2. The keyword in verse 18a is "grow" *auxanete*, connoting "increase" or "progress" in Christian living. The subject matter relates to internal development. The sentiments recall some key ideas in Chapter 1. The final closing words in verse 18ᵇ are a benediction, a replacement of the usual health wish in secular letters of the day. Here, the keyword is a concluding "glory" *doxa*. The sentiments enlarge on matters at issue in Chapter 3.

The following format arises as we conclude our study of Second Peter:

WATCH	(v17)
GROW	(v18ª)
GLORY	(v18ᵇ)

EXPOSITION

WATCH

"You therefore, beloved, knowing this beforehand, take care that you are not carried away with the error of lawless people and lose your own stability" (3:17)

"You therefore, beloved" Each of these three words significantly introduces Peter's conclusion to his letter. **"You"** *humeis* is first in the sentence and emphatic. It contrasts Peter's readers with the ignorant and unstable people who twist Paul's writings (v16). **"Therefore"** *oun* strikes the final reasoning note of this summary conclusion. **"Beloved"** *agapētoi* picking up on vv1, 8, 14, recalls Peter's warm, affectionate address to his readers to encourage them, contrasting his condemnation of the false teachers and scoffers. From the slight but relevant digression about Paul's writings, Peter returns to his main theme at verse 14 as he concludes his letter.

"Knowing this beforehand" is *proginōskontes* from which comes our English "prognosis". Peter has outlined the future. This is the fourth occasion he mentions what will occur later, after his "departure" and presumably death (1:15). Those times will be marked by false teachers (2:1-3), scoffers (3:3-4) and, now, by **"lawless people"** (3:17). The fact that some of these things are already taking place is similar to Paul's "future prognosis" regarding coming events both after he will leave the church at Ephesus mentioned in Acts and later in his remarks to Timothy in his first letter (Ac. 20:29-31 cf. 1 Ti.4:1-10). **"Knowing this beforehand"** is not synonymous with **"knowing this first of all"** *touto prōton ginōskontes* at 1:20 and 3:3. The latter is knowing something of importance as a priority, the former is knowing something in advance[247]. Peter's expression here **"knowing this beforehand"** *proginōskontes* is not, as R.J. Bauckham seems to suggest, the literary device of a pseudepigrapher.[248] Rather, primarily the reference seems to be to the Scriptures, namely, the words of the holy prophets and the commandment of the Lord through the apostles and also to the information contained in Second Peter. D. J. Moo puts it well:

---

[247]   T. R. Schreiner, *1, 2 Peter, Jude,* p399.

[248]   R. J. Bauckham, *Jude, 2 Peter,* p337.

If, as we think, Peter is writing this letter, he is then referring generally to the early Christian teaching about eschatology and its moral implications that his readers had received. Peter's point is that the readers have been amply warned about the danger of false teaching. Forewarned should mean that they are forearmed – ready to resist the perverse attractions of the false teachers' heresies.[249]

"**Take care**" or "guard" is *phulassesthe*. As to meaning, it can connote "keeping" the law (Mk. 10:20 par Mt. 19:20 par Lu. 18:21 cf. Ac. 7:53; 21:24; Ro. 2:26; Ga. 6:13), "guarding someone or something in prison" or "guarding one's house" (2 Pe. 2:5; Lu. 2:8, 11:21; Ac. 22:20, 28:16). It can be used metaphorically of "guarding someone spiritually" so that they will not fall away irretrievably (Jn. 12:25; 17:12; 2 Th. 3:3; 2 Ti.1:12; Jude 24). In this case, God is often the one doing the guarding. The nuance of meaning, here, has an edge of urgency about it, akin to Luke 12:15 "Watch out! Be on your guard against all kinds of greed" NIV; 1 Timothy 6:20 "guard what has been entrusted to your care" NIV; 2 Timothy 4:15 "You too should be on your guard against him" NIV; 1 John 5:21 "Dear children, keep yourself from idols" NIV.[250] The term has a particularly strong, military thrust of meaning.

"**Take care**" or "guard" is the main verb in the sentence and constitutes the concluding negative warning of Peter in his letter. The present tense of the imperative suggests a continual state of watchfulness, alert to the probability of attack. Peter obviously assumes that they are already watching or on guard but urges them to do so yet more. This recalls both the urgency and continuity of Jesus' frequent exhortations to his disciples to watch and be alert. With what information Peter is giving them in his letter and has

---

[249] D.J. Moo, *2 Peter, Jude*, p213.
[250] P. H. Davids, *The Letters Of 2 Peter And Jude*, p310.

reminded them of in Scripture, there should be no danger of them falling away. All he has been saying to them has been to induce this vigilance. Now, he rounds it off finally and peremptorily. Simon J Kistemaker puts it succinctly:

> The command in the Greek indicates that the believers are indeed guarding themselves. Nevertheless, Peter deems it necessary to reinforce them by describing the consequences of failing to heed his command.[251]

"That you are not carried away" **"Carried away"** is *sunapachthentes* and means "to be carried away", "to be led astray". The same verb is used of Barnabas at Galatians 2:13 when he, though a colleague of Paul, was drawn aside from eating with Gentiles at Antioch through the influence of James, Peter and the circumcision party. It illustrates well the danger of getting into the wrong company and being swayed by the crowd toward a questionable course of action, whether as a non-Christian or as a Christian. It is so easy for others to influence and lead us away from the truth as it is in Christ, for Barnabas had so many fine qualities.

"With the error of lawless people" **"Error"** is *planē*. As a noun it means, literally, "wandering" or "error" from a true or correct path. When used metaphorically, in its verbal form it carries the nuance of "to err, wander or depart from the truth". It could be taken either, negatively, of those being led astray from the truth or, positively, of those distracting others from the truth or, indeed, of both, in which case it could imply both those influenced by the false teachers and scoffers or these errant leaders themselves. Intriguingly, the very word-root recalls the false teachers particularly in respect of those who had left the straight path and "gone astray" (*eplanēthēsan*) to

---

[251] S. J. Kistemaker, *James, Epistles of John, Peter, and Jude*, p347.

follow the way of Balaam (2:15) and who "live in error" (2:18 – *planē*). Jude 11 speaks similarly of "Balaam's error" (*planē tou Balaam*). "**Lawless**" is *athesmōn*, that is, men who live "without law" and again recalls the false teachers who are so described by that very same word at 2:7. The language, in both these instances, "**error**" and "**lawless**", is clearly that of recall going back quite definitively to descriptions in Chapter 2.

"**And lose**" "**Lose**" is *ekpesēte*. The simple form of the verb is used in the New Testament literally as at Acts 12:7 for Peter's chains falling from his wrists and at Acts 27:26, 29 in a context of shipwreck. Both in its simple and compound forms, it is frequently used metaphorically for "falling from faith" or "apostasy" as, for example, at Romans 11:11, 22; 14:4; 1 Corinthians 10:12; Hebrews 4:11; Revelation 2:5 in the simple form and as a compound both here at 2 Peter 3:17 and Galatians 5:4, in which latter case it literally reads, "fallen away from the grace".

"**Your own stability**" is the crucial aspect of this point. Here "**stability**" translates *stērigmou*. This is the only occurrence of the noun in the New Testament but verbally and adjectivally the term seems to be a favourite of Peter's. The term harks back not only to this second letter but to First Peter as well and, indeed, perhaps to Jesus' personal relationship with Peter himself. Its meaning can be gauged from the fact that, in secular Greek circles, the word was used to describe the fixity of the stars, the stations of the planets and the steadfastness of a beam of light. Kindred occurrences of the word-group are found metaphorically elsewhere in the New Testament as, for example, at Luke 22:32; Romans 16:25; 2 Thessalonians 3:3 cf. 1 Peter 5:10. Within a Petrine context, it was used to describe the scoffers and false teachers and also, perhaps, those under their influence as "unstable" *astēriktoi*, the negative adjectival form at 3:16 and 2:14. Earlier in the letter, if Peter's readers would follow his advice to make their calling and election sure, they would never "fall" (*ptaisēte*) (1:10). Peter goes on immediately to remind them of things, which they already know, and in which they are "established" (1:12 – *estērigmenous*). Intriguingly, in his first letter, Peter urges his readers, how, after they have suffered a little time, the God of grace "will himself restore, confirm (*stērixei*), strengthen and establish you" (1 Pe. 5:10). Previously, Christ commanded Peter when he had repented and recovered from his own instability of denial to "strengthen" (*stērison*) his brothers (Lu. 22:32). A catena of this word-group, thus, stretches back through Peter's two letters to Jesus' himself. It is difficult to avoid both the poignancy and passion of Peter's own personal experience in all of this.

T.R. Schreiner, clarifying the nature of this falling, helpfully comments:

> Those who are on their guard will not fall from their secure position, while those who are careless are apt to slip away because they ignored warning signals. We should add here that any who finally do turn aside and fall away reveal that they were never part of the people of God (1 Cor. 11:19; 1 John 2:19). But Peter's purpose in a warning was not to handle that question. The warning is prophylactic and prospective, not a retrospective analysis of those who have departed.[252]

Watch means to be forewarned, forearmed, guarded from wandering or losing one's stability. However long on the Christian road, we need to be careful and watch all this.

---

[252]   T.R. Schreiner, *1, 2 Peter, Jude*, p400.

GROW

"But grow in the grace and knowledge of our Lord and Saviour Jesus Christ" (3:18ᵃ)

"But grow in the grace and knowledge of our Lord and Saviour Jesus Christ". **"Grow"** is *auxanete* meaning "to advance or increase in the sphere of". Peter implies here that his readers continue to grow, for the verb, as previously with "guard" or "watch", is the present tense of the imperative.

There are, however, a number of ways of taking the reference to **"grace"** and **"knowledge"**, which are both, here, *anarthrous*, that is, without the definite article. There are three major options and we are indebted to Thomas R Schreiner for his excellent discussion of the matter, which clearly identifies the issues so well.[253]

1. Both **"grace"** and **"knowledge"** might be construed as parallel and both connected to Jesus Christ as the source of these attributes. This is meaningful but leaves the objective side to **"knowledge"** wanting.

2. Jesus Christ could be the source of **"grace"** in the first instance and the object of **"knowledge"** in the second. This, too, is helpful but leaves the parallelism somewhat disjointed, and lacks a subjective side to the meaning of **"knowledge"**.

3. **"Grace"**, in this sentence, is not to be connected with Jesus Christ in terms of syntactical meaning but rather treated as a separate entity: **"but grow in grace"**. **"Knowledge"**, on the other hand, is specifically expanded in the phrase **"our**

---

[253] T.R. Schreiner, *1, 2 Peter, Jude*, p401.

Lord and Saviour Jesus Christ" and is largely objective though not exclusively so.

While the difference between *gnōsis* for "**knowledge**" (here and at 1:5-6 and verbally 1:20; 3:3) and *epignōsis* similarly for "**knowledge**" (1:2, 3, 8; 2:20 and in 2:21 twice verbally) has been differentiated by some, the former implying continuing objective knowledge and the latter converting or initial subjective knowledge, and while there is some merit in these distinctions, they do not seem strong enough to determine the issue here. Further, Peter has elsewhere used the titles "**Lord and Saviour**" together as here (1:11; 2:20; 3:18) as, of course, also separately "**Saviour**" (1:1) and "**Lord**" (1:16) to highlight respectively Christ's power to save and to judge. Both attributes, saving and judging, are implicit in "**grace**" and in "**knowledge**" and though, perhaps, more indicative of the former than the latter again are insufficient to warrant a definitive decision on the issue under discussion.

In all, our preference for option 3 is really, as with Schreiner along the lines that it provides a fitting closing summary for "**grace**" and "**knowledge**", since Peter speaks about them at the beginning of his letter. It is, in this sense, one of a number of final *inclusios* closing Peter's correspondence.

GRACE

Peter begins his letter by showing how the grace of God in Jesus Christ is primary. Grace is expressed in God's saving righteousness through which God bestowed faith on believers (1:1). Grace is sought in prayer to be multiplied to these same believers (1:2). Grace provides believers with everything they need to live a godly life (1:3-4). How apt for Peter to close his letter by urging his readers to grow in this same grace given them (3:18).

KNOWLEDGE

Peter also begins by mentioning the saving knowledge of Christ, upon which they subjectively latch in an objective way. Grace and peace are increased by knowing Jesus Christ as God and Saviour (1:2). Everything for life and godliness is available *through* knowing God (1:3). Growing in such knowledge is necessary for the Christian life (1:5-6). Only those who so progress prove that such knowledge is fruitful (1:8). Conversely, those who renounce Christ after apparently coming to know him are worse off than those who never profess faith at all (2:20-22). True knowledge of our Lord Jesus Christ is necessary to begin the Christian life and equally necessary to continue in it. This is why Peter makes this true knowledge a final and grand conclusion to his letter, and it is largely an objective knowledge of Christ both empirically and experientially which believers should covet in Christian growth.

Calvin seems to see this conclusion in a similar way and, as usual, puts succinctly what we perhaps put more expansively:

> The word *grace*, I take in a general sense, as meaning those spiritual gifts we obtain through Christ. But as we become partakers of these blessings according to the measure of our faith, *knowledge* is added to grace; as though he had said, that as faith increases, so would follow the increase of grace.[254]

Growing in the grace of our Lord and Saviour Jesus Christ invariably leads to knowledge of him. This brings the initial doublet, grace and knowledge, to a final *inclusio* at the end of the letter. The two run in tandem. Subjective and objective aspects unite both grace and knowledge.

---

[254]   J. Calvin, *Commentaries on II Peter*, p426, (Emphasis his).

We must come to truly know and continue within a true knowledge of God in Christ. We need to avoid, at all costs, false or spurious knowledge, which perverts both understanding and living. Rather, particularly in the light of Christ's return and the coming final judgement, we should grow in a practical knowledge of God in Christ, which gloriously transforms character and behaviour. This brings Peter's teaching about true, false and practical knowledge of God to a majestic climax, as he concludes has letter.

GLORY

"To him be the glory both now and to the day of eternity. Amen" (3:18ᵇ).

"To him be the glory" "Glory" is *doxa* arising from the Hebrew *kabod* meaning literally "heaviness". Both words connote the "solemnity" "awe" and "majesty" of God. The idea is of divine reputation, perfection of attributes and character, supreme impressiveness of person. Peter's description is remarkable in at least four ways. First, a doxology, a hymn of praise in terms of glory, from the Greek *doxa* **"glory"**, is an unusual ending for letters, including those in the New Testament. Greetings, references to fellow-workers, prayer requests and grace wishes all closed both secular and sacred letters of the day but rarely doxology. The only New Testament examples, apart from this, where a doxology actually closes a letter are Romans 16:25-27 Jude 24, 25 and, possibly, though not found at the very end of the letter, Philippians 4:20. The suggestion has even been made that this implies a letter intended for circulation, a 'circular letter', but this is hardly necessarily so.

Secondly, a doxology in praise of Jesus Christ *alone* is unusual. The only other concrete examples are 2 Timothy 4:18 (possibly) and Revelation 1:5-6, with which Hebrews 13:21 and 1 Peter 4:11 have been compared. Of course, ascription of deity to Christ is a common feature throughout the New Testament, for example Matthew 28:9, 17; John 5:23; Philippians 2:10; Hebrews 1:6. Here, however, we are thinking specifically of doxological format and that at the close of a letter. Michael Green remarkably suggests the impact of the effect of this in the particular area to which these letters were addressed, when he writes:

> For it was in the Asiatic churches of Bithynia, to which 1 Peter (1:1) and perhaps 2 Peter were written (if we are to infer from 3:1 that it was sent to the same destination), that the Roman governor, Pliny, about A.D.112 noticed that Christians 'sing a hymn of praise to Christ as God' (*Ep. x. 96*).[255]

As mentioned above, while a high Christology is of general note throughout the New Testament, it is particularly in later books of the canon, such as 2 Peter, 2 Timothy and Revelation, that we find expressed examples of such Christology, as well as poignant comments on the doctrine of revelation.

Thirdly, and equally remarkably, within Second Peter itself, this doxology concludes, in one of two *inclusios*, the theme of Christ's divinity prominent at the beginning of the letter and prevalent throughout. At 1:1-2, Christ is hailed as God and Saviour. At 1:17, Peter recalls the voice from the Majestic Glory (*megaloprepous doxēs*) affirming Christ's divine sonship. Here, at the close at 3:18, Christ is ascribed glory, which is due to God alone (cf. Ro. 11:36; Jude 25), quite natural, of course, since Christ is God. The remarkable divine glory of Christ stands complete.

"Both now and to the day of eternity"

---

[255] M. Green, *2 Peter and Jude*, pp164-165, Compare with R. J. Bauckham, *Jude, 2 Peter*, p338.

Fourthly, the doxology remarkably climaxes both now and in eternity. Peter says that this glory belongs to Jesus Christ both in the present age and for ever. But the phrase he uses for "for ever" is not just the usual one *eis tous aiōnas,* literally, for the eternity (cf. Ph.4:20). The Greek here literally reads: *eis hēmeran aiōnos* "to the day of eternity".

The introduction of "the day" is strikingly difficult if remarkably significant. For how can a day last forever? Peter had written earlier in his letter of that day: "to which you will do well to pay attention as to a lamp shining in a dark place, until the day dawns and the morning star rises in your hearts" (1:19). Towards the end of his letter, that "day" pounds his mind and he pounds his readers' minds with it. It is the day of judgement, the day of the Lord, the day of God (3:7, 10, 12). Now, it is "the day of eternity", the day that ushers in the new heavens and the new earth, the judgement of God and the return of Christ. This is Peter's final *inclusio* of all and it is the glorious beginning of a new world for the believer and the eternal glory of God in Christ. Hallelujah! Whether the "Amen" at the close is original or not – some maintain it to be a secondary scribal gloss – it is the glorious covenant oath cry affirmed by all God's people who shout and sing Amen, Amen and Amen, "to the day of eternity". And we all gladly join with them in their anthem.

Calvin, as ever, closes majestically:

> *To him be the glory.* This is a remarkable passage to prove the divinity of Christ; for what is said cannot belong to any but to God alone. The adverb of the present time, *now,* is designed for this end, that we may not rob Christ of his glory, during our warfare in the world. He then adds, *for ever,* that we may

> now form some idea of his eternal kingdom, which
> will make known to us his full and perfect glory.[256]

The *Glory* is of Christ as divine, as unique, as climactic, and as eternal. It is the glory of God alone in Christ.

APPLICATION

Peter ends his letter where he started it, with the grace of God and the knowledge of our Lord and Saviour Jesus Christ through which God is pleased to communicate that grace. Peter set out that very stall at the outset of his letter: the true knowledge of God. That grace and knowledge not only brought his readers to faith in Jesus, it progressed them along the line of that faith. They added to their faith. They must make their calling and election sure. They would eventually receive a rich welcome into the kingdom of all who hold a like precious faith with them. The basis of that faith was in what God said. The voice from the Majestic Glory not only announced the Word made flesh; it recalled the Scriptures of the holy prophets and brought the commandment of the Lord through the holy apostles. Peter, whose life in this world was almost over, would remind them of that.

Peter too would remind them all the more forcefully of these things because of the possibility of false knowledge. The false prophets had their modern counterpart in false teachers. These teachers were not only errant in doctrine, they were sinful in lifestyle. It was just as the Master had taught: by their fruits, you would know them. Of course, the whole Old Testament story recalled this: God and angels, Noah and the Flood, Lot and the people of Sodom and Gomorrah, righteousness and wickedness vying with each other, the Son and the Serpent replayed again and again and again.

---

[256] J. Calvin, *Commentaries on II Peter*, p426, (Emphasis his).

So a very practical knowledge of God was necessary. That would be played out through true doctrine and godly living. Those were the handmaidens of this practical knowledge, fought out on the battlefield of Christ's return. The scoffers were virtually synonymous with the false teachers and that was their field of combat, their weapons of choice. They scorned the promise of his coming. If there were a God, he had reneged on his promise, they claimed. It was all a tissue of lies. But Peter said: No! Peter himself had been through the horrendous of denial and knew all about it. They must recall, remember, re-live Scripture – the words of the holy prophets, the commandment of the Lord through the apostles. The present world would be destroyed, Christ would return and wrong would be righted. A heaven was to be gained and a hell to be shunned and, after the destruction of the old, there would be a glorious new heavens and new earth, where righteousness dwells. This was the word of the Lord, Old and New Testament, prophet and apostle, Isaiah and Paul centred on the Lord Jesus Christ, the cornerstone of the church and her returning king. They must watch and beware of the false teachers and their false knowledge, but grow in grace and in the knowledge of their Lord and Saviour Jesus Christ until the day dawns and the shadows fly away. Second Peter, whatever else, is primarily about this: Christ and Scripture, the grace and knowledge of God. Peter's readers needed to watch and grow till the day dawns. So should we. Even so, come, Lord Jesus. Amen and Amen.

Bibliography

COMMENTARIES

BAUCKHAM, R.J.	*Jude, 2 Peter* (U.S.A., Nelson/Word 1983).
BIGG, C.	*The Epistles of St. Peter and St Jude,* International Critical Commentaries, (Edinburgh, T.&T. Clark, 1901).
CALVIN, J.	*Commentaries Hebrews, I Peter, I John, James, II Peter, Jude* – Volume XXII, U.S.A., Baker, (1989).
CRANFIELD, C.E.B.	*I & II Peter and Jude,* (London, SCM, 1960).
DAVIDS, P. H.	*The Letters Of 2 Peter And Jude,* (U.S.A.,- Eerdmans, England,- Apollos, 2006).
GREEN, M.	*2 Peter and Jude,* England, and U.S.A., Inter-Varsity and Wm. B. Eerdmans, (1994).
HELM, D.R.	*1 & 2 Peter and Jude,* U.S.A., Crossway, (2008).
KELLY, J.N.D.	*A Commentary On The Epistles Of Peter And Of Jude,* (London, A. and C. Black, 1969).
KISTEMAKER, S.J.	*James, Epistles of John, Peter, and Jude,* U.S.A., Baker Academic, (1986, 1987, 2007).

LUCAS, D. & GREEN, C.	*The Message Of 2 Peter & Jude*, (England, U.S.A., Inter-Varsity, 1995).
MacARTHUR, J.	*2 Peter & Jude*, (U.S.A., Moody Publishers, 2005).
MOFFATT, J.	*The General Epistles: James, Peter and Jude, The Moffatt New Testament Commentary.* (London: Hodder and Stoughton; 1928).
MOO, D. J.	*2 Peter, Jude, The NIV Application Commentary*, (U.S.A., Zondervan, 1996).
NISBET, A.	*1 & 2 Peter*, (1658; Great Britain, U.S.A., Banner of Truth, 1982).
SCHREINER, T.R.	*1, 2 Peter, Jude*, (U.S.A., Broadman & Holman Publishers, 2003).

OTHER LITERATURE

BAUER, W.; ARNDT, W. F. and GINGRICH, F. W. *A Greek-English Lexicon of The New Testament and Other Early Christian Literature* (U.S.A., London, University of Chicago Press, Zondervan, 1957).

BENGEL, J.A.	*Gnomon Novi Testamenti (1773), Gnomon of The New Testament*, Edited by Andrew R. Fausset. Translated by William Fletcher, 5 vols. 7th Ed. Vol 5. Edinburgh: T. and T. Clark 1877.
CARSON, D.A.	*Exegetical Fallacies*, (U.S.A. Baker, 1984).
DONNELLY, E.	*Heaven and Hell*, (Great Britain, U.S.A. Banner of Truth, 2001).
GUTHRIE, D.	*New Testament Introduction*, England, Tyndale Press (1970).

GUTHRIE, D.	*New Testament Theology*, England, U.S.A. Inter-Varsity Press (1981).
HOEKEMA, A.A.	*THE BIBLE AND THE FUTURE* (U.S.A., Wm. B. Eerdmans Publishing Company, First Edition, 1979; Jointly Paperback with, U.K., The Paternoster Press, First Edition, 1994).
KÄSEMANN, E.	*Essays on New Testament Themes* (London: SCM; Naperville; A.R. Allenson, 1964).
LEAHY, F.S.	*Satan Cast Out,* A Study in Biblical Demonology (Great Britain, U.S.A. Banner of Truth, 1975)
LEWIS, C.S.	*The Four Loves,* (London, Geoffrey Bles Ltd, 1960).
LLOYD-JONES, D.M.	*Expository Sermons On 2 Peter,* (England, U.S.A., Banner of Truth, 1999).
PHILLIPS, J.B.	*The New Testament In Modern English*, (Great Britain, Geoffrey Bles Ltd. Collins, 1958).

The Psalter and Church Hymnary, Revised Edition, The Presbyterian Church in Ireland, Scotland, Oxford University Press, (1997).

The Septuagint with Apocrypha: Greek and English, L.C.L. BRENTON, U.S.A., Hendrickson Publishers (2007).

Westminster Confession of Faith, First published (1646), Glasgow, Free Presbyterian Publications, (1995).

Printed in the United States
by Baker & Taylor Publisher Services